WAR
BLACKS

MATT ELLIOTT

HarperCollins*Publishers*

HarperCollins_Publishers_

First published in 2016
by HarperCollins_Publishers_ (New Zealand) Limited
Unit D1, 63 Apollo Drive, Rosedale, Auckland 0632, New Zealand
harpercollins.co.nz

HarperCollins_Publishers_

Unit D1, 63 Apollo Drive, Rosedale, Auckland 0632, New Zealand
Level 13, 201 Elizabeth Street, Sydney NSW 2000
A 53, Sector 57, Noida, UP, India
1 London Bridge Street, London, SE1 9GF, United Kingdom
2 Bloor Street East, 20th floor, Toronto, Ontario M4W 1A8, Canada
195 Broadway, New York NY 10007, USA

National Library of New Zealand cataloguing-in-publication data:

Elliott, Matt.
  War Blacks : the extraordinary story of New Zealand's
  World War I All Blacks/Matt Elliott.
  ISBN 978-1-77554-036-6 (paperback)— 978-1-77549-072-2 (e-book)
  1. All Blacks (Rugby team) 2. Soldiers—New Zealand.
  3. World War, 1914-1918—New Zealand. I. Title.
940.41293—dc 23

Cover design by Darren Holt, HarperCollins Design Studio, from an original
idea by Matt Elliott
Index by Frances Paterson
Typeset in Historical Felltype and Sabon LT Roman by Kirby Jones
Printed and bound in Australia by Griffin Press
The papers used by HarperCollins in the manufacture of this book are a
natural, recyclable product made from wood grown in sustainable plantation
forests. The fibre source and manufacturing processes meet recognised
international environmental standards, and carry certification.

This book is dedicated to my wife, Melissa,
ever supportive and enthusiastic,
especially during a 'three-book year'

Contents

Introduction   1
Author's note   3

Before the War   5

1914   11
Sergeant Frederick Harold 'Skin' Masters MM   12
Trooper Karl Donald Ifwersen   16
Private Charles McLean MM   21
Driver Andrew 'Son' White   24
Sergeant Henry 'Norkey' Dewar   27
Lieutenant Charles Theodore Gillespie MC   29
Lieutenant Colonel Henry Esau Avery CMG, CBE, DSO   32
Sergeant Hubert Sydney 'Jum' Turtill   36
Second Lieutenant Hohepa 'Harry' Jacob MC   39
Driver Charles Napoleon 'Nipper' (or 'Nap') Kingstone   42
Gunner Peter Williams   43
Captain John Elliott 'Jock' Cuthill   45
Lieutenant Sergeant William Ernest Smith   49

1915   51
Sergeant Albert Joseph 'Doolan' Downing   51
Second Lieutenant Frank Reginald Wilson   55
Camp Quartermaster Sergeant Edward
    'Teddy' James Roberts   57
Lance Corporal Reginald Taylor   60
Sergeant Charles 'Chas' (or 'Charlie') Brown   61
Corporal Lynley Herbert Weston   64
Private Thomas William 'Tiger' Lynch   65
Sergeant Richard Fogarty MM   69

Sergeant James 'Jim' Edward Moffitt MM   71
Major William McKail Geddes MC   73
Sergeant Beethoven 'Beet' Algar   79
Driver Alfred 'Alf' Hubert West   83
Major William 'Billy' Spiers Glenn MC   86
Rifleman William August 'Jockey' Ford   90
Corporal Edmond Ryan   91
Bombardier John Alexander McNab   92
Private Eric McDonald 'Fritz' Snow   94
Rifleman Ernest Arthur 'Moke' Belliss   97
Trooper Cyril James Brownlie   100
Corporal Albert Robert 'Mick' Lomas   104
Private Robert 'Bobby' Stanley Black   106
Lieutenant Eric Arthur Percy Cockroft   107
Corporal Leslie 'Les' Frank Cupples MM   110
Sergeant Bernard Francis 'Frank' Smyth   112

1916   115

Sapper George 'Bear' Loveridge   115
Private William Robert Hardcastle   116
Lieutenant Colin MacDonald Gilray MC, OBE   118
Sergeant Nathaniel Arthur 'Ranji' Wilson   126
Driver Edward 'Ned' Hughes   129
Gunner Edward William 'Nut' (or 'Nuts') Hasell 132
Second Lieutenant Cyril Edward 'Scrum' Evans   134
Sapper John Gerald 'Jack' O'Brien   135
Private George Maurice Victor Sellars   137
Private James 'Jim' McNeece   138
Private Michael 'Mick' Joseph Cain   139
Private Richard John 'Jock' McKenzie   142
Private James Alexander Steenson Baird   143
Sergeant David 'Dave' Gallaher   145
Sergeant Percival 'Percy' Wright Storey   148
Corporal Maurice John Brownlie   150
Corporal Harold Vivian 'Toby' Murray   154
Lance Corporal Johnstone 'Jock' Richardson   156
Trooper James Hislop Parker MM, CBE   159

Trooper 'Dean' Eric Tristram Harper   165
Lieutenant Stanley Keith Siddells   168
Private Eric Leslie Watkins   175
Gunner Charlie Edward 'Bronco' Seeling   176
Staff Sergeant Major James Ryan   178
Sergeant John Victor Macky   179

1917   183
Private Robert Graham Tunnicliff   183
Corporal Cecil 'Ces' Edward Oliver Badeley   184
Second Lieutenant John 'Jack' Ormond/Tiaka Omana   187
Private Henry Gordon 'Abe' Munro   190
Driver Brian Verdon McCleary   191
Trooper Charles John Compton Fletcher   195
Private Frances 'Frank' Beresford Young   196
Trooper James 'Buster' Barrett   197
Second Lieutenant Robert Gemmell Burnett
    'Jimmy' Sinclair   199
Lance Sergeant Ernest 'Ernie' Henry Dodd   200
Corporal William Charles Francis   202
Sapper Sidney 'Sid' David Shearer   204
Private Leonard Frederick 'Jack' Stohr   206
Rifleman Alfred 'Alf' Lewis Kivell   207
Private David Lindsay 'Scotty' Baird   209
Driver William Richard 'Bill the Bull' Irvine   210
Private Samuel William Gemmell   216
Sapper John Alexander 'Peppy' Bruce   219
Private Donald Cameron Hamilton   225
Lance Corporal Alfred 'Alf' Henry Netherwood Fanning   227
Private Jack Douglas Shearer   228
Corporal Henry Morgan Taylor   229
Rifleman Lancelot Matthew Johnson   230
Private James Burt Douglas   232
Rifleman Richard 'Dick' William Roberts   233
Rifleman Alexander James 'Jimmy' Ridland   239
Gunner William Frankham Snodgrass   241
Corporal Francis 'Frank' Turnbull Glasgow   243

1918   249

Staff Sergeant Major Frederick 'Fred'
    Elder Birbeck Ivimey   249
Rifleman William Rognvald Fea   251
Corporal Alexander 'Alex' McDonald   258

After the War   263

Back Home   275

Bibliography   286
Acknowledgements   292
Index   293

The horror and strains that this war would impose on the human spirit were unknown, and never contemplated. There is an air of unreality in looking back on the sailing of the Main Body of the New Zealand Expeditionary Force [NZEF] in October 1914. It was more like the start of an international tour by an All Black team rather than soldiers embarking for a war.

– Christopher Pugsley, military historian

Another of New Zealand's best known footballers has made the supreme sacrifice after playing the game for the Empire on a wider field.

— widely published newspaper item noting the death of
1913 All Black Reginald Taylor

I left my best rugby years on the desert.

– Beethoven 'Beet' Algar, All Black captain (1920)

Introduction

The sad fate of 13 men who had worn the black jersey and silver fern in representing their country as All Blacks has been the subject of numerous newspaper and book mentions in the century since their deaths during World War I. Such is the place of rugby football in our country's psyche that those men are remembered today because of their place in the history of rugby, in a way that many of our other sporting champions tend not to be. This book sets out to record the contributions of All Blacks, both famous and forgotten, to the war effort of 1914–18. Some men were All Blacks, then soldiers. Others were soldiers, wearing the double silver fern of the New Zealand Expeditionary Force (NZEF), then All Blacks. Most spent much longer in khaki than they did in black.

For a long time I had wanted to know just how many All Blacks experienced Samoa, Gallipoli, Sinai and Palestine, the Western Front, base depots in England or training camps at home. In 1981, esteemed rugby historians Rod Chester and Neville McMillan published their first *Encyclopaedia of New Zealand Rugby*, containing potted profiles of every man who had taken the field as an All Black to that point. In it, the service records and decorations from World War I were included in the biographies of about a third of the 93 men included in this book. There were, of course, many more men whose war experiences were not mentioned, so in the last months of 2014 I began searching for them and, by the time of the centenary of the Anzac (Australian and New Zealand Army Corps) landings at Gallipoli, I had compiled the list that makes up this book.

Our rugby history is recorded in detail that is not matched anywhere in the world, which means that it is easy to chart the careers of our All Blacks. The history of our involvement in World War I, and the men and women who were among the 110,000 who served, is a different matter. While there has been a plethora of new material available in recent years (to which this author has been a contributor), official regimental or battalion histories written in the years after the Armistice were about the respective groups of men, rather than individuals. So, I have tried to, where possible, situate soldiers in the specifics of their service rather than just within the larger group.

At the same time, this book charts the effect of the Great War on our great game and the role our national sport played as recreation for servicemen. Where our soldiers went, so did rugby football. From there, Services rugby and war veterans were an integral part of the revival of the game and made up one of New Zealand's greatest-ever football teams, the 1924–25 'Invincibles'.

When it comes to army service, I have included the time men spent in training rather than just the time spent overseas. There are two reasons for this. Firstly, some men spent up to a year at Trentham and Featherston camps before sailing overseas. Thus, their time overseas would not be properly representative of their military service. Secondly, one or two conscripted men (towards the end of the war) spent time in camp and did not go overseas. That tells a story in itself of the final stages of the war, and to exclude them when they did serve their country would not be fair to their memory.

Today, rugby, like no other sport, is described in the terminology of war. At the beginning of the Great War, that escalating conflict was being described as 'the game'. The reality became something very different. My then 19-year-old grandfather wrote in his 1917 diary while fighting on the Western Front that the war was 'a living hell'. Today's players may talk about other players they would want 'to go to battle with' or 'have in the trenches' with them, but you never hear a rugby game being described as 'a living hell'.

The experiences of war were unspeakable for many who endured them, whereas the exploits of rugby players on the field have been told and retold for decades. I hope this book adds to the history of our national game and our consideration of the men who played and fought. As Richie McCaw said of Victoria Cross winner Willie Apiata, who was involved with the All Blacks during the 2015 Rugby World Cup, 'He's a good man to have around, and the boys enjoyed hearing a few of his stories and calming words. If you talk about being in pressure environments, he's probably been in environments that are a damn sight more pressurised than we end up with.'

Author's note

The enlistment date for each man is taken from his service record as the day he entered training camp. The rank is that attained by the end of the war and decorations are included. Some soldiers embarked with one group but ended up serving with others, and that is noted in the profiles. The playing records list known clubs, provinces and other selections, such as for the North Island or the short-lived North and South Island Country teams. Surprisingly, it was less than 20 years ago that the number of men who had played for the All Blacks was finally counted by rugby historian Ron Palenski. By the end of the 2015 season, 1,146 men had worn the black jersey, and a player's representative number has become an integral part of their biographical details.

In consideration of the descendants of the men herein, it was decided not to include some of the more intimate details of a number of medical conditions, illnesses or wounds.

Before the War

The All Blacks (as we now call them) had their inauguration in 1884 when a nationally selected side visited New South Wales, reciprocating a visit from their hosts in 1882. Following the formal establishment of the New Zealand Rugby Football Union (NZRFU) in 1892, there were further visits across the Tasman — in 1893 and 1897. New South Wales were welcomed again in 1894 and 1901, while Queensland undertook a tour in 1896.

Wellington was the home of the NZRFU, and, being in the middle of the country, was where the All Blacks assembled before sailing away on tour. A farewell match would often be played at Athletic Park against Wellington. When the All Blacks returned home a match would usually be staged in Auckland, too, before the players drifted off to their home towns.

In 1902, what would become the most prized and keenly contested trophy in New Zealand provincial rugby, the Ranfurly Shield, was gifted to the NZRFU by the then Governor of New Zealand, the Earl of Ranfurly. The NZRFU decided that the Shield would be a challenge trophy, and Auckland were chosen to be the first holders. They had been the champion side of 1902, as well as being unbeaten in 22 matches (although they had played 3 drawn games) stretching back to 1897. In 1903, Auckland were undertaking a southern tour, meaning that none of their seven games would be in Auckland, so the first defence was not until 6 August 1904.

Challengers Wellington won a tight contest 6–3 in front of 9,000 spectators at Alexandra Park. The gate-takings topped £500, then the highest amount for any inter-provincial match in New Zealand. A member of the victorious Wellington team, William Hardham, was the only New Zealand soldier to be awarded the Victoria Cross in the Boer War, where he served as a farrier. A well-known club player and Wellington representative between 1897 and 1910, Hardham would rise to the rank of major during World War I, serving with the Wellington Mounted Rifles at Gallipoli and in the Middle East. He donated a trophy in his name to the Wellington Rugby Union to be awarded to the winner of the second-division club competition.

So Wellington carted the Shield off to the capital and repelled Canterbury, Otago, Wairarapa and Hawke's Bay until Auckland won it back in 1905. Their first defence was the following year, and the Shield would stay in the Queen City until August 1913, when at their twenty-fourth defence they lost to Taranaki. This was the first great Shield era, and from the beginning the Shield clashes played an important role in allowing local spectators to see many All Black stars — and those in the making — in the flesh and at their best.

It wasn't until 1903 that the All Blacks played their first test match, against Australia in Sydney, winning 22–3. That game was part of an unbeaten 10-match tour. The following year, the first international was played in New Zealand when the Great Britain team was hosted at Athletic Park in Wellington. The All Blacks won 9–3.

The year of 1905 saw a monumental 35-game tour of the British Isles, France and North America, prefaced by a tour to Australia, in part to help the NZRFU fund the trip 'home'. After the amateur touring party (who all had to secure unpaid leave from their various jobs) had sailed from Wellington, an Australian team toured New Zealand, playing seven matches. They lost the only test, against what could be considered a third-string All Black side, 14–3.

Meanwhile, the All Blacks on the other side of the world, captained by Dave Gallaher, lost only one match on tour. That defeat was inflicted by Wales at Cardiff by 0–3. Some controversy was attached to the game, in the question of whether All Black centre Bob

Deans had in fact scored a try that had been disallowed by the referee. Regardless, the constancy of victories by the team, and the inventive and at times dazzling way in which they played the game, cemented rugby firmly in the national psyche. Not only that, their play on that tour became the stuff of legend.

Gallaher and teammate Harold 'Bunny' Abbott had both served in South Africa during the Boer War (1899–1901). Abbott, then a blacksmith, was a sergeant farrier who left with the Fifth Contingent and remained in South Africa for further service, joining the Eighth Contingent. Likewise, Gallaher extended his service, which began with the Sixth Contingent and ended with the Tenth and the close of the conflict.

All Black tours to Australia (namely New South Wales and Queensland) were undertaken again in 1907 and 1910 — with Boer War veteran Fred Ivimey playing one match for the All Blacks on the latter trip — while the Anglo-Welsh visited in 1908.

That same year Northern Union, or what we now call rugby league, was first played in New Zealand, twelve years after a group of rugby clubs in the north of England had broken away from their governing body and devised new rules of play.

Australia toured New Zealand in 1913 and played three tests, the first of which overlapped with the first-choice All Blacks departing for a tour of North America. That trip was very much an exercise in rugby football empire-building, promoting the game at a time when American football was losing spectators and players due to the high rate of injuries (and even deaths) being suffered on the field. When American football was banned for a time in the state of California, the California Rugby Union invited the NZRFU to send a rugby team to play a number of university teams.

In July 1914, the All Blacks set off for a 10-match tour of Australia.

The rugby year would begin after Easter with club football, followed by inter-provincial games at which the Ranfurly Shield could be at stake, then the inter-island game between North and South, which had begun in 1897 and was used as something of a trial by the All Black selectors, followed by matches for the All Blacks at home against a touring side or away.

The 14 inter-island matches up to and including 1914 (none had been played in the four years between 1898 and 1901) had seen the North win seven times, the South six, and 1904 was a 3–3 draw.

Peculiar to New Zealand football until 1930 was the 2-3-2 scrum (as opposed to the modern 3–4–1 formation), which consisted of two front-row hookers, then a single lock (who was very much in the build of the modern-day prop) flanked by two side-row forwards and behind them a back-row forward. The eighth man played as a wing-forward, a controversial position wherein he would feed the scrum but could remain in a blocking position to prevent the opposing halfback advancing as the ball was heeled through the scrum, as long as he had one hand on the scrum.

Kicking duties often fell to the forwards, too, with the hefty blokes booting the heavy leather ball with the toe of their boots (rather than the instep) at kick-offs or when taking shots at goal. The ball also spent a lot of time on the ground, with the forwards indulging in what were known as 'dribbling rushes'. The ball was dribbled ahead in a manner more akin to today's soccer. Many serious shin and ankle injuries were suffered by players when they attempted to counter-dribble, and defending players needed some mettle to try to go down on the rolling ball as a group of burly forwards wearing heavy boots thundered behind it.

Between 1883 and 1914, the All Blacks played 134 games, winning 126, losing 6 and drawing 2. Of the 134 games, 24 were internationals, with 20 won, 2 drawn and 2 lost. Remarkably, a third of the internationals had been played in Sydney, at the Sydney Cricket Ground or Sydney Sports Ground, while only one had been played in Auckland (Potter's Paddock) or Christchurch (Lancaster Park). Other venues were Athletic Park (Wellington), Tahuna Park and Carisbrook (Dunedin), Inverleith (Edinburgh), Landsdowne Road (Dublin), Crystal Palace (London), Cardiff Arms Park (Cardiff), Parc des Princes (Paris), Woolloongabba/Brisbane Cricket Ground (Brisbane) and California Field (Berkeley). Eden Park did not become the home of Auckland rugby until the beginning of the 1914 season, rugby having previously been based at Potter's Paddock in Epsom, which was renamed Alexandra Park in 1901.

At the time of the outbreak of World War I, the number of men who had represented their country in the national rugby football team, from James Allan in 1884 through to Lyn Weston in 1914, stood at 214.

From the mid-1800s, citizen-soldiers had made up a national Volunteer Force that could be quickly called up to defend New Zealand from an invading force and from the 1890s All Blacks were involved. One example is Samuel Cockroft (All Black #21), who represented New Zealand as a hooker on the 1893 tour to Australia and in 1894, playing a total of 12 games. After making his provincial debut in 1887 for Wellington, he had also played for Manawatu, Hawke's Bay and the North Island in 1894. Returning to Australia in 1895, he captained the 1896 Queensland side to New Zealand, then moved back to New Zealand and joined the New Zealand Permanent Artillery Force.

The Defence Force Act of 1909, similar to that introduced in England two years earlier, subsumed the volunteers who became known as the Territorial Army. It also introduced compulsory military training for junior cadets (aged 12–14), senior cadets (14–18) and territorials (18–21). Later legislative changes, in part prompted by a visit from Lord Kitchener in 1910, removed the junior cadets and extended the age of territorials to 25, from which men would be part of the Reserve for a further 5 years.

Englishman Major General Alexander Godley became the first Commandant of the New Zealand Military Forces, arriving in December 1910, and with great effect and speed a national defence force came into being. Four military districts were established: Auckland, Wellington, Canterbury and Otago. Each had infantry battalions and mounted rifles regiments. Within them were four sub-districts overseen by officers in the region. Regular meetings, training courses and appearances by cadets and territorials became a feature of communities throughout the country.

The Mounted Rifles were not intended to be a fighting force that charged on horseback with their swords drawn; such warfare was becoming obsolete. They were considered a branch of infantry who, thanks to their equine friends, could quickly get to the scene of a battle.

Edward Millton (All Black #16) was a forward in the very first New Zealand football team, that of 1884, which visited Australia. His brother, William, was captain of the side. Edward played football for Canterbury until 1886, and in 1889 took over Birch Hill Station in North Canterbury, which had been owned by his father, Captain William Millton. A keen horseman, Edward conducted mounted infantry training for those working on the station. He enrolled in the Cust Mounted Rifles in 1900, and in 1911 became Lieutenant-Colonel, 8th (South Canterbury) Mounted Rifles. (After World War I, in which workers and horses from Birch Hill served overseas, he was awarded the Colonial Auxiliary Forces Officers' Decoration for his long service. He later built a monument to the horses of the 8th Regiment New Zealand Mounted Rifles in the family cemetery.)

Godley, all too aware of rising political tensions in eastern Europe that could result in a wider war, requiring a New Zealand expeditionary force to support the British army, recruited 14 professional British soldiers as instructors, and the first training camp for permanent officers and non-commissioned officers took place at Tauherenikau in 1911. Battalion camps were held the following year, and a divisional camp in 1914.

Then, following the June 1914 assassination of Austro-Hungarian Archduke Franz Ferdinand, Austria-Hungary's declaration of war against Serbia, sabre-rattling by Germany and Russia, and finally Germany's declaration of war against France on 3 August 1914, the mobilisation of New Zealand soldiers to fight overseas became a reality.

1914

5 August 1914

Horowhenua were undertaking their first ever challenge for the
Ranfurly Shield, against Taranaki in Stratford. Approaching
halftime they were behind by 0–11. (They would eventually
lose, 3–14.)

Meanwhile, at 3 p.m. in Wellington, the Governor of New
Zealand, the Earl of Liverpool, announced from the steps of
Parliament that Britain had declared war against Germany. Premier
William Massey told the assembled crowd to 'Keep cool, stand
fast, do your duty to your country and your Empire.' Leader of
the Opposition Sir Joseph Ward added that 'Everyone recognises
the horrors of war. The time arrives in the affairs of nations as of
individuals when they must fight in the defence of honour and for
their existence, when the blessings of peace have to be foregone
and all the grief that the sacrifice of human life entails has to be
borne with fortitude and resignation. The loss of treasure will be
stupendous, but that is a secondary consideration.' In response, the
throng sang 'God Save the King' and 'Rule Brittania'.

Later that evening, Defence Minister James Allen announced
the requirement for a 7,000- to 8,000-strong expeditionary force.
Training camps were then established in Auckland (Alexandra
Park), Palmerston North (Awapuni Racecourse), Christchurch
(Addington then Sockburn Park) and Dunedin (Tahuna Park). The
initial force, commanded by Major-General Godley, consisted of a

Mounted Rifles Brigade (three regiments of three squadrons from Auckland, Canterbury and Wellington), an independent Mounted Rifles unit, a Field Artillery brigade, Infantry Battalion (of four battalions, one each from the four main centres and their regions), a Signal unit company, Field Ambulance, Veterinary Corps, Chaplains' Department, a company of divisional train, headquarters' staff and an Army Pay Depot. Personnel totalled 354 officers, 7,412 of other ranks and 3,753 horses.

At this time, the All Blacks were 8 matches through what would be an unbeaten 10-game tour of Australia. At halftime in their match against Metropolitan Union in Sydney, a sign reading 'War Declared' was posted on the scoreboard.

The call to arms had been sounded. Young men from around the country rushed to enlist. Among them would be past, current and future All Blacks.

10 August 1914

ENLISTED: **Sergeant Frederick Harold 'Skin' MASTERS MM (1895–1980)**

AGE AT ENLISTMENT: 18 years, 7 months, 21 days

ARMY NUMBER: 4/469

EMBARKATION: Wellington, 16 October 1914; Royal New Zealand Field Engineers, Main Body

LENGTH OF SERVICE: 3 years, 226 days

PLAYED FOR: Stratford, Tukapa and College Rifles clubs; Taranaki 1919–22; North Island 1919, 1922; New Zealand Trials 1921

ALL BLACK NUMBER: 254

POSITION: Lock

APPEARANCES: 1922; 4 matches

Born in Brunnerton, near Greymouth on the West Coast, but educated in Taranaki, Masters was living in Auckland, working as a chemist for Hutcheson Brothers and playing for the College Rifles Rugby Football Club when war was declared.

The club had been formed in 1897, and its players originally came from the College Rifles Volunteers, old boy cadets from the Auckland Grammar, King's and St John's colleges. The Volunteers had been established by Colonel Charles T. Major, with their coat of arms adopting aspects of the three educational institutions' insignia.

In the days after the declaration of war, the College Rifles club rooms were busy with men signing up for service, among them Masters. (One of his brothers also served and was wounded in action, while a second was ruled unfit for service.)

A Methodist, Masters left New Zealand as a sapper with the Main Body's Divisional Signal Company bound for Gallipoli in October 1914, and was part of the landing on 25 August 1915. At 10.30 a.m. he and his fellow sappers scrambled off a transport barge and, having retrieved their load of equipment from the infantrymen who were unloading it from the barge and carrying it further along the beach, set up a signal office 50 yards (45 metres) from the beach. With initial supplies of 8 miles (13 kilometres) of heavy D.1. wire and 2 miles (3 kilometres) of the lighter D.3. wire, as well as signalling equipment which included eight heliographs, eight Begbie lamps, two bicycles, signalling flags, telescopes and field glasses, they had a line set up to the Divisional Headquarters further along the beach within two hours.

For the next two days, setting up further lines of communication had nothing of the speed or success of the initial arrival. The Australians and New Zealanders struggled to hold and then establish positions on the poorly mapped coast under the dizzying assault of shrapnel bursts, bombardments and gunfire from Mustafa Kemal's forces. A concerted effort went into positioning the Anzac brigades, with the New Zealanders on the left, the 4th Australian Brigade in the middle, and the Australian Division on the right. A day later, cables were finally run between the Divisional Headquarters and the brigades, and then from there to the battalions who were still entrenching.

In his 1968 account of being a sapper, Roy Ellis (who was the recipient of a Military Medal) wrote that:

The Turks overlooked most of the country the wires ran over, so they were duplicated, and laddered wherever possible ... Corporal Harold Masters (Skin) and Harry Field had a hectic time running a line from the 4th Australian Brigade to the 1st Australian Brigade on their right. They were in full view of the Turks, who sniped at them as they ran from mound to shell-hole. Half way they decided to wait for an hour or so, and then managed to get across — Johnny Turk must have been having his evening meal. They received a cool reception from the Aussies however, who said they had no telephone, and nobody to man one. 'Skin' rang up Captain Edwards, who told him to man it for the night. It was a vital link in a desperate situation.

Masters was twice wounded in action on the Turkish peninsula, in May and then again during the August Offensive of 1915. He initially remained with his unit, but after the second incident was evacuated from Gallipoli and admitted to the military hospital in Pont de Koubbeh for treatment to an injured left foot. He rejoined his unit for the final two months of the Gallipoli campaign, then sailed for France in April of 1916.

In July of 1916 his actions during the Gallipoli campaign were mentioned in despatches: 'For distinguished and gallant services rendered during the period of Gen. Sir C. Monro's command of the Mediterranean Expeditionary Force.' Promotion to sergeant came in April 1917, while he was receiving hospital treatment for septic sores, which was indicative of the dire lack of hygiene being endured by soldiers in the field.

Wounded in action for the third time in mid-June 1917, at Messines, Masters suffered, among other things, injuries to his right hand.

While a patient in the No. 2 New Zealand General Hospital in Walton, he was awarded the Military Medal 'for acts of gallantry in the field'. In November 1917, he set sail for New Zealand aboard the hospital ship *Devonport*, and was discharged from the army in March 1918, as he was no longer physically fit for war service on account of wounds received in action. He returned to his family in Stratford, where he worked in the family hardware store.

A 15-stone (95-kilogram) lock, he was a big man for the time. His provincial debut came at the age of 24 in 1919, and he was part of the Taranaki team that drew 0–0 with the 1921 Springboks, proving himself a match for South African forwards who were considered 'giants' by the New Zealand public and press.

He captained the Stratford senior team, and was part of a sub-committee that established a list of club members who had been on active service for the Taranaki union's Honour Roll.

In 1922, Masters gained All Black honours as the only specialist lock in the 24-man team that played 5 games in Australia and 3 in New Zealand. One was a warm-up match against Wairarapa, and two were played on their return, against a Manawatu–Wellington XV and a New Zealand Maoris XV. He played in the first 'international' against New South Wales (the NZRFU was not awarding test caps for those matches), which was won 26–19, but he was not a part of the teams that lost the next two encounters with the Waratahs. Of those in the touring party, 11, including Masters, were never chosen for the All Blacks again.

Having retired from playing, Masters became a Taranaki selector and also served in 1936–37 as a seventh (co-opted) member of the national selection panel. A year later, he moved to Australia to take up a position with a public accounting firm, but he continued to be involved in rugby from junior level (coaching Sydney Grammar School) through to state and national level (as a selector for New South Wales and Australia).

11 August 1914

The first New Zealand Expeditionary Force (NZEF) of 1,400 men sailed from Wellington for German Samoa, under the command of Colonel Robert Logan. Their main objective was to capture a wireless station, seen by the British government as of strategic importance should Germany decide to make their island territory a Pacific base for soldiers and naval vessels.

ENLISTED: **Trooper Karl Donald IFWERSEN (1893–1967)**
AGE AT ENLISTMENT: 21 years, 7 months, 5 days
ARMY NUMBER: 1/672
EMBARKATION: Wellington, 15 August 1915; 3rd (Auckland) Regiment, Samoan Advance Party
LENGTH OF SERVICE: 2 years, 91 days
PLAYED FOR: College Rifles and Grammar Schools' Old Boys clubs; Auckland 1912, 1921–24; Auckland–North Auckland 1921
ALL BLACK NUMBER: 249
POSITION: Second five-eighth
APPEARANCES: 1921; 1 test

Such is the reputation of Ifwersen — still spoken of as one of the most gifted backs this country has produced — that it comes as a surprise to many to learn that he played only one game for the All Blacks, and that in a match where no points were scored.

Having been a member of the Territorial Force with the College Rifles, the young warehouseman of Danish extraction played for the Rifles club and was part of a junior side that won the Auckland competition two years in a row.

He was brought into the Auckland senior team in 1912, and played in all seven matches that season, including three Ranfurly Shield defences (in combination with two of his College Rifles teammates, Lynley Weston and Clifton Webb), kicking a goal in the first match, a 6–5 win over Taranaki. The following year he was lured to 'the league code', leaving Rifles for the North Shore Albions, who played at the domain at Devonport, which was also home to the North Shore Rugby Club.

In 1913, he played for the Auckland and New Zealand league teams. The latter went to Australia and, although he was the top points-scorer on tour, he did not make the test selections. International honours came the following year when England visited New Zealand.

Ifwersen began his war service as part of the Samoan Advance Party. Following his time in the Pacific, he re-enlisted with the 8th Reinforcements and then was transferred to the 11th Reinforcements, but was discharged from Trentham in April 1916, on account of being medically unfit.

Curiously, Ifwersen then turned out that season for his Grafton Athletic league club. At an Auckland club championship semi-final between City and Newton, a public ballot was taken to find the public's favourite player. Ifwersen attracted only 230 votes, well behind another code-convert, City's Albie Asher, and the winner, Scotty McClymont, who was captain of Ponsonby. Nonetheless, Ifwersen was a very popular footballer, whether under union or league rules, because he was exciting to watch. He was one of those players whose every touch of the ball had spectators leaning forward expectantly. A natural runner with ball in hand, he also possessed great vision and, where other players only saw tacklers in front of them, Ifwersen saw the space between the defenders. The best way for a five-eighth to create opportunities for the backs outside him is to run straight, and that was a trademark of Ifwersen's play. Combining this with great pace from a standing start, jinks and swerves, and a wonderful passing action, Ifwersen made the play of an inside back look ridiculously easy.

Eleven months after being rejected as not medically fit to continue his army training, he re-enlisted and entered Tauherenikau Camp (where he was promoted to sergeant) before leaving with the Mounted Rifles as part of the 26th Reinforcements in May of 1917. He was at the training camp of Moascar, Egypt, for little more than a month before being diagnosed with ancylostomiasis, or hookworm. Those infected can experience unrelenting abdominal pains, intestinal bleeding and severe diarrhoea, causing them to quickly become malnourished, dehydrated and anaemic. In the case of Ifwersen, dysentery was to be the scourge for him. After two months in hospital, he was invalided back to New Zealand at the end of December 1917.

At war's end, rugby unions were inviting former players who had turned to the professional game to return to their ranks. But Ifwersen refused to be drawn back into the union fold, captaining the national league side in three tests in Australia in 1919, and playing further internationals at home against the green-and-golds and England in 1920.

Finally, in 1921 his arm was twisted enough for him to return to union, and he joined the Grammar club. It was suggested in newspapers that he was to take part in the Possible versus Probables trial match in Wellington to decide the make-up of the first test team to face the Springboks in the first ever international between the two sides, but could not make his way to the capital as he was away from Auckland at the time. He did, however, captain an Auckland–North Auckland side against the tourists, scoring a try in the 8–24 loss.

A month later he was chosen for the third test team in the deciding match played at Wellington. The All Blacks had won the first test in Dunedin 13–5, but South Africa claimed the second at Eden Park by 9–5. There was a raft of changes to the All Blacks that even saw captain George Aitken dropped from the side. The new five-eighths combination of William Fea and Ifwersen was expected to create running for the All Black backs, but atrocious weather put paid to that. Rain pummelled Wellington the night before the game and was still constant by the time of kick-off, making the ground more pond than football field. Over 18,000 hardy fans braved the conditions for the series decider in what became known as the 'the umbrella test'.

Despite the weather, Ifwersen — who had overcome a poisoned leg in the days before the game — tried to remain inventive and nearly created a try for one of his wings when he cross-kicked behind the Springbok outside backs, but it was knocked away in a spray of water. After the match, some rugby writers found the greatest fault in his play was his lack of desire to go to ground to recover the loose ball.

A curious footnote to the game was that the referee, Mr A.E. Nielson, fell ill during the match and required medical attention immediately afterwards. Rumours quickly circulated among the departing spectators that he had died!

Ifwersen continued to turn out for Auckland until 1924. A lovely striker of the placed ball, he became the first New Zealand player to kick eight conversions in a game (which he did against a

Wellington XV in 1922, when he actually kicked nine in a game won 54–0).

Even though he hadn't been chosen for the All Blacks since that lone 1921 test, Ifwersen would probably have toured Australia in 1923 had he been available. Many in Auckland considered he would be included in the squad to tour Britain, Ireland, France and Canada in 1924–25. However, the English Rugby Union declared him ineligible as he had previously played rugby league. The Auckland Rugby Football Union protested, on the grounds that he had played an international match since reinstatement without any protest from the South African opponents then, and a number of other local unions supported them. However, the harsh edict remained.

The local hero had become something of a bureaucratic martyr, which led to unique scenes when a tour trial match between two combination teams (Hawke's Bay–Poverty Bay–East Coast–Bay of Plenty and North Auckland–Auckland–Thames–Waikato) met at Eden Park. During the game, Auckland inside back Vic Badeley was seriously injured, and some time was taken to remove him from the field. As the crowd waited and the replacement player from Waikato prepared to take the field, a chant began among a group of spectators and it quickly spread around the ground: 'We want Iffy! We want Iffy!'

Ifwersen was sitting in the stand watching the match, and such was the intensity of the chant that he was ushered to the changing rooms, where he donned a borrowed kit and took to the field. Not only did this delight his fans, but it seemed to have a positive effect on the team he joined. Trailing 0–6 before Ifwersen took the field, they played with new zest and ran away winners, 18–9.

If it could be said Ifwersen was ahead of his time in the way he played on the field, off the field he made the headlines for reasons that seem all too familiar in the lives of a number of modern, professional sportsmen. In 1919, he was co-respondent in a divorce trial with a Florence Hodder. Her husband, Gordon, won custody of the children, a decree nisi, and costs from Ifwersen and Florence of £53.

Ifwersen worked for a time in the family-owned warehouse, until he apparently strained his heart while lifting tins of paint.

He married, had a child, and spent a period of time unemployed before taking up a low-paid job as a commercial salesman for a cordial manufacturer.

In 1927 he was the subject of a bankruptcy hearing, at which it was noted that he owed £411 to unsecured creditors, including a large debt to a doctor; accusations of renting flats under assumed names were also revealed.

Securing a job with Cadbury, Fry and Hudson in Whangarei in 1934, Ifwersen moved north and became sole selector and coach of North Auckland. The province's biggest match during that time was against the 1937 Springboks (their final tour match of 17), to whom they lost 6–14.

In 1943, at the age of 50, Ifwersen ran into trouble over money again. He had been working as a meter reader for the Auckland Electric Power Board for three years, and it was discovered that in the two months before he left his position portions of customer payments had found their way into his pockets. He was charged with theft as a servant — which he admitted with great frankness — the amount totalling £66 (the equivalent of his wage for 10 weeks).

At trial, Ifwersen acknowledged the thefts, but insisted that he had always intended to repay the money. His defence lawyer, Mr W.W. King, spoke of Ifwersen's outstanding sporting career and that 'he found it difficult to settle down to make a serious living'.

The judge, Mr Justice Fair, showed some leniency to Ifwersen, who was already on probation for obtaining credit without disclosing he was a bankrupt. Justice Fair declared that, being the war years, men were of better use outside prison than in. A suspended sentence was imposed with conditions that he would serve three years' probation, had to repay the monies at the rate of £1 per week, accept work outside the city and 'refrain from entering hotels'.

The post-football life of Ifwersen was probably best summed up by the Official Assignee, Mr G.N. Morris, when he declared 'Iffy' bankrupt in 1927:

Ifwersen was almost a national hero, and through that notoriety it made it easier for him to get money. If I was satisfied his bankruptcy was a case of bad luck, I would have nothing to say. But I am not so sure. He said he had certain expectations, but I don't know about that. I don't think that there is a question of any criminal charge being made, but at the same time I am not convinced that the money was spent legitimately. In a way, I am sorry for him. He is a man who achieved fame too young, and that has contributed to the position in which he finds himself.

In 2000, Karl Ifwersen was admitted into the New Zealand Rugby League's Legends of League.

12 August 1914

ENLISTED: **Private Charles McLEAN** MM (**1892–1965**)
AGE AT ENLISTMENT: 21 years, 10 months, 23 days
ARMY NUMBER: 6/690
EMBARKATION: Lyttelton, 16 October 1914; Canterbury
    Infantry Battalion, Main Body
LENGTH OF SERVICE: 4 years, 245 days
PLAYED FOR: Westport; Buller 1919–23; South Island 1920,
    1921
ALL BLACK NUMBER: 221
POSITION: Loose-forward
APPEARANCES: 1920; 5 matches; 21 points (7 tries)

A sawmill-hand for the Westland Sawmilling Company at Ruatapu, McLean enlisted in Hokitika having previously undertaken compulsory military training in Westport as part of the 13th Regiment's A Company.

McLean saw action at Gallipoli before being evacuated and treated for dysentery in May 1915. On his return to the peninsula he suffered a gunshot wound to the back and buttocks in the August Offensive.

In April 1916, he was transferred to the 2nd Battalion of the Wellington Regiment for service in France, and in August 1916 was hospitalised suffering badly from the effects of poisonous gas which was being used as a weapon by both sides.

In the middle of February 1918, he joined the New Zealand Cyclist Corps. A Cyclist Company had been formed early in 1916, made up of men from Featherston Camp who had been part of the New Zealand Mounted Rifles (NZMR) reinforcements. Such a company had not existed in the Territorials, and a badge was designed featuring winged handlebars and front wheels, which was made and sold to those in the company. However, the men still wore NZMR shoulder titles.

In France, in July 1916, the company became part of the 2nd Anzac Cyclist Battalion. Colour patches — a two-inch (five-centimetre) white diamond overlaid with a one-inch (two-and-a-half-centimetre) red diamond — were to be worn on both sleeves.

A year later, new badges were issued bearing the words 'N.Z. Cyclist Corps' and featuring a wheel behind which were crossed rifles and on top of which sat a crown. Shoulder badges of 'NZCC' were also distributed.

The work of the corps was varied, and not too dissimilar to that of the engineers. One of their most exacting jobs was laying cables to the front lines up to eight feet (two-and-a-half metres) below the ground, so as to give them some protection from exploding shells. Much of that work was done at night. They repaired trenches, felled trees, carried out reconnaissance, were involved in advances as mounted troops and even, famously, held a section of the line at Vierstraat in April 1918, an action McLean was in the thick of.

The *Regimental History of the Cyclist Corps* records events:

On the morning of the 25th we received orders to move forward, and after reporting at Ouderdom received orders to 'stop a gap' near Vierstraat. We accordingly moved off (with the Mounted men) and reached Hallebast Corner amid awful shelling. We proceeded in small parties and on arrival at Swan and Edgar Corner, three enemy planes followed and peppered us with their M.G.'s. It was decided by Captain McHugh to leave the cycles on Vierstraat Road and proceed on foot in artillery formation. We were advised by a returning officer that the enemy had advanced in huge numbers. Our patrols soon reported this fact, and it was impossible to get within 600 yards of the line given us to take up, owing to the enemy having advanced in such numbers it was beyond our power to push him back. The Companies took up a defensive line astride the Vierstraat Road, filling a gap of 1,000 yards, and for four days held the enemy off with determination and with such success that he did not advance past the point where our men stopped him. That night small organised out-flanking movements gained us prisoners, from whom valuable information was obtained ... Up to the 28th instant the Battalion held on to their positions. The enemy made no further progress, although he made several attempts which were held off by our troops. On the evening of the 28th we were relieved, and moved into support slightly right of our original line. The position was open and swampy. The men dug in during the night and remained in these slit trenches for the next two days. During the daytime no movement was allowed, so the inevitable was to remain up to the knees in water, wishing for the night to speedily come so that cramped limbs could be revived. Our cycles were still on Vierstraat Road, and received a fair amount of shellfire and were badly damaged. On the nights of the 29th and 30th small parties of men who could be spared from the line were engaged in moving the cycles back to the rear, and this saved the total loss of several: as it was some 90 cycles were so badly damaged as to be totally useless.

McLean was awarded the Military Medal in the King's Birthday Honours 1918, 'for acts of gallantry in the field' which took place under intense shelling and machine-gun fire during the five days of fighting at Vierstraat.

In 1920, McLean was part of the South Island team that lost 3–12 to the North in Wellington, but nonetheless he was chosen for the All Blacks' seven-match tour that was at the invitation of the New South Wales Rugby Union (and was book-ended by three matches in New Zealand).

Remarkably, in the 27-year-old loose-forward's five appearances he scored seven tries: one in the 11–11 draw with Auckland; two in the 39–0 win over Manawatu–Horowhenua–Wanganui; two in the 70–9 win over the Manning River District side at Taree; and two against the Metropolitan Union in Sydney, a game won 79–5.

For some unknown reason, he was not part of the West Coast–Buller side that played the 1921 Springboks (losing 33–3), but a month later he captained Buller in their match at Westport against the New South Welshmen. The tourists won, 25–11.

When he retired from the game, McLean had made a mere 22 first-class appearances.

15 August 1914

The All Blacks finished their 10-match tour of Australia with a 22–7 win over Australia in Sydney. They had been unbeaten, scoring 246 points and conceding only 50. But, with war the focus of attention now, crowds at their final three matches had noticeably ebbed away. And with talk of German warships in the Pacific, their boat-trip home was a somewhat nervous one.

17 August 1914

ENLISTED: **Driver Andrew 'Son' WHITE (1894–1968)**
AGE AT ENLISTMENT: 20 years, 4 months, 27 days
ARMY NUMBER: 9/352
EMBARKATION: Port Chalmers, 16 October 1914; Otago
  Mounted Rifles, Main Body
LENGTH OF SERVICE: 4 years, 158 days
PLAYED FOR: Waikiwi and Christchurch clubs; Southland 1919–
  23; Canterbury 1927; South Island 1921, 1922, 1924
ALL BLACK NUMBER: 235
POSITION: Back-row forward
APPEARANCES: 1921–25; 38 matches, including 4 tests;
  3 games as captain; 48 points (10 tries, 9 conversions)

A farm labourer from Grassmere, White was the only brother to six sisters. His first three months of service overseas with the Otago Mounted Rifles were marred by intestinal illness. He fought at Gallipoli until diarrhoea brought about his evacuation to Lemnos, and then spent time in Malta recovering. He was then sent back to Egypt and Lemnos, but did not set foot on Gallipoli again.

At the Western Front he was transferred to the 4th Howitzer Battery of the New Zealand Field Artillery from the end of August 1916 through to May 1917, working as a driver. Then came an incident when he was charged with drunkenness, violently resisting a member of the military police, and being absent from his billet without permission. He was 'awarded' 21 days' Field Punishment No. 2, which meant three weeks of extra hard work and heavy duties.

When at Mailly-Maillet on the Somme in April 1918, he was admitted to hospital with cordite burns to his face and left wrist caused by 'an unexpected blaze' when he was throwing an armful of rubbish onto a fire when cleaning his billet. This was recorded as 'in performance of military duty and [he was] in no way to blame'.

In July 1918, he was deemed 'unfit' due to shell-shock, believed to have been caused by a shell exploding near him in October the previous year. He was still finding breathing painful following the fire, too. Diagnosed with hearing difficulties as a result of concussion (persistent tinnitus in both ears), shortness of breath and getting shaky and nervous when excited, a month later he was on his way back to New Zealand on the *Paparoa* for a recommended 12 months' rest, during which time the war ended.

At a medical board hearing in Invercargill on Christmas Eve 1918, he was diagnosed as 'greatly infirmed'.

A member of the Auckland Infantry, George Tuck, wrote of just what effects shelling could have on those who were amidst the barrage:

One shell landed in the trench near us and gave one of the healthiest and strongest of men shell-shock ... he was half-dazed and jumping at every sound of shell or gun. I told him he would have to go back. He said he wouldn't. That the boys would call him cold-footed. I insisted and after a moment's silence he broke down and wept. A nice thing shell-shock, when it makes a half-witted snivelling kid of a hard-headed man. And 'tis knowledge of these things and of seeing good men flinch from duty when their nerve is gone — that, hangs like a waiting beast on its opportunity, that darkens the soul of a man.

White's recovery once back in New Zealand appears to have been swift, which was most fortunate for him. Hundreds of men suffered from the effects of shell-shock for their rest of their lives, some easily identified as 'nerve cases' while others were sent back to the horrors of their youth mentally whenever they were startled by any sudden loud noise.

White turned out for the Southland football team a year after returning home, and played for the South Island in 1921, 1922 and 1924.

One of his great attributes as a player, in the days when forward packs would go on dribbling rushes with the ball at their feet, was White's control of the ball on the toe. He was considered to be without peer in that facet, as well as being highly regarded for the way he could discuss the more technical aspects of forward play with his fellow pack members.

Rugby writer Morrie Mackenzie, who covered more than 50 years of domestic football, wrote in a recollection of White that he could

> dribble the ball up to a much bigger opponent, trap it like a soccer player, and push it through his legs to retrieve it and go on again. When Son got the ball spinning end over end like a cross-cut saw, he was unstoppable and uncatchable. Two dribbles in which he took the ball half the length of the field in the inter-island match in 1924, one of which resulted in a try were as memorable as the brilliance of Nepia.

White's All Black debut came in the first test against the 1921 Springboks, and after appearances for the men in black over the next two seasons he was selected for the 1924–25 tour of Britain, Ireland, France and Canada. Once on board ship, White was elected part of the team's management committee, alongside manager Stan Dean, captain Cliff Porter, vice-captain 'Jock' Richardson and Maurice Brownlie.

He played 23 games on tour, including the tests against Ireland, England and France, and captained the side in 3 matches (Hampshire, Vancouver and Victoria).

18 August 1914

ENLISTED: **Sergeant Henry 'Norkey' DEWAR (1883– 1915)**

AGE AT ENLISTMENT: 30 years, 10 months, 5 days
ARMY NUMBER: 11/448
EMBARKATION: Wellington, 16 October 1914; Wellington Mounted Rifles, Main Body
LENGTH OF SERVICE: 357 days
PLAYED FOR: Melrose, Hawera, Star and Stratford clubs; Wellington 1907–08; Taranaki 1910–14; North Island 1913
ALL BLACK NUMBER: 175
POSITION: Back-row forward
APPEARANCES: 1913; 16 matches, including 2 tests; 3 points (1 try)

Foxton-born, Dewar began his first-class rugby career with Wellington in 1907, and was a member of the team that beat the touring Anglo-Welsh the following year, 19–13. Also in the side were three veterans of the 'Originals' tour — 'Mona' Thomson, the great Billy Wallace, and halfback Fred Roberts — as well as Victoria Cross recipient William Hardham. Dewar was part of the Melrose side that won the Wellington club championship in 1908.

Moving to Taranaki, he eventually settled in Stratford, where he worked as an iron-moulder for a Mr Harkness in Juliet Street. Playing for Taranaki, he was part of the amber-and-blacks' 1913 side that ended Auckland's Ranfurly Shield tenure, which had reached its eighth season. He scored a sensational try in the 14–11 win when he ran at pace onto an inside pass from one of the wings, Dick Roberts, and charged up the centre of the field, breaking tackles and plunging over between the posts.

The same year he turned out for the North Island in their resounding 0–25 loss to the South, and for his province against the touring Australians in their narrow 9–11 loss at the Sports Ground in New Plymouth. He was then chosen — just shy of his thirtieth birthday — for the All Blacks who were to tour North America.

The Australians had arrived just as the main group of All Blacks was about to depart for North America, so they, including Dewar, turned out against the visitors (who were wearing the light blue jerseys of New South Wales) at Athletic Park. An interesting feature of the match was that it was played in 20-minute quarters rather than 40-minute halves. In the Australian side were 'Twit' Tasker, who would be killed in action in 1918, and 'Doss' Wallach, who saw action at Gallipoli and France, won the Military Cross, lost both of his legs and ultimately died of his wounds.

The All Blacks won handsomely, 30–5, but four days later they sneaked home 19–18 against Wellington before boarding their ship, the *Willochra*, bound for North America. The vessel would later be used to transport troops during World War I.

On the North American tour, Dewar proved a highly valuable asset as a player of versatility, appearing in every forward position except for lock in 14 of the 16 games. He scored his only points for the All Blacks in the second match of the tour, a 31–0 victory over the University of California at Berkeley.

Dewar's All Black career looked set to continue when he was chosen for the 1914 tour of Australia, but he had to excuse himself from the prospective touring party as he could not get time off work for the six-week trip.

Having spent four years with the Wellington Naval Artillery Volunteers Machine Gun Section of the Wellington Mounted Rifles, Dewar was promoted to sergeant on 1 September 1914. The Wellington Mounted Rifles were based at the Awapuni Racecourse in Palmerston North under the command of Lieutenant-Colonel

W. Meldrum, and, following training there, of horses and men, they travelled down to Wellington for their departure. They were farewelled at Newtown Park, and then marched to the wharves for embarkation.

Aboard ship, a newspaper called *The Arrower* was printed and distributed throughout the seven-week journey. Like most such publications at the start of the war, its contents were a mix of levity and bravado:

We'll soon fall in 'midst battle din
To see what we can do.
With leaders right, we're bound to fight
And see the business through.
You'll find we stand for Maoriland
And play the game of war,
And fill the gaps for the British chaps
When the guns begin to roar

Dewar reportedly captained the Wellington Mounted Rifles in several football matches as the troops waited in Egypt for their call-up to the fighting, and he served four months as a gunner at Anzac Cove, where his old teammate William Hardham was severely wounded. The peninsula was to hold a more tragic fate for Dewar. (See page 77.)

24 August 1914

ENLISTED: **Lieutenant Charles Theodore GILLESPIE** MC
  (1883–1964)
AGE AT ENLISTMENT: 31 years, 2 months
ARMY NUMBER: 2/263
EMBARKATION: Wellington, 16 October 1914; Field Artillery,
  Main Body
LENGTH OF SERVICE: 4 years, 306 days
PLAYED FOR: Oriental; Wellington 1905, 1911–13; Wellington–
  Wairarapa–Horowhenua 1905; North Island 1913

ALL BLACK NUMBER: 196
POSITION: Lock
APPEARANCES: 1913; 1 test

At the age of 14, Gillespie began a three-year carpenter's apprenticeship for a Mr Albert Hoar in Masterton, earning £1 per week. When he had completed that, he took up a six-month contract at Whatatutu, Gisborne, working for station-holders the Tulloch brothers as a farm labourer. This paid him £2/8 per week. When that contract was complete he returned to Masterton, but it was March of the following year before he was again employed. In that instance it was a local drainlayer, Mr J. Cottiss, who hired the 19-year-old Gillespie as a labourer and paid him 8/- per day.

Gillespie became a member of the New Zealand Permanent Militia in 1902, and made his debut for the Wellington rugby team in 1905. The same year he played in the Wellington–Wairarapa–Horowhenua side that defeated the visiting Australians, 23–7, on a very greasy Athletic Park. Also in the combined side's forward pack were William Hardham and Ernie Dodd (who had played for the All Blacks in 1901 and would be called up to play in the one-off test against the visitors).

In 1907, Gillespie was, for some unknown reason, subject to a court of inquiry at the Alexandra Military Depot after scraping his shin(!) while on duty, carrying equipment down some stairs.

He was part of the 1910 Oriental team that won the Wellington senior club championship, and the following year he again donned the jersey of his province. A tall man at six feet two inches (188 centimetres), he played as a side-row forward for the North Island in July 1913.

Newspapers reported that he had been included in the touring team to North America in place of West Coaster Henry Atkinson, who had apparently withdrawn from the party. However, that report was quickly rebuffed by Atkinson, and it was discovered that his 'withdrawal' was a curious case of a fake letter being sent to the NZRFU.

So, as the main group of players set sail for California, 30-year-old Gillespie was a part of another All Black side that contested the second test against Australia at Carisbrook. The hosts won 25–13, but Gillespie, having played at lock, wasn't included in the team for the final test a week later.

When war broke out the following year, he was the first of 10 of the playing XV from that day to enlist.

Gillespie was promoted to second lieutenant in March 1916, and in June of the following year it was announced that he was to be awarded the Military Cross for 'conspicuous gallantry and devotion to duty in extinguishing burning boxes of ammunition under heavy hostile shell fire. Assisted by two of his men, he worked amidst the burning shells with total disregard of danger, thereby saving a large amount of ammunition and averting a heavy explosion.'

Late in October 1917, he reported that he had been slightly wounded at Passchendaele but remained on duty. Six months later, Gillespie was admitted to hospital suffering severe bronchitis as a result of having been gassed. He spent four months in hospital, but a month after his discharge was admitted again suffering from appendicitis. A month later he was promoted to lieutenant and then granted temporary rank of captain which he held until March 1919.

In December 1919, he attended a ceremony at Buckingham Palace where King George V presented him with his Military Cross. At the war's end he received a report on his service from Lieutenant-Colonel Symon, which stated that he was 'Very courageous, always has his men in hand. Reliable. Lacking in education for an Artillery Officer, but persevering. Suitable for Battery Captain for an Expeditionary Force but no higher.' After the war he remained with the regular army until 1938, when he retired to a farm outside Masterton.

In 1931, he was made a life member of the Oriental rugby club.

Three weeks after he passed away in January 1964, the War Pensions Board declared that his death was 'due to his war service with the forces', which raises the question whether Gillespie can be counted as the fourteenth All Black casualty of World War I.

29 August 1914

The NZEF arrived at Apia, where it quickly overwhelmed the German constabulary (of about a dozen men!) guarding the wireless station. A Lieutenant Cotton commandeered a German flag from the home of the governor, Dr Schultz, and legend has it that was one of the first flags, if not the first flag, taken by New Zealanders. When Cotton returned to New Zealand he presented it to the College Rifles football club, where it remained for many years until being returned to his family. In 2004, the club purchased it from Cotton's family and, after some careful restoration work from conservators at Auckland Museum, it now holds a proud place in the club's memorabilia.

9 September 1914

ENLISTED: **Lieutenant Colonel Henry Esau AVERY CMG, CBE, DSO (1885–1961)**
AGE AT ENLISTMENT: 28 years, 11 months, 6 days
ARMY NUMBERS: 5/420a, 11/420
EMBARKATION: Lyttelton, 16 October 1915; Canterbury Mounted Rifles, Main Body
LENGTH OF SERVICE: 4 years, 324 days
PLAYED FOR: Wellington College Old Boys; Wellington 1905–06, 1908–10; North Island 1910
ALL BLACK NUMBER: 170
POSITION: Wing-forward
APPEARANCES: 1910; 6 matches, including 3 tests

Upon leaving school, Avery worked as an accountant and company secretary in partnership with his brother at offices in Wellington's Featherston Street. He served with the D Battery of the New Zealand Field Artillery Volunteers, commencing as a gunner in July 1904, and winning a special prize as the best gunner in the battery. Over the next four years he progressed through the ranks as a bombardier, corporal, sergeant and sergeant-major. He gained certificates in gun-laying, gunnery, signalling (Morse and semaphore) and field range finding. He also had a good knowledge of field sketching, and passed the examination to become a lieutenant in March 1910.

In May 1910, he applied for appointment as an adjutant in the New Zealand Defence Force. Included in his application were two testimonials written for him in December 1901. The first was from the headmaster of Wellington College, Mr J.P. Firth, who wrote of Avery — who had gained a scholarship to the college to complete his schooling — that 'his conduct has been excellent throughout; his ability is distinctly good and he has worked to the entire satisfaction of his masters. He is now sitting for the Matriculation examination of the University of N.Z. I have no doubt of his success.'

The second referee was the Reverend Richard Coffey, who had been the vicar of St Mark's Church in Wellington. Coffey (who had since passed away) had written: 'I have much pleasure in testifying to the excellent moral character borne by Henry E. Avery, who has been brought up almost under my eyes. His parents are respectable citizens and one of his brothers is doing good service in the Post Office.'

A handwritten note in his file added:

This is a most promising officer who has passed through each grade of his battery. He is hardworking and reliable. His battery officers speak highly of him and my personal knowledge of him points to him as being one of the best types of officer produced. I am sure his inclusion in the staff would be most beneficial to efficiency.

A month later, having been called up as a replacement for the All Blacks' tour to Australia, he wrote to the commanding officer of the Wellington District: 'Herein I beg to ask for leave of absence from the Dominion for three weeks. I am going to Sydney on Friday 10th inst to join the NZ Football team there and will be leaving Sydney on the return trip on June 25th.'

This stalwart and eventual life member of the Wellington College Old Boys club (whose 1909 senior team also included Bernard Freyberg, who would win a Victoria Cross in World

War I and command the 2nd NZEF in World War II) had played for Wellington between 1905 and 1910. He was one of nine Wellington players in the 1910 North Island side, and when the All Blacks were about to depart for their seven-match tour of Australia (taking in Sydney and Brisbane) he captained Wellington against the All Blacks in their traditional farewell fixture. The match was played at Athletic Park on a Friday afternoon and was won by the national side, 26–17.

Avery received a very late call-up to join the team following a handful of withdrawals, and arrived in Sydney on the day of the first tour match, against New South Wales. He proceeded to play in all of the remaining six games, three of which were internationals against Australia. All three tests were played in Sydney. The first was won 6–0. The second was lost 0–11, the first-ever win for Australia over the All Blacks. The third was won convincingly, 28–13.

Avery's rugby career came to an end when he was only 25, upon him receiving a permanent appointment to the Defence Force in January 1911. The position, which paid him an annual salary of £250, saw him posted to Nelson with the rank of captain, as an adjutant for the Canterbury Mounted Rifles.

In April 1913, he married Alice Draper in Blenheim, and a son, Henry, was born in July 1914.

Two months after the declaration of war — with young Henry a mere three months old — and having been put in charge of requisitioning duties for Colonel Russell's Mounted Rifles Brigade, Avery sailed from Lyttelton aboard the *Athenic* with the Main Body of the Canterbury Mounted Rifles, bound for Suez.

During the 260 days Avery spent at Lemnos and Gallipoli, he was promoted to major in the Army Service Corps and received the Distinguished Service Order in June 1916, for his work as senior supply officer. The commendations published in the *London Gazette* stated:

> November 26–30 1915. During a period of very bad weather when roads were nearly impassable for mules it was only by constant supervision and the most careful arrangement that a supply of water and food was maintained.

December 18–19 1915. Also during the evacuation of the Anzac position, Major Avery, though thrown on his own resources, by his skilful manipulation of the means at his disposal and his untiring efforts, kept the troops of the division supplied up to the end. This officer has done very good work ever since he took up the work of Senior Supply Officer, and is deserving of special mention.

The 'very bad weather' began as a southwesterly gale which grew in force and sank several ships and barges. On shore, troops sought whatever shelter they could find from thunderstorms. Trenches flooded, which saw dozens of men drown, while mud slips and cascading rivers of water washed down the hills, collecting anything in their paths. Snow then fell and overnight temperatures plunged to below zero. Soldiers unable to find space huddling in dugouts cut from the faces of the hills froze to death, while thousands of others suffered frost-bite.

The evacuation from the peninsula three weeks later was an exercise in deception, as the Australian and New Zealand forces made their night-time retreat while giving the Turkish army the impression that more troops were actually landing. Crude but clever devices were attached to rifles left in trench positions to make them self-firing. The last to leave were several officers and 24 men from the Mounted Rifles, early on the morning of 20 December 1915.

The following month, Avery was again mentioned in despatches: 'For distinguished and gallant services rendered during the period of Gen. Sir C. Monro's command of the Mediterranean Expeditionary Force.' In January and June of 1917, while serving as assistant adjutant and quartermaster general at Divisional Headquarters in France, he was twice more mentioned in despatches.

In June of 1919, having served for 1,088 days at the Western Front, he was made an Additional Member of the Third Class, or Companion of the Chancery of the Order of St Michael and St George, 'for services rendered in connection with military operations in France and Flanders'.

As quartermaster general for the New Zealand Division, who were part of the British army of occupation in Germany, he was mentioned in despatches for the sixth time by Field Marshal Sir Douglas Haig 'for distinguished and gallant service and devotion to duty during the period 16–9–18 to 15–3–19'.

At the conclusion of the war he continued to work for the regular army and represented New Zealand at the War Office in London during 1920–21. On his return to New Zealand he was quartermaster general until his retirement in 1924.

Having secured a Ford franchise, he then established Avery Motors, which quickly became one of Wellington's largest and best-known dealerships. He served as President of the Motor Trade Association, Vice President of the Rongotai Boys' College Parents Association, and continued to be involved with veterans' affairs, holding the office of President of the Wellington Returned Services Association from 1929 to 1933.

Avery was general manager of the 1940 Centennial Exhibition before again returning to army service as quartermaster general at Army Headquarters in Wellington. In 1943, he was promoted to brigadier.

After World War II, he ran Avery's Book Depot in Eastbourne.

10 September 1914

Wellington won the Ranfurly Shield from Taranaki, 12–6, at the Stratford Showgrounds. It would turn out to be the last such match until 1919.

14 September 1914

ENLISTED: **Sergeant Hubert Sydney 'Jum' TURTILL (1880–1918)**
APPROXIMATE AGE AT ENLISTMENT: 34 years
ARMY NUMBER: T6959/426516

EMBARKATION: unknown; 422nd Field Company, Royal
    Engineers
LENGTH OF SERVICE: unknown
PLAYED FOR: Christchurch; Canterbury 1902–03, 1905; South
    Island 1903, 1907
ALL BLACK NUMBER: 139
POSITION: Fullback
APPEARANCES: 1905; 1 test

Born in England, the tubby boy initially nicknamed 'Jumbo'
moved to Christchurch with his parents when he was four years
old. His only match for the All Blacks was in 1905 when, with the
Originals on the boat to Britain, another national team was fielded
against Australia in Dunedin. Also in that side, which was won
14–3, were Colin Gilray and Ernie Dodd.

Turtill switched to Northern Union and played in the 'All
Golds' tour to Britain and Australia in 1908. In England, he was
spotted by club scouts, and in 1909, a year after marrying Edith
Hancock at St Mary's Church in Riccarton, the couple and young
son, Alan, moved to Lancashire, with Turtill having signed with
the St Helen's rugby league club. More than 10,000 fans packed
the Knowsley Road ground for the match against Hull Kingston
Rovers to see Turtill's first appearance for the club on 2 September.
He would go on to become the first player from the club to kick
more than 50 goals in a season, and he finished his career having
landed 200 goals and scored 3 tries for 409 career points.

The St Helen's club headquarters was the Talbot Hotel, where
players changed for matches before being taken to the ground on
a horse-drawn wagon. After time as a tobacconist, Turtill himself
became proprietor of a hotel named the Nelson Hotel, and the last
of his 137 appearances for St Helen's was against Warrington in
February 1914.

Across countries and sporting codes, the pipe-smoking Turtill,
who always looked as though he was about to break into a grin,
was renowned for his sportsmanship and was hugely popular.

The exact date of Turtill's enlistment is not known, due to
many English service records having been damaged or lost during

World War II, but it could not have been later than 14 September 1914. The date of embarkation and exact length of service are not on record either. He initially had the service number of T6959, indicating that he had enlisted with a Territorial Force Field Company — the 422nd Company — which in November 1915 merged with the 55th 2nd West Lancashire Division.

As a Royal Engineer he would have seen action at Hallencourt, Bretencourt, Guillemont, Ginchy, Ribemont, Flers-Courcelette and Morval. In 1917, his regiment spent the first six months of the year in the Ypres salient. He survived the battles of Pilckem Ridge and Menin Road Ridge, until the 55ths were relieved by the 39th Division. They then moved south to an area near Cambrai, which, on 30 November 1917, was the scene of a devastating tank attack by the Germans. Turtill survived that epic battle and, after a period of instruction at Bomy, near Fruges, returned with his regiment to the frontline at Givenchy around March 1918. A month later, the German Army began their Spring Offensive.

16 September 1914

Prime Minister Massey announced that a Maori Contingent of 200 men would be sent to Egypt. They were later formed into two companies: A, made up of four platoons of soldiers from Northern Maori and the West Coast-South Island; and B, also consisting of four platoons, from Rotorua and the East Coast.

14 October 1914

Due to the presence of two German cruisers in the southern Pacific, the departure of the Main Body, with men and horses from Christchurch and Dunedin having been made to encamp in Wellington, was delayed until the arrival of the HMS *Minotaur* and the Japanese battleship *Ibuki*, which were to accompany the 10 transport ships: *Arawa*, *Athenic* (on which the Anglo-Welsh footballers had sailed to New Zealand in 1908), *Orari*, *Ruapehu*,

Waimanu, Maunganui, Hawke's Bay, Star of India, Limerick and *Tahiti*. The wait was hugely frustrating for the soldiers who were raring to see action.

The same month, Trentham Camp was established by the Ministry of Defence as the central training camp for all recruits.

20 October 1914

ENLISTED: **Second Lieutenant Hohepa 'Harry' JACOB MC (1894–1955)**
AGE AT ENLISTMENT: 19 years, 11 months, 4 days
ARMY NUMBER: 16/268
EMBARKATION: Wellington, 14 February 1915; A Company, 1st Maori Contingent
LENGTH OF SERVICE: 4 years, 197 days
PLAYED FOR: Levin-Wanderers; Horowhenua 1911, 1913–14, 1919–25; Manawatu–Horowhenua 1921, 1922, 1924; Manawhenua 1921, 1922, 1924–27; North Island 1919–21, 1923; New Zealand Maoris 1913–14, 1922–23; New Zealand Trials 1924; Wellington–Manawatu–Horowhenua 1925
ALL BLACK NUMBER: 220
POSITION: Wing-forward/loose-forward
APPEARANCES: 1920; 8 matches; 25 points (7 tries, 2 conversions)

In a centennial history of the Horowhenua Rugby Union titled *In Jacob's Shadow*, the noted rugby historian Clive Akers described Jacob as 'A gifted athlete, inspiring captain and a gentleman[,] he is perhaps the most outstanding sportsman the region has ever produced.' That was written in 1993, one year before the audaciously talented Carlos James Spencer had made his debut for the province while still at Waiopehu College and set a record for most individual points in a match, with 22 versus East Coast. Much had changed in the world of rugby between Jacob retiring in 1927, having played 101 first-class matches, and Spencer appearing. So much so that Spencer's playing career began as an amateur with his province and ended as a seasoned professional with South African Super Rugby side the Lions. In between, he starred for Auckland in 93 games, the Blues in 96 matches and the All Blacks in 44 games, including 35 internationals.

Jacob enlisted for service shortly before his twentieth birthday and departed from New Zealand four months later, bound for Gallipoli with the A Company of the Maori Contingent. Captain Buck of the Contingent wrote in his diary of an act of heroism by Jacob during the disastrous three days of the assault on Chunuk Bair: 'Sergeant-Major Hill of A Company Maoris, was carried over by Sergeant Jacob but was practically dead when he arrived, shot through the spine with shrapnel.'

Fighting at the Western Front, Jacob was promoted to second lieutenant in April 1918. He was awarded the Military Cross in the King's Birthday awards of 1919 for 'distinguished service in connection with military operations in France and Flanders'. (It was presented to him by the governor-general at a public service in Levin two years later.) The same year he played in the Pioneer Battalion football team, which played a series of matches around New Zealand.

The Manawatu and Horowhenua unions amalgamated between 1925 and 1932, but continued to play each other annually as a trial for the combined team. Jacob captained the side until his retirement at the end of the 1927 season, and had the honour of receiving the Ranfurly Shield following the union's 'provisional shield challenge' success over Wairarapa in 1927. (Wairarapa had won the Shield from Hawke's Bay 15–11, then lost it back to them a month later, 21–10. But a player ineligibility issue surrounding Jacob's old Pioneer football teammate Wattie Barclay meant the Appeal Council of the NZRFU awarded the latter match to Wairarapa.) Subsequent Ranfurly Shield challenges for the 'log o' wood' from Taranaki and Wanganui were repelled, before a strong Canterbury team, with a backline boasting five All Blacks, defeated the determined Manawhenua side 25–6.

At the end of Jacob's playing days, he remained heavily involved in the union and his club, of which he was president in 1929, and was inaugurated as a life member in 1948. He also took up the whistle and refereed for a decade.

When arthritis began to trouble Jacob, he ceased farm work and took on the role of custodian of the Otaki Maori Racing Club. At the outbreak of World War II, his application to be an army training officer was rejected on medical grounds. He was, however, able to take up a position as a Maori recruiting officer.

After the war, and suffering evermore with painful arthritis, he was well known as a welfare officer with the Department of Maori Affairs in Levin. Harry Jacob died in 1955. A year later his wife Lucy (née Winiata) was awarded the MBE for her own tireless community service. One of the Jacobs' four children, Ranfurly ('Ran'), played as a halfback for Horowhenua, Wellington, New Zealand Universities and New Zealand Maoris. While studying in Sydney he was selected for a Sydney Metropolitan XV to play the touring British Lions, and the next year turned out for an Australian XV against the All Blacks in Melbourne.

The Harry Jacob Memorial Trophy for the Best and Fairest remains a coveted senior award in Horowhenua club rugby.

SLING CAMP

With news of the outbreak of war, a small number of New Zealanders who were in England at the time signed up for service. They were assembled at Sling Camp, where they went about the business of construction, preparing for the expected arrival of soldiers from New Zealand bound for France. They worked closely with a similar group of ex-pat Canadians. In the course of their work, competition raised its head, and the two groups competed on the drill ground, undertaking platoon and ordering drills, for a challenge cup. They also took to the field in a game of rugby, the Kiwis winning, 3–0.

3 December 1914

The NZEF Main Body arrived in Egypt at the port of Alexandria. While the men had expected to continue to France, Winston Churchill had devised a plan to secure the vital shipping route of the Suez Canal. Allied forces, including the New Zealanders and Australians, would attack Turkish forces at the Dardanelles.

From Alexandria, the Kiwis entrained to a large camp which had been set up at Zeitoun, a short distance from Cairo. Training began — hard training at that — with hours of attack drills, musketry, trench-digging, route-marching with full packs, begun in the cool of morning and ending under the blaze of the hot afternoon sun.

14 December 1914

ENLISTED: **Driver Charles Napoleon 'Nipper' (or 'Nap') KINGSTONE (1895–1960)**
AGE AT ENLISTMENT: 19 years, 5 months, 12 days
ARMY NUMBER: 2/1283
EMBARKATION: Wellington, 17 April 1915; New Zealand Field
    Artillery, 4th Reinforcements
LENGTH OF SERVICE: 4 years, 160 days
PLAYED FOR: Grafton and Clifton clubs; Auckland 1920;
    Taranaki 1921; North Island 1921; New Zealand Trials
    1921
ALL BLACK NUMBER: 231
POSITION: Fullback
APPEARANCES: 1921; 3 tests

The brown-haired, blue-eyed blacksmith from Mount Eden was the essence of a fullback and was almost faultless as a defender. He covered ground from one side of the field to the other stealthily, was sure under high kicks in any conditions, and his own personal safety was never a consideration when bringing ball-carriers to the ground.

Serving with the Field Artillery, Kingstone fractured his collar-bone while playing rugby in a brigade tournament in March 1917. After treatment in England and retraining with the New Zealand Field Artillery Reserve at Aldershot, he returned to the front serving with the 5th Battery.

He suffered another accidental injury in November 1918, while lifting a container of boiling water from a fire. The water spilt on his legs and feet, causing burns, but the incident was described on his service record as 'a trivial matter'.

Kingstone played in all three tests against the touring South Africans in 1921. (The second test of the series was the first to be played at Eden Park, seven years after the Auckland Union had moved there from Alexandra Park.) After his play in Taranaki's 0–0 draw with the tourists, in which he gave a great display of line-kicking and devastating tackling, there was no dispute that he was the best fullback in the country.

A car accident in 1922 cut short Kingstone's rugby career, but he did make a return to the sports field. He represented Taranaki at cricket as early as 1924, when he turned out against the touring New South Wales side. He played as wicket-keeper for The Rest of New Zealand against a national XI in a three-day match at the Basin Reserve in 1927. Batting at number 10, he top-scored for The Rest with 43 out of a total of 267. The New Zealand side replied with 369, which included centuries to Charlie Dempster and Roger Blunt.

For Taranaki's Hawke Cup fixtures in 1926–27, Kingstone captained the side and in 1928 turned out against the touring Australians, a side that contained the likes of Vic Richardson, Clarrie Grimmett, Bill Ponsford and Bill Woodfull.

In 1930 when the MCC (Marylebone Cricket Club) side touring the country played Taranaki at Pukekura Park, Kingstone had the satisfaction of catching the great Duleepsinhji (the 'Wisden Player of the Year' that year) for two.

ENLISTED: **Gunner Peter WILLIAMS (1884–1976)**
AGE AT ENLISTMENT: 26 years, 7 months, 22 days
ARMY NUMBER: 2/1221

EMBARKATION: Wellington, 17 April 1915; New Zealand Field
   Artillery, 4th Reinforcements.
LENGTH OF SERVICE: 1 year, 89 days
PLAYED FOR: Alhambra; Otago 1908, 1910–14; South Island
   1912–14
ALL BLACK NUMBER: 184
POSITION: Front-row forward
APPEARANCES: 1913; 9 matches, including 1 test; 3 points
   (1 try)

Williams possessed the ideal build for a front-row forward of his
day standing five feet six inches (168 centimetres) and weighing
160 pounds (73 kilograms). His consistent play for Otago, for
whom he debuted in 1908, was acknowledged by his selection
for the South Island side three seasons in a row, beginning in
1912.

The following year he became an All Black, playing in the
first test against the visiting Australians, before leaving for North
America with the first-choice All Blacks. A number of rugby
scribes could not fathom how Williams had made the side ahead
of Southland's Jimmy Ridland. Nonetheless, on tour he played in
8 of the 16 games.

He was again chosen for the All Blacks in 1914 to tour
Australia, but had to withdraw due to work commitments.

Williams was a wire-worker employed by Chas. Bills & Co
in Dunedin's George Street. His war service was cut short due to
the disabling effects of dysentery and enteric fever contracted in
Egypt. While convalescing, he contracted typhoid and was sent
back to New Zealand in September 1915, only six months after
initially departing. The proceedings of the medical board which
recommended his discharge in March 1916 noted that he had
not been at Gallipoli and that he was by then 'quite well' but
that he occasionally felt 'a funny feeling in his neck. Undoubtedly
neurotic.'

After the war he took to farming and lived out his days at
Mosgiel.

21 December 1914

ENLISTED: **Captain John Elliott 'Jock' CUTHILL (1892–1970)**

AGE AT ENLISTMENT: 22 years, 3 months, 27 days

ARMY NUMBER: 8/1724

EMBARKATION: Wellington, 17 April 1915; Otago Infantry Battalion, 4th Reinforcements

LENGTH OF SERVICE: 2 years, 325 days

PLAYED FOR: Taieri and University clubs; Otago 1911–14; South Island 1913; New Zealand Universities 1913

ALL BLACK NUMBER: 174

POSITION: Fullback and wing

APPEARANCES: 1913; 16 matches, including 2 tests; 31 points (7 tries and 5 conversions)

Scottish-born Cuthill (hence his nickname) came to New Zealand with his family as a four-year-old, and was later schooled at Otago Boys' High School, where he had three years in the First XV and the same length of time in the school's cadets. Upon leaving school he enrolled at Otago University and joined the 4th Regiment of the Otago University Training Corps.

Broad-chested, standing six feet (183 centimetres) tall and weighing 182 pounds (83 kilograms), he had a build comparable to many of the forwards of the day. When he captained the New Zealand Universities team in 1913 on a short tour of Australia, the Sydney *Daily Telegraph* wrote glowingly of his play:

Much of the spectacularity of the game on the Black side was provided by the light-haired Cuthill, the unassuming University captain. He has got beautiful 'hands', he takes the ball like an angel, and he kicks quickly, strongly and irritatingly far. He is a powerful chap, much more so than he looks, runs with his knees well up and his legs in a swervy fashion, which makes it puzzling for the enemy how they are going to take him, and, above all in these days of machine-like running and passing to the side, he goes straight ahead, keeps the fun going merrily, and to the unbounded admiration of his own side and the envy of the others, gets his wings into delightful scoring positions.

In the 1913 inter-island match, won by the South 25–0, Cuthill scored 10 of the team's points through a try, a goal from a mark, and 2 conversions. Having just turned 21, he was duly chosen to play the first test against the visiting Australians in Wellington (a match won 30–5) before departing with the All Blacks to North America. Although known as a centre, he turned out at fullback in 10 of his 14 tour appearances, including the lone test against All America.

The following year he was asked to captain the All Blacks on their 1914 tour of Australia, but chose to turn the honour down to concentrate on his university studies (having had to seek a leave of absence to tour the previous year).

Highly regarded on and off the field, Cuthill enlisted for service at the end of 1914 and passed the examination to become commissioned as a second lieutenant. He sailed with the Otago Infantry Battalion as part of the 4th Reinforcements in April 1915. On arrival in Egypt, he qualified as a Lewis gun instructor, before moving off to the Gallipoli peninsula.

The Lewis gun was a new addition to the Allies' military hardware. It was gas powered and fired .303 bullets from a circular 'pan' that could hold 47 or 97 bullets and sat atop the gun. It eventually replaced the heavier, more awkward Vickers machine gun.

When the operation to take Chunuk Bair was under way, Cuthill reportedly noticed enemy movement to the extreme right of his battalion's position. With great stealth, he made his way forward to where he could observe large numbers of Turkish soldiers readying themselves for a surprise attack. Cuthill made his way back to his unit and spread word of his observation, giving the New Zealand soldiers time to prepare for the Turkish assault. Despite the forewarning, Cuthill himself was wounded as the battle raged later in the day, suffering a bullet wound to the buttocks.

Recovered and with the division in France, he served as a Lewis machine-gun officer with the 2nd Otago Infantry Battalion at the Somme. On 15 September 1916, he was originally listed as missing presumed wounded before being found four days later. He had suffered a gunshot wound to his right shin-bone, which, though it had shattered part of the bone, had not severed it.

While incapacitated in the Royal Herbert Hospital in Woolwich, he was mentioned in despatches in January 1917 and promoted to the rank of captain.

In June 1917, he underwent further surgery at the No. 1 New Zealand General Hospital. A piece of dead bone was removed from his wound, which by this stage was nine months old. The initial diagnosis was that movement of the knee was very limited and the muscles around the wound were 'much wasted'. His post-surgery recovery noted that the wound remained very tender to touch and Cuthill could not walk without pain or a limp.

His active service over, he sailed from England on the hospital ship *Marama* in August 1917, destined for Dunedin and outpatient treatment. In November 1917, New Zealand newspapers were carrying an item about Cuthill having been 'struck off strength', meaning he had been removed from his unit on account of the injury. 'According to what a Home writer had to say a few months ago, the New Zealand [Universities] skipper will never again play football. At that time he was reported to be limping around London, wearing his old smile and retaining a shrapnel souvenir in his leg.'

Two years later, while working as a grain broker and general commission agent, he was still receiving treatment for the injury, at Dunedin Hospital. Fluid was still seeping from the wound, and X-rays showed that there was serious infection in the bone, so further surgery was undertaken and more of the tibia bone removed.

Despite his disability, he was absorbed into the Territorial Force, joining the 2nd Battalion of the Otago Infantry Regiments in 1921, but was posted to the Retired List in 1926 as he was deemed to be one of those officers of the Reserve who had 'been unable to attend Camps or have taken no active interest whatever in the welfare of their units'.

At the outbreak of World War II he enlisted to serve with the Home Guard, and in October 1941 was appointed to the rank of major in command of the Invercargill Battalion. In the middle of 1943 he resigned and was discharged as being medically unfit.

ARMY DISCIPLINE

Soldiers were punished for all manner of offences, from failing to appear on parade through to refusing to fight. The manner in which they were disciplined fell under the following 'Rules for Field Punishment' in Section 44 of the *Army Act*:

1. A court-martial, or a commanding officer, may award field punishment for any offence committed on active service, and may sentence an offender for a period not exceeding, in the case of a court-martial three months, and in the case of a commanding officer twenty-eight days, to one of the following field punishments, namely:—

   Field Punishment No. 1
   Field Punishment No. 2.

2. Where an offender is sentenced to field punishment No. 1, he may, during the continuance of his sentence, unless the court-martial or the commanding officer otherwise directs, be punished as follows:—

   A. He may be kept in irons, i.e., in fetters or handcuffs, or both fetters and handcuffs; and may be secured so as to prevent his escape.

   B. When in irons he may be attached for a period or periods not exceeding two hours in any one day to a fixed object, but he must not be so attached during more than three out of any four consecutive days, nor during more than twenty-one days in all.

   C. Straps or ropes may be used for the purpose of these rules in lieu of irons.

   D. He may be subjected to the like labour, employment, and restraint, and dealt with in like manner as if he were under a sentence of imprisonment with hard labour.

3. Where an offender is sentenced to field punishment No. 2, the foregoing rule with respect to field punishment No. 1 shall apply to him, except that he shall not be liable to be attached to a fixed object as provided by paragraph of Rule 2.

4. Every portion of a field punishment shall be inflicted in such a manner as is calculated not to cause injury or to leave any permanent mark on the offender; and a portion of a field punishment must be discontinued upon a report by a responsible medical officer that the continuance of that portion would be prejudicial to the offender's health.

5. Field punishment will be carried out regimentally when the unit to which the offender belongs or is attached is actually on the move, but when the unit is halted at any place where there is a provost marshal, or an assistant provost marshal, the punishment will be carried out under that officer.

6. When the unit to which the offender belongs or is attached is actually on the move, an offender awarded field punishment No. 1 shall be exempt from the operation of Rule 2, but all offenders awarded field punishment shall march with their unit, carry their arms and accoutrements, perform all their military duties as well as extra fatigue duties, and be treated as defaulters.

30 December 1914

ENLISTED: **Lieutenant Sergeant William Ernest SMITH (1881–1945)**

AGE AT ENLISTMENT: 33 years, 9 months, 21 days

ARMY NUMBER: 6/1722

EMBARKATION: Wellington, 14 February 1915; Canterbury Infantry Battalion, 3rd Reinforcements

LENGTH OF SERVICE: 1 year, 266 days

PLAYED FOR: Nelson club; Nelson 1900–08; South Island 1902; Marlborough–Nelson–West Coast–Buller 1905; Nelson–Golden Bay–Motueka 1908

ALL BLACK NUMBER: 138

POSITION: Five-eighth

APPEARANCES: 1905; 1 test

Smith played only one match for the All Blacks, the 1905 test against the Australians, after the Originals had departed for England, but was a seasoned captain of Nelson. He stood out on the football field because at over six feet (183 centimetres) tall and weighing nearly 200 pounds (91 kilograms) he was bigger than many forwards. (Also in the winning 1905 test team for the Tahuna Park match were the first set of brothers to play a test together for the All Blacks, Charles and Edward — known as 'Pat' — Purdue.)

Smith had enjoyed his Marlborough–Nelson–West Coast–Buller selection, beating the tourists a week earlier at Trafalgar Park, 12–3. Nelson–Marlborough had no such luck at the same venue three years later when the Anglo-Welsh triumphed 12–0. However, the home side did keep the visitors scoreless in the first half, in front of a then record crowd of 4,000, but, despite outstanding play by Smith and his wings Saunders and Costello, they could not reply to the Anglo-Welsh scores.

Prior to active service, Smith had served for six years with the New Zealand Volunteers, while working as a clerk with the Anchor Shipping Company. On 28 July 1915, he was shot in the chest at Gallipoli, and was hospitalised in Alexandria before being moved to England, where he spent seven months in the American Women's War Hospital. The 'hospital' was the converted mansion of the Singer family, who had made their fortune through the sales of sewing machines. The building was known as 'Oldway', and its design had been based on the Palace of Versailles. The ballroom, where once members of high society had danced and cavorted, now housed rows of beds, where men who had undergone all manner of operations for wounds lay receiving care.

Smith's convalescence did not see him recover enough to return to active service, so he was sent back to New Zealand on the *Rotorua*, along with 55 other men, a dozen of whom were from the Canterbury Battalion. Declared medically unfit, he was discharged from the army in August 1916.

1915

2 February 1915

NZEF soldiers had their first experience of combat when they defended a section of the Suez Canal against Turkish forces. Serving with the NZEF was a Lietenant Colonel Arthur Plugge, who had emigrated from England to New Zealand in 1899, and taught science at King's College before assuming the role of headmaster at Dilworth College. When the orders came to entrain from Zeitoun for the battle, Lietenant Colonel Plugge told his troops: 'Men, there is just one thing I want to say to you. I know it is not necessary; yet I want to say it. It is probable that we shall be scrapping within the next twenty-four hours from now. *Play the game.* Let Auckland and New Zealand be proud of you.' There, the first New Zealand soldier fell, Private William Ham, who died of wounds.

13 February 1915

ENLISTED: **Sergeant Albert Joseph 'Doolan' DOWNING (1886–1915)**

AGE AT ENLISTMENT: 28 years, 7 months, 1 day

ARMY NUMBER: 10/2119

EMBARKATION: Wellington, 13 June 1915; Wellington Infantry Battalion, 5th Reinforcements

LENGTH OF SERVICE: 177 days

PLAYED FOR: Marist; Hawke's Bay 1909–12; Auckland 1913;
North Island 1911–12, 1914; North Island Country
1911–12
ALL BLACK NUMBER: 176
POSITION: Side-row forward and lock
APPEARANCES: 1913–14; 26 matches, including 5 tests;
21 points (7 tries)

Legend has it that the 1914 All Blacks who were in Australia when the war broke out vowed to a man that they would sign up for service. The first to enter camp, some six months after the players returned from their unbeaten tour, was 'Doolan' Downing, so nicknamed due to his schooling under the Marist Brothers in Napier, the town where he was born ('Doolan' being New Zealand slang for a Roman Catholic, especially one of Irish origin or connection).

Norman McKenzie, who went on to coach Hawke's Bay for 30 years, including during their glorious Ranfurly Shield reign from 1922 until 1926, was his club captain and wrote of Downing being

> a real attacking forward. Once we were playing in a club match, and after we had lost the toss and were to play against a very strong wind, I said to the team, and to Albert in particular, 'Now we'll have to hug the touchline all through this first half and then do our best with open football in the second half.' Albert agreed, but from the kick-off he forgot all about his instructions. His idea was to create openings, carry on and never mind about the wind, and it amazed me how successful he was.

Downing made his first-class rugby debut for Hawke's Bay in 1909, and after four seasons, which included representation for the North Island and all nine matches for the North Island Country (a two-season initiative of a domestic touring team made up of players from outside the Auckland, Taranaki, Wanganui and Wellington unions), he moved to Auckland. He was immediately selected by Dave Gallaher for the Auckland side, playing in six of their seven matches that season, including the loss of the Ranfurly Shield to Taranaki. In the visitors' forward pack that day was 'Norkey' Dewar (see page 27). The two faced each other again less than a month later in the final representative match of the season. While the Shield was not at stake, Auckland did restore some pride by winning the encounter in New Plymouth.

Downing was not in the Auckland side that beat the 1913 Australians 15–13 at their then home-ground of Alexandra Park, but his form had been such that he was named in the All Black side to tour North America, and prior to departure he was one of the most prominent forwards in the 30–5 first test win for the 1913 Auckland side over Taranaki. In North America, Downing relished playing on the hard, dry grounds and scored 6 tries in the 14 games he appeared in.

All who played with him admired the spirit in which he approached the game. He could take hard knocks with some playfulness, but was also unhesitating in helping up from the ground an opponent he had driven into the dirt seconds before.

Having spurned approaches to turn to league, Downing left Auckland to return to Port Ahuriri in Napier in 1914, commemorating his time in the Shield-holding side by having a tattoo of the sporting trophy inked on his right forearm. It was not the only colour he sported on his skin — that forearm also bore a tattoo of a star, a heart and a dragon.

Selected again for the All Blacks to tour Australia in 1914, he scored a try in the farewell game against Wellington (lost 14–19) and missed only one of the 10 matches across the Tasman. His work in securing the ball from lineouts and play in the loose had some observers and journalists comparing him to Charlie 'Bronco' Seeling, one of the stars of the 1905–06 All Blacks.

Having worked as a clerk or storeman for the Excelsior Dairy Company Limited and Barry Brothers Limited, he was employed by wholesale merchants Ellison and Duncan at the time of enlisting in February 1915.

Downing had his only appearance at the new home of the Auckland Rugby Union — Eden Park — representing Trentham in a match against Auckland shortly before sailing for Gallipoli. (The soldiers, all of whom had experience of first-class football, had recently beaten Wellington in a fund-raising match for the Belgian Relief Fund, and three camp teams played in the Wellington club competition.) The fund-raising game, won by the visiting soldiers 15–5, contributed over £220 to the Hospital Ship Fund. The match was refereed by George Nicholson, who had been a member of the 1905 All Blacks to Britain. Other All Black soldiers to turn out were Thomas 'Tiger' Lynch, 'Teddy' Roberts, Lynley Weston, Frank Wilson and Reginald Taylor for Trentham, while George Sellars started for Auckland.

At the end of June 1915, Downing was promoted to sergeant. Years later, one old soldier recalled seeing Downing arriving at Gallipoli as part of the reinforcements, looking even larger in his uniform, and certainly more robust than the men who had been on the peninsula since the landing and were rapidly losing weight due to the lack of food and the ravages of dysentery. (See page 76.)

FOOTBALL IN THE LAND OF THE PHARAOHS

One of the first football matches in Egypt by members of the NZEF was recorded by Ormond Burton in his post-war history of the Auckland Battalion. It took place after the New Zealand soldiers returned to Zeitoun from fighting at the Suez Canal at the end of February 1915.

> ... the ranks of the Battalion were full of first-class athletes; and so when the Artillery sent in a challenge to play Rugby football, there was not the slightest difficulty in picking a very fine team. The Auckland representatives were Fitzgerald, Les. Hill, Roy Lambert, McGeehan, Fox, Jock McKenzie, Moki, Fordyce, Savory, Frank McKenzie, Ted Lambert, Smith, Gasparich, and two others. Two great games resulted, the first ending in a draw, neither side scoring, and the second in a win for Auckland, six to three. Never in all its history had the Egyptian Railway Ground seen such struggles.

14 March 1915

ENLISTED: **Second Lieutenant Frank Reginald WILSON (1885–1916)**

AGE AT ENLISTMENT: 29 years, 9 months, 14 days
ARMY NUMBER: 12/2616
EMBARKATION: Wellington, 14 August 1915; Auckland
   Infantry Battalion, 6th Reinforcements
LENGTH OF SERVICE: 1 year, 191 days
PLAYED FOR: Ponsonby and University clubs; Auckland
   1906–10; North Island 1909
ALL BLACK NUMBER: 166
POSITION: Wing
APPEARANCES: 1910; 2 matches; 4 points (1 dropped goal)

An unmarried teacher working at Newtown West School who lived with his parents on Ponsonby's Pompallier Terrace, Wilson was the first All Black from Auckland's University club. A product of Auckland Grammar School, he actually began his rugby career with the Ponsonby club and was a well-respected and familiar figure in the suburb, attending All Saints church, where Dave Gallaher was also a member of the congregation.

In the summer months, Wilson had played cricket for the Ponsonby Cricket Club, captaining the side to their first Auckland Championship win in 1915. A man of many talents, he was also an outstanding amateur sprinter and pianist, a member of the All Saints' choir and the Orpheus Glee Club, and the secretary of the Ponsonby Swimming Club; he had also won prizes for champion roses at the 1913 Auckland Exhibition. On top of all that, he ran a well-attended gymnasium for boys in the All Saints' hall.

The amiable Wilson had been brought into the Auckland rugby team in 1906 by Gallaher, who had just retired from playing but had taken on the role of selector-coach for the blue-and-white hoops. Over the next five seasons, Wilson represented Auckland 22 times.

He was a replacement in the All Blacks touring group to Australia in 1910, appearing against Wellington before the team departed, and then in the first match in Australia against New South Wales. He revelled in sprinting on the hard, dry ground, showcasing his impressive speed. Unfortunately, he badly twisted his knee so found himself replaced and he returned home.

While the injury brought about the end of his All Black and representative appearances, it was not the end of his footballing days. He was a member of the 6th Reinforcements football team and turned out for Trentham in their match against his province of Auckland in June 1915, scoring a try in their 15–5 win.

Wilson left New Zealand holding the rank of private, but was promoted to acting sergeant and then corporal while at Mudros, waiting to sail to Alexandria in September 1915.

He wrote a letter to a mate in Auckland, Bert Hayson, in which he mentioned that he had captained the Auckland Infantry team in their 11–0 win over Canterbury while in Egypt. The match was, he wrote, 'a good go right through. The sand was a bit heavy and slackened the play but our forwards played like tigers and were irresistible.'

At Gallipoli, he was, according to one biographical note written during the war, one of the last 14 New Zealanders left to hold their trench position (under Lieutenant J. McKenzie) as the evacuation was carried out. At the end of August 1916, he was promoted to second lieutenant while in the field in France. (See page 160.)

19 April 1915

Having travelled south by train from Taranaki together, three All Black mates, Teddy Roberts, Reginald Taylor and Charles Brown (who would all have been teammates at the Clifton club in 1915 had war not intervened), walked through the gates of Trentham Camp. The trio's enlistment was noted in *The Free Lance*, with an additional comment that 'those who say that Rugby footballers are not doing their share in this great war don't know what they are talking about'.

ENLISTED: **Camp Quartermaster Sergeant Edward 'Teddy' James ROBERTS (1891–1972)**

AGE AT ENLISTMENT: 33 years, 11 months, 9 days

ARMY NUMBER: 8/2714

EMBARKATION: Wellington, 14 August 1915; Otago Infantry Battalion, 6th Reinforcements

LENGTH OF SERVICE: 3 years, 287 days

PLAYED FOR: St James and Athletic clubs; Wellington 1910–14, 1919–21, 1923; North Island 1910, 1912–14, 1919; New Zealand Trials 1921

ALL BLACK NUMBER: 207

POSITION: Halfback

APPEARANCES: 1913–14, 1920–21; 26 matches, including 5 tests, 2 games as captain; 110 points (13 tries, 34 conversions, 1 penalty)

Educated at Brooklyn School in Wellington, Teddy was the first son of an All Black to don the black jersey, his father Harry having played for New Zealand in 1884, scoring the first-ever try by the team in their match against Wellington. Harry coached the St James senior side, from which Teddy made the Wellington provincial team at the age of just 19 in 1910, and he also made the first of his five appearances for the North Island that year.

Possessed of what one might call the typical halfback build, Teddy Roberts was only five feet six inches (168 centimetres) tall, but he used his lack of height to great effect. He could be an elusive scurrier, and had a particular fondness for using the blindside. A handy goal-kicker, he was adept at the 'corkscrew' punt a few years before George Nepia dazzled the rugby world with the distances he could kick a ball using that technique.

In the summer months he could be found crouched down behind cricket stumps. He played in a YMCA junior boys team in 1907–08, a team which also contained Clarrie Grimmett, who later crossed the Tasman and became Australia's highest wicket-taker in tests bowling his mesmerising spinners. In one match, the two young lads opened the batting and put on an unbroken stand of 114. Wellington selection came Roberts's way in the 1910–11 season.

Roberts was first chosen for the All Blacks in 1913, as the understudy to Cantabrian Henry Taylor, but illness and injury meant he didn't play until the eighth match of the tour (against the University of Nevada) and only appeared in four of the remaining eight games.

When the 1914 All Blacks were announced for the tour of Australia, rugby writers around the country had a field day questioning selections. Roberts's name was not among the touring party, despite the fact that he had been in superb form for his club and for Wellington. Perhaps the selectors were wary of taking him away again given the lack of match-time he'd had in North America the previous year. Henry Taylor, who had played in 10 of the 16 games on that tour, was seen as out of form, despite being deemed to have outplayed Roberts in the inter-island match. Taylor was named in the side, as was the bustling, consistent Buller halfback, Clem Green.

Unfortunately for Green, he had to withdraw from the touring party (and never again got the opportunity to play for the All Blacks). This meant that Roberts was called into the side captained by his namesake Dick Roberts, and he went on to be one of the stars of the tour, playing in all 11 games. One Australian report described him as 'a wonder'. The only other player to appear in every game was, funnily enough, Henry Taylor, who secured himself a place as a wing! Roberts was the second-highest points-scorer on the tour, scoring only 3 tries but kicking 17 conversions and a penalty goal.

The history of the Ranfurly Shield shows that it is often the exceptional play of one man that can break the stranglehold a team has on the trophy. One of Roberts's finest displays was Wellington's 1914 challenge against Taranaki in Stratford. There, he directed much of the play when the challengers had the ball, and never seemed hurried when passing, kicking or choosing whether to run to the blind- or open-sides. Add to that his tackling of the imposing Taranaki forwards when required, and people could see just what an assured all-round footballer he was.

By the time of his enlistment, Roberts had moved north from Wellington and was living and working in Waitara, as a bookkeeper and salesman for George & Johnston Motor Engineers.

After sailing from Wellington in August 1915, he joined his unit, the Otago Infantry Battalion, at Lemnos in October. He was transferred to the Wellington Infantry Battalion in February of the following year at Moascar, with which he left for France two months later. With little more than two months' service in France, he was promoted to corporal and played for the Wellington Battalion football team. (His brother, 'Little' Len, played football in France with the 1st Light Trench Mortar Battery team.)

Roberts was admitted to the No. 2 Australian General Hospital with a gunshot wound to the thigh, suffered on the Somme in July 1916. From there he was transferred to England and the convalescent camp at Hornchurch.

At the start of 1917, Roberts was at Codford Camp where he took up the position of quartermaster sergeant (QMS) and later a temporary appointment as Camp QMS. He was a noted and popular captain of the camp's football team.

While being able to scamper about a football field, at the beginning of 1918 he was returned to New Zealand on the SS *Arawa*, having been deemed 'no longer physically fit for war service on account of wounds received in action'.

However, he was not discharged, and instead returned to Trentham as a quartermaster sergeant, and in the winter months of 1918 was a member of the camp's football team that played a series of matches against Auckland, Wellington and Canterbury. His discharge from the army finally came at the end of January 1919. Eighteen months later he married his sweetheart, Myrtle Hanlon, and the couple settled in Wellington.

In his twentieth match for the All Blacks, against Metropolitan Union in Sydney in 1920, Roberts became just the fifth man to accumulate 100 career points for the team when he kicked the team's only conversion in a 20–11 win. Those who had also passed the milestone were Billy Wallace (367), Jimmy Hunter (141), 'Tiger' Lynch (107) and Dick Roberts (101).

Roberts's omission from the side to face the Springboks in the first test of 1921 — when Petone's Ginger Nicholls got the nod for the halfback role — is said to have so incensed some of the Athletic club's more 'influential' members that their appeals to the selectors saw him brought into the side for the remaining two tests and named as captain for the match with New South Wales. For a player of such skill and profile, his All Black days did not have a fairy-tale finish; those three matches were a loss, a draw and a loss.

In 1929, Roberts was seriously ill for some months with pleurisy and pneumonia (all too frequent illnesses for veterans of the Western Front who had been exposed to gas), but was still turning out for Petone in the Wellington senior club cricket competition in the 1930s.

ENLISTED: Lance Corporal Reginald TAYLOR (1889–1917)

AGE AT ENLISTMENT: 26 years, 27 days

ARMY NUMBER: 8/2738

EMBARKATION: Wellington, 14 August 1915; Otago Infantry Battalion, 6th Reinforcements

LENGTH OF SERVICE: 2 years, 63 days

PLAYED FOR: Waimate and Clifton clubs; Taranaki 1910–14; North Island 1914

ALL BLACK NUMBER: 202

POSITION: Wing-forward

APPEARANCES: 1913; 2 tests; 3 points (1 try)

The Waitara labourer boarded a troopship bound for Gallipoli as news broke at home that his Ranfurly Shield-winning teammate 'Norkey' Dewar had perished in the attempt to capture Chunuk Bair.

The 1913 match in which Taranaki broke Auckland's long, firm embrace of the Ranfurly Shield was one of Taylor's finest. Playing at wing-forward, he was one of the reasons the yellow-and-blacks were utterly dominant in the first half, although a late try just before the interval saw Auckland lead by 5–3. Taylor harried the Aucklander inside backs from set-play, was almost omnipresent in the loose and unflinching in the tight, wrestling contests that nuggety forwards of the day revelled in. (One such forward was Auckland's solid lock, Bill Cunningham, who was playing his one-hundredth first-class game that day, having debuted way back in 1899. His tally included 39 games for New Zealand, including 9 internationals. Without question the greatest lock of the pre-war period, his inclusion in the 1905 team to Europe proved crucial to the success of the All Black scrum throughout the tour.)

Although not selected for the All Black tour of North America, Taylor did play against the visiting Australians for Taranaki and in the final two tests, scoring a try on his debut in the 25–13 win in Dunedin.

The following season Taylor played in Taranaki's six successful defences of the Shield and scored a try in the 6–12 loss to Wellington, putting the holders in the lead for a time when he swept on to a loose ball near the Wellington try-line and threw himself over to make the score 6–4. He was included in the North Island team, but did not make the All Blacks touring party to Australia.

Taylor's grandfather, James Hill, was a 'Die Hard', a British soldier who had served with the 57th Regiment in Taranaki during the New Zealand Wars. Reginald had been a cadet with the Hawera Mounted Rifles, and began his service overseas training with the Otago Infantry Battalion firstly at Mudros, from where he was briefly hospitalised at Ismaïlia, and then at Moascar. On departing for France in April 1916, he was transferred to the 1st Battalion of the Wellington Regiment. (Two of his brothers also served, one having left with the Main Body as one of Brigadier-General Russell's orderlies, while the other would later depart with the 18th Reinforcements.)

Vice-captain of the New Zealand Divisional XV in France, he was promoted to lance-corporal while in the field in July 1917. (See page 222.)

ENLISTED: Sergeant Charles 'Chas' (or 'Charlie') BROWN (1887–1966)

AGE AT ENLISTMENT: 27 years, 4 months
ARMY NUMBER: 4/890
EMBARKATION: Wellington, 13 June 1915; New Zealand Field Engineers, 5th Reinforcements
LENGTH OF SERVICE: 4 years, 209 days
PLAYED FOR: Star and Tukapa clubs; Taranaki 1909–14, 1920–22; North Island 1911, 1920

ALL BLACK NUMBER: 192
POSITION: Halfback
APPEARANCES: 1913, 1920; 11 matches, including 2 tests

Although renowned as a halfback, Brown was a very versatile player, as evidenced by his participation in the 1920 All Black tour to Australia where he played in five matches as halfback and one at fullback. Upon the tourists' return, when they lined up to play Wellington at Athletic Park, Brown slotted in as hooker!

In 1913, Brown made something of an honorary appearance for the New Zealand Maoris XV when they played the touring Australians, faced the tourists again in two tests, and captained Taranaki in their Ranfurly Shield win over Auckland.

A corporal (later sergeant) with the New Zealand Field Engineers, Brown had worked as a wheelwright in peacetime. He played in the New Zealand army's Divisional Football Team and was slightly wounded in November 1917, but remained with his unit. Three weeks later he was wounded again, and was removed to the convalescent depot at Rouen.

Making a quick recovery, Brown was back to fighting and playing for the Divisional team when it won the King's Cup. He then captained the Services side to South Africa. That appointment was something of a surprise to observers, given that James Ryan had captained the King's Cup team.

The vagaries of appointing captains rose again when the All Blacks resumed playing in 1920. Many assumed Brown would captain the side, containing as it did other members of the Services team. Surprisingly, that was not to be, and, although he did make the side, it was under the captaincy of Jim Tilyard.

After hanging up his boots in 1922, 5 matches short of joining the select group who had played 100 first-class matches, he coached Tukapa (who honoured him with life membership in 1924) for 17 years. He also held a number of management and selectorial positions at provincial and national levels, including Taranaki selector in 1925 and then again from 1932 to 1946. He was a New Zealand selector in 1944, and on the panel for the North Island in 1947–48.

During World War II, having worked as a joiner for Boon Bros. in New Plymouth, he was made a sergeant with the 2nd Taranaki unit of the Home Guard, but he was pensioned off, suffering from arthritis of his right knee.

Upon his death, a New Plymouth newspaper obituary described him thus: 'A modest and unassuming character, this genial gentleman endeared himself to countless thousands of Rugby followers who were fortunate enough to know him.'

Brown's 1913 All Black cap is held by the National Army Museum at Waiouru.

25 April 1915

Before sunrise, the First Australian Division landed on the coast of Turkey, followed nearly six hours later by the Auckland Infantry Battalion, under the command of Lieutenant Colonel Plugge. (The first hilltop they took was named Plugge's Plateau.) They had been briefed by the commander of the Anzac Corps, General W.R. Birdwood:

> OFFICERS AND MEN — In conjunction with the Navy, we are about to undertake one of the most difficult tasks any soldier can be called on to perform, and a problem which has puzzled many soldiers for years past. That we will succeed I have no doubt, simply because I know your full determination to do so. Lord Kitchener has told us that he lays special stress on the role the Army has to play in this particular operation, the success of which will be a very severe blow to the enemy — as severe as any he could receive in France. It will go down to history to the glory of the soldiers of Australia and New Zealand. Before we start, there are one or two points that I would like to impress on all, and I must earnestly beg every single man to listen attentively and take these to heart.
>
> We are going to have a real hard and rough time of it until, at all events, we have turned the enemy out of our first objective. Hard, rough times none of us mind, but to get through them successfully we must always keep before us the following facts. Every possible endeavour will be made to bring up transport as often as possible; but

the country whither we are bound is very difficult, and we may not be able to get our wagons anywhere near us for days, so men need not think their wants have been neglected if they do not get all they want. On landing it will be necessary for every individual to carry with him all his requirements in food and clothing for three days, as we may not see our transport till then. Remember then that it is essential for everyone to take the very greatest care not only of his food, but of his ammunition, the replenishment of which will be very difficult. Men are liable to throw away their food the first day out and to finish their water bottles as soon as they start marching. If you do this now, we can hardly hope for success, as unfed men cannot fight, and you must make an effort to try and refrain from starting on your water bottles until quite late in the day. Once you begin drinking you cannot stop, and a water bottle is very soon emptied.

Also, as regards ammunition, you must not waste it by firing away indiscriminately at no target. The time will come when we shall find the enemy in well entrenched positions, from which we shall have to turn them out, when all our ammunition will be required; and remember,

Concealment whenever possible

Covering fire always

Control of fire and control of your men

Communications never to be neglected.

Despite having spent several weeks preparing for the landing at Lemnos, 40 miles away on the island of Mudros, the assault was the beginning of a great disaster. Kiwi soldiers killed in action that day totalled 149, with 4 others dying of wounds.

5 May 1915

ENLISTED: **Corporal Lynley Herbert WESTON (1892–1963)**

AGE AT ENLISTMENT: 22 years, 8 months, 4 days

ARMY NUMBER: 4/1017

EMBARKATION: Wellington, 14 August 1915; New Zealand Field Engineers, 6th Reinforcements

LENGTH OF SERVICE: 1 year, 73 days

PLAYED FOR: College Rifles and Whangarei United clubs; Auckland 1912–14; North Island 1914; North Auckland 1920–22; Auckland–North Auckland 1921

ALL BLACK NUMBER: 213

POSITION: Five-eighth

APPEARANCES: 1914; 1 match

The first All Black from the College Rifles club, Weston had been a player of great promise, joining the ranks of senior football when still a teenager as part of the first Rifles side to play in the first-grade competition, having won the second-grade banner the previous two seasons. His Auckland debut came in 1912 and he chalked up 13 appearances in the backline over three seasons. Weston played for the North Island and toured with the All Blacks to Australia in 1914 but, due to injury, appeared in only 1 of the 11 games, the seventh match, against Queensland, which the All Blacks won, 19–0.

Weston served with the No. 2 Company of the New Zealand Engineers at Gallipoli from October 1915. Two days before Christmas, and four days after the last Anzacs left the Turkish peninsula, he was evacuated to Cairo suffering from catarrh (excessive mucus in the sinuses or chest) and jaundice. Three months later he was invalided back to New Zealand due to dislocated cartilage in his right knee.

After the war he moved to Whangarei, playing football for Whangarei United, and became the first captain of the North Auckland union when it came into being in 1920. He also played in the North Auckland–Auckland team against the 1921 Springboks.

8 May 1915

ENLISTED: **Private Thomas William 'Tiger' LYNCH (1892–1950)**

AGE AT ENLISTMENT: 23 years, 2 months, 2 days

ARMY NUMBER: 3/2559

EMBARKATION: 10 November 1916; Merchant Navy, Hospital
   Ship *Marama*
LENGTH OF SERVICE: 4 years, 120 days
PLAYED FOR: Celtic and Northern clubs; South Canterbury
   1911–14, 1919–20; South Island 1911–14; Southland
   1921–22
ALL BLACK NUMBER: 177
POSITION: Wing
APPEARANCES: 1913–14; 23 matches, including 4 tests;
   113 points (37 tries, 1 conversion)

After leaving school, Lynch began playing club football for
Timaru's Celtic Club in 1907, and the following year, according
to some oral accounts, he made his representative debut for South
Canterbury aged just 16. His father, also called Tom, had played
four times at centre against the Great Britain side that toured in
1888: three times for Otago and once for the South Island. All
matches were held at the Caledonian Ground in Dunedin, and the
scores were 3–8, 3–4, 0–0 and 3–5.

Lynch scored three tries for the South Island in the 1913
inter-island match, a hint of what was to come as an All Black
over the next two years. On test debut, against Australia at
Athletic Park in September 1913, he had another three-try haul,
a remarkable achievement given that the weather was foul and
the ground was quickly churned up into a muddy morass. (It was
only the second time an All Black had scored three tries in a test,
the first being the electric Wellington centre Frank Mitchinson,
also against Australia, in 1907.) Four days later on the same
ground Lynch collected two more tries, as the All Blacks, in their
farewell game before departing for California and Canada, lost
18–19 to Wellington. On the North American tour he played in
11 of the 16 games, relishing running on the mostly hard, dry
grounds, scoring 17 tries. During the 1914 tour of Australia he
was the All Blacks' highest points-scorer, collecting 16 tries in
10 matches, including a bag of 4 against Queensland. So, in 23
games for the All Blacks he had scored an incredible 37 tries! Of
these tries, 33 were scored overseas, at the time the third highest

number behind 1905 Originals legends Billy Wallace and Jimmy Hunter.

A clerk with Dalgety & Co. in Timaru, Lynch sailed for the front as a member of staff on the hospital ship *Marama*, but ended up spending time in bed himself due to illness. In October 1918, he was at the front with the Canterbury Infantry Regiment when his left shoulder was fractured by a bullet. While supposedly recuperating in hospital, and waiting to return to New Zealand, he was absent without leave for a night and refused to obey orders upon his return, which saw him face a regimental court-martial hearing. His punishment was forfeiture of 23 days' pay.

The shoulder fracture suffered in war closed the door on Lynch's All Black representation, but remarkably he was still able to turn out for South Canterbury during the two seasons immediately after the war, and then for Southland for a further two years.

Lynch was a key participant in Southland's win over Canterbury in 1921, 12–8. By then he was playing at fullback, and it was reported for some years afterwards that he gave one of the great displays of a defensive fullback as well as a masterclass in line-kicking.

He captained the Northern District Sub-Union side in 1923, and was very much a local identity as a farmer in the Balfour district.

14 May 1915

The 1914 annual report of the Wellington Rugby Union had carried the comment that:

> The great European war disorganised the latter part of the club fixtures and the whole of the representative games. No complaint, however, is made as it was felt that the first thought and care of every citizen should be for the Empire. The answer to the nation's call by members of rugby clubs, players, officials and ex-players, has been gratifying in the extreme, some clubs having lost nearly all their members who were eligible for service.

By mid-May 1915, the New Zealand Rugby Football Union (NZRFU) estimated that over 2,000 rugby players had enlisted to serve. Volunteers from Wellington club football were approximately 400. Wanganui had sent 120 men. Rugby officers from the Otago Province believed they had farewelled 800 players and ex-players. The relatively new South Auckland union saw off 170 players, while 240 sons of Canterbury were fighting or preparing to. Outgoing NZRFU President John Arneil said that, 'All would be glad that the union had such a fine lot of men who were ready to offer their services for the honour of the Empire ... It is without question that we are all under a great debt of gratitude to those who have given their lives at the front.' He also wondered if the new committee could 'devise some scheme of co-operating with the Defence Office for the further stimulation of recruiting among Rugby men'. Management committee member George Fache added that, 'Every man who went to the front gave his life, or did what was equal to that — offered his life. The flower of Rugby had enlisted.'

The NZRFU suspended the annual inter-island match and Ranfurly Shield challenges in 1915. Only 15 first-class games were played throughout the country. Auckland fans were fortunate to have had three games to attend, and Hawera, Dunedin and Wellington hosted two, while other centres such as Invercargill, Christchurch, Westport, Carterton and Wanganui saw only one fixture in the season. Two of the matches featured a Trentham Military Forces side, who turned out against Wellington (17–0) and Auckland (15–5). Apart from the Trentham side, teams fielded players who were under the age of enlistment (20). While the colloquialism of the NZRFU's stance was 'fit to play, fit to fight', the emphasis fell on school-boy competitions to uphold the profile of the game.

The union's stance, patriotic as it was, did not meet with unanimous approval from players, spectators and sportswriters, such as the *New Zealand Free Lance* columnist, Touchline, who wrote on 14 May 1915:

> 'They're off!' — the Rugby football season of 1915 has commenced, and, whatever may be the result of playing the game during this period

of tension within the Empire, I am perfectly satisfied that many of us — participants as well as onlookers — will all feel the better for the game having been played. The country may call many of those who took the field on Saturday — and my hope is that the players may hear the call to arms in preference to the call to Rugby, if needs be — still the games can go on, mainly because the training and discipline required for the playing of Rugby will stand the men in good stead when the more serious business comes their way.

There are few who place sport of all sorts on a higher pedestal than I do, yet, even with me, the call of Empire is stronger than the call of pleasure, and if I was a younger man with no ties I would be prepared to shoulder my gun and go forth with the desire to place Old England at the head of the nations of the world. And I am sure a similar feeling is present with the players of the present today. Therefore, I say, play the game while there are players left, and as long as such playing does not interfere with the call to arms.

29 May 1915

ENLISTED: **Sergeant Richard FOGARTY** MM **(1891–1980)**
AGE AT ENLISTMENT: 23 years, 5 months, 17 days
ARMY NUMBER: 23/1048
EMBARKATION: Wellington, 9 October 1915; 1st Battalion, New Zealand Rifle Brigade
LENGTH OF SERVICE: 4 years, 171 days
PLAYED FOR: Union, Hawera and College Rifles clubs; Otago 1914; Taranaki 1920–22; New Zealand Trials 1921; Auckland 1923–24
ALL BLACK NUMBER: 230
POSITION: Loose-forward and hooker
APPEARANCES: 1921; 2 tests

Fogarty's first-class rugby career had just begun for Otago when war broke out. A year later he sailed with D Company, 1st Battalion of the New Zealand Rifle Brigade, bound for Gallipoli. Famous rugby commentator and rugby writer Winston McCarthy described Fogarty as 'hard as they make them'. That appraisal may have been based on Fogarty's time with the New Zealand Rifle Brigade, which saw him wounded in action three times. He also bore a large scar on his left forearm, the result of a pre-war accident, which probably added to his repute as a man of some endurance.

He was selected for the Divisional Football Team in November 1916, then suffered a gunshot wound to his left shoulder in June 1917. After being hospitalised at Brockenhurst and convalescing at Hornchurch, he returned to France in September 1917. In the middle of April 1918, Fogarty was wounded in the face and hand by shrapnel, but remained with his unit. A week later he suffered multiple shrapnel wounds to his chest and abdomen. He was first treated by field ambulance, then moved to a casualty clearing station, then to a general hospital before winding up once again at Brockenhurst General Hospital.

A month into his recuperation, he received news that he had been awarded the Military Medal for 'acts of gallantry in the field'.

He recovered swiftly enough to again be included in the Divisional Football Team that contested the King's Cup. From there he travelled with the Services team to South Africa, playing in 11 of the 14 tour games.

Once back in New Zealand, he moved to Taranaki and was one of the stars of that province's scoreless draw with the 1921 Springboks, reacquainting himself with a number of players he had found in opposition teams in the Republic in 1919. He was added to the first test side (won 13–5) when Les McLean withdrew, was dropped like many of his teammates from that match for the second test, and then was recalled for the third test, which was a scoreless draw, too. Curiously, he was asked to play at hooker rather than loose-forward. Few footballers of the era could claim to have played the Springboks three times and never lost, as Fogarty had.

On the move again, Fogarty settled in Auckland and represented that province seven times in the 1923–24 seasons. His club allegiance was with College Rifles as a player, and later as a coach.

As late as 1929 a newspaper report on Auckland club rugby noted that:

Dick Fogarty the veteran of the team [then aged 38] is getting well down the road of years but there is a chance he may again pull on a jersey. Although he is hardly possessed of the stamina of some of the youngsters he is always in good condition and has a football brain that is too often lacking among the younger players.

Fogarty worked as a carpenter at the naval dockyard at Devonport before returning to Dunedin to live once he had retired.

5 July 1915

ENLISTED: **Sergeant James 'Jim' Edward MOFFITT** MM **(1889–1964)**
AGE AT ENLISTMENT: 26 years, 1 month, 2 days
ARMY NUMBER: 5/436
EMBARKATION: Wellington, 13 November 1915; Army Service Corps, 8th Reinforcements
LENGTH OF SERVICE: 4 years, 132 days
PLAYED FOR: St James and Oriental clubs; Wellington 1910– 12, 1914–15, 1920–24, 1926; North Island 1920–21
ALL BLACK NUMBER: 222
POSITION: Lock
APPEARANCES: 1920–21; 12 matches, including 3 tests; 14 points (4 tries, 1 conversion)

Moffitt's rugby career extended either side of the war, beginning in 1910 and ending in 1926. Although a regular in the Wellington team, the sturdy lock (considered by many observers to be the perfect scrum-anchor at lock in the 2–3–2 formation) didn't join the ranks of the All Blacks until after the war, by which time he had featured in the Services rugby side.

A tailor by profession, Moffitt was a member of the 1914 Wellington side that took the Shield from Taranaki. Originally with the Army Service Corp, he later served with the Auckland Infantry Regiment and was awarded the Military Medal for gallantry in April 1918.

When inter-services rugby was being played during World War II, the *Auckland Star* reminisced on the personnel of the Services side in 1919:

> Jim became the best-known soldier in Great Britain. While the Mother Country fifteen was comprised of 14 'brass hats' and a solitary sergeant-major, the New Zealand personnel consisted of 14 N.C.O.'s and Lieutenant James Moffitt! So, hilariously dubbed 'Gentleman Jim', Moffitt was ever a popular figure at Twickenham, Inverleith and Bradford, besides on many other subsidiary grounds where games were played. Both on and off the field, Jim's popularity followed him on to the Rugby Kingdoms of France, South Africa, New Zealand and New South Wales.

Although he had played five seasons of first-class football prior to the war, it was the quality of his play with the Services side that saw his elevation to the first All Black team post-war. He was indisputably the top-ranked lock in the country for two seasons, playing in all seven matches on the 1920 tour of Australia, and then all three tests against the 1921 Springboks.

As late as 1933, when he was into his forties, he was attached to the Wellington team as trainer, baggage man and their emergency forward reserve when on tour. Even so, when an opportunity arose for him to take the field in a game at Taihape, he deferred to a younger team member.

A brother, Joe, refereed a 1936 test between the All Blacks and Australia.

When the Oriental club celebrated its silver jubilee in 1938, Moffitt arranged for a special commemoration to players from the club who had served and lost their lives in World War I. (It was estimated that 300 men from the club enlisted, 45 of whom lost their lives overseas.) The parade was held at the Citizens' War Memorial in Lambton Quay, with Moffitt leading the laying of wreaths and flowers.

12 July 1915

ENLISTED: **Major William McKail GEDDES** MC (1893–1950)
AGE AT ENLISTMENT: 22 years, 2 months, 21 days
ARMY NUMBER: 2/2023
EMBARKATION: Wellington, 9 October 1915; Field Artillery, 7th Reinforcements
LENGTH OF SERVICE: 4 years, 23 days
PLAYED FOR: University; Auckland 1911, 1913–14; North Island 1913
ALL BLACK NUMBER: 195
POSITION: First five-eighth
APPEARANCES: 1913; 1 test

Geddes was just 21 when the war began, but he had already played 11 games for Auckland, one for the North Island and a solitary test against the 1913 Australians.

Working as a merchant for Brown Barratt & Co., he was a single man who lived with his parents in central Auckland's Wynyard Street. An experienced territorial soldier, he had three years' training with senior cadets and an additional three years' service with the Field Artillery Brigade in Auckland under his belt.

In February 1915, he was informed that the commander of the Auckland Military District had requested of the New Zealand Defence Force headquarters in Wellington that Geddes be appointed second lieutenant (on probation) of the G Battery Field Artillery:

In recommending Mr. Geddes for appointment to 'G' Battery as an officer, I would like to state that I have every confidence in his making a success as an officer, he is well up in gunnery and competent to impart instructions, he intends volunteering for service with the Expeditionary Force Reinforcements and when the time comes I will have much pleasure in recommending him.

The response on behalf of the Commander of the Auckland District stated that: 'I recommend that this be treated as a special case, in view of the depletion of establishment of Officers caused by transfers to the Expeditionary Force, and owing to there being no N.C.O.'s available who have passed the necessary examination.'

At the beginning of July, having received instructions to report to Trentham, Geddes again corresponded with District Headquarters: 'I beg to bring before you notice of the addition of McKail to my baptismal name, my full name is now William McKail Geddes. I will be leaving for Trentham by 8.50pm Express Friday 9th inst.'

Geddes first saw action in France in the summer of 1916, having joined the New Zealand troops in Moascar before sailing north.

When Sapper Roy Ellis wrote in 1968 about the circumstances of his being awarded the Military Medal, he was quick to acknowledge other linesmen whose feats were not recognised, as well as a story about Billy Geddes who

> had two guns up close to Flers. The Huns were driving back the 41st Division who had taken some land in front and east of Flers. The two guns were really close to the front line, and dealt severely with the Germans. However the retaliation of the latter was heavy. Of the twenty-two men who manned the guns nineteen were killed, but Billy Geddes and the other three men kept one gun firing until the German attack petered out. Nobody received a medal — chiefly because all the Senior Officers of the Battery were casualties, and their replacements became casualties also.

Geddes was awarded the Military Cross at the beginning of June 1917, but it is uncertain as to whether it was for his gallantry in the incident recalled by Ellis (many years later) or for a separate event. The citation read:

> For conspicuous gallantry and devotion to duty. As forward observing officer he displayed the greatest courage in reconnoitring enemy country under very heavy shell-fire. He sent back information of great value to his Brigade, and throughout the operations his daring and resourcefulness contributed in a large degree to the success of our artillery.

A confidential note written by his commanding officer in April 1918 noted that he was 'very zealous has good ability with force of character would make a good captain'. To this, Brigadier-General Johnston added 'I agree'.

In August 1918, Geddes received a wound bullet to the neck. Where the bullet had entered his neck healed quickly, so Geddes (having been promoted to major) rejoined his unit. However, over the next few days he began to suffer from very uncomfortable neck pain, below his Adam's apple, so he was invalided to Brockenhurst. A medical board reported the cause of the pain:

> On admission to this hospital 14/9/18 the entering wound was soundly healed. Bullet seen by x-rays to be lying posterior to left Sterno-Clavicular joint. Operation 17/9/18 incision along lower 1/6ths inner aspect of Sterno-mastoid muscle (L) Parts dissected and retracted. Bullet found lying on latero-internal aspect of L. innominate vein, removed, wound closed by suture.

In March 1919, as he waited to return to New Zealand, he had an operation for a long-standing problem with his adenoids, but his hospital stay was slightly prolonged as he then contracted measles. He finally left England in May 1919, but remained with the Territorial Force.

When attesting to join the Remuera Battalion of the Home Guard at the start of World War II, Geddes was living at 738 Remuera Road with his wife, Mary, and was the managing director of Brown-Barrett, food processors.

15 July 1915

The hospital ship *Willochra* berthed at Glasgow wharf in Wellington, carrying the first large group of Gallipoli wounded. It was the same vessel that the All Blacks had sailed on to North America two years earlier. The men were then dispersed to their home towns through the North Island. When soldiers from Auckland arrived at the central railway station, the *New Zealand Herald* reported:

> The people cheered those men who were able to hobble to the motor cars provided for them, but when the sick men on stretchers were carried past … the cheering broke off suddenly, and in the absolute silence which followed, women sobbed openly, and men's faces hardened in the effort of self-control.

8 August 1915

The attack on the summit known as Chunuk Bair was the high-point in terms of geographical and territorial advance for the New Zealand soldiers at Gallipoli, but it was the absolute low-point in terms of the numbers of men who lost their lives, or were wounded, claiming a hill-top for a matter of only hours before a furious Turkish riposte.

† DIED: **Sergeant Albert Joseph 'Doolan' Downing** †

According to his service record, Downing (see page 51) had been at Gallipoli for only three days when he became the first former All Black to lose his life in combat. He had been with a group from the Wellington Infantry Battalion, who, as part of the 5th Reinforcements B Company, managed to reach the top of Chunuk Bair and was part of a fierce bayonet charge against the Turks. Their next job was to maintain, under heavy fire, the position his unit had captured. Lance-Corporal Hill of the Auckland Infantry reported that:

They only lasted 12 hours however. The Turks went for them with bombs and what with these awful weapons and the high explosive shells it was not long before the trench was a shambles. It is hard to find out who fell there but I know that Downing, Lieutenant AJ Clark and Joe Daniel fell. Downing I believe was blown to pieces.

His overseas service had lasted just 57 days. (Such was the chaos of those August days that groundbreaking Gallipoli historian Richard Stowers has speculated that Downing may have actually been killed on 9 August.) Downing was one of 297 members of the Wellington Infantry Battalion to be killed in action during a dreadful day that saw 484 New Zealanders lose their lives in combat.

9 August 1915

† DIED: **Sergeant Henry 'Norkey' Dewar** †

The Chunuk Bair offensive claimed the life of Downing's 1913 fellow forward and teammate on the North American tour the very next day. One story reported that Dewar (see page 27) was initially seriously wounded but was determined to fight on and reluctant to part with his gun.

His commanding officer, Lieutenant Colonel Meldrum, reported to headquarters that the casualties 'were very heavy in my Regiment, 110 officers, N.C.O.'s and men being killed or wounded (out of 173 engaged)'. The actual total of those killed in action that day was 88.

In July of the following year, a benefit match for Dewar's mother was played between New Plymouth Boys' High School and Technical College. This came about after it became known in Taranaki rugby circles that Mrs Dewar, a widow and old-age pensioner, was suffering financial hardship following the death of Norkey, who had given £1 per week

of his wages to her. Her other son had also contributed 15/-
per week, but had been paralysed due to a diseased spine,
and as an invalid had come to rely on his mother for support
and to pay their rent. Representations by members of the
Stratford War Relief Association had been made on her behalf
to the Pensions Board, who paid her a mere 10/- per week,
and even to Defence Minister Sir James Allen when he was
visiting Stratford. His answer to the advocates seemed to be
to approach patriotic committees for financial support.

The matter was discussed at a meeting of the Taranaki
Rugby Union, around the time of the first anniversary of the
landing at Gallipoli. A Mr McLeod spoke of the character of
Norkey as 'one of the straightest fellows that played football'.
In conclusion a resolution was passed that they:

> strongly protest against the inhuman treatment by the
> Pensions Board in failing to make adequate allowance
> for Mrs. Dewar (aged 65) who[se] son lost his life in
> the defence of his country, and the Union asks that
> she be placed at least in the position of comfort that
> existed prior to the death of her son.

For a number of years, on the anniversary of Dewar's death,
his mother (until her passing in 1925) and the families of his
brother and sister would place an In Memoriam piece of verse
in the *Evening Post* newspaper. This one from 1921 read:
'A precious one from us is gone/A voice we loved is stilled/A
place is vacant in our home/Which never can be filled'.

In 1941, 'J.H.' wrote a tribute to both Downing and
Dewar in the *Auckland Star*, which concluded: 'The wonderful
sunsets may continue over Thrace eternally, but that night we
climbed the iron sides of the troopships to join our Gurkha
friends, leaving Gallipoli for ever, we left behind two of the
best. May they rest in peace.'

There are no known graves for either man. Their names
are carved on the Chunuk Bair Memorial along with 854 other
New Zealand soldiers who lie somewhere on the peninsula.

23 August 1915

ENLISTED: **Sergeant Beethoven 'Beet' ALGAR (1894–1989)**
AGE AT ENLISTMENT: 21 years, 2 months, 26 days
ARMY NUMBER: 11/1884
EMBARKATION: Wellington, 13 November 1915; Wellington Mounted Rifles, 8th Reinforcements
LENGTH OF SERVICE: 3 years, 97 days
PLAYED FOR: Poneke; Wellington 1914–15, 1919–22; North Island 1919–21
ALL BLACK NUMBER: 214
POSITION: Utility back
APPEARANCES: 1920–21; 6 matches, 1 as captain; 9 points (3 tries)

Algar's family was what in modern parlance would be called 'dysfunctional'. His father was a tailor's cutter, while his mother was a composer. Such was her love of music, she named one of her five children Beethoven. Sadly, she also had a love of liquor, and that was one of the reasons his parents separated when Beet was a young boy.

Algar said that he hated his father, whom he went to live with at Wellington's Worser Bay. Having completed schooling to Standard 6, he ran away from home and secured a job in a Masterton hotel as what was known as 'a buttons boy', a messenger for management and guests. On receiving news of his father's death, he returned to Wellington, reunited with his mother, brothers and sister, and took up an apprenticeship as a joiner in a factory his eldest brother owned.

His first outing for the Wellington provincial rugby team was in 1914 and he quickly established himself as a key figure in the team that season. When they claimed the Ranfurly Shield off Taranaki on 10 September 1914, Algar put the challengers in the lead 4–3 when he kicked a dropped goal early in the first half, and 15 minutes after the interval Algar made what would be the winning score. The Wellingtonians returned a kick, passes going from Teddy Roberts to Jim Moffitt to Jim Tilyard and on to Algar, who, nearing the sideline, cut back past a lone Taranaki defender and dotted down under the posts. The conversion was a formality for Teddy Roberts, to make the score 12–6 in their favour.

Algar told historians Nicholas Boyack and Jane Tolerton that on hearing the proclamation of war he and a group of mates rushed to the recruitment hall in Buckle Street. 'I felt it was my duty to go. Couldn't think of anything else really. It came before everything.'

Somehow confusion arose over Algar's age, even though he was 20 and of the legal age to enlist. A year later, and after three more games for Wellington, Algar tried again and was finally able to sign up. He left New Zealand with the Mounted Rifles, but transferred to the Imperial Camel Corps in July 1916. The Corps functioned exactly the same as their horse-riding colleagues, but their new mounts were more suited to the desert conditions.

There was initial humorous disdain for the camels by the soldiers, who found mounting the animals most ungainly at Firstly, and the pace and way in which they walked caused a lot of discomfort until riders became more relaxed and experienced in handling them. Riding at speed, however, was never deemed comfortable. One noted advantage was the height the men sat at. The air up there was cooler than when sitting closer to the blazing hot desert sands in horse saddles.

Cameleers fed their camels durra, which was millet, and an issue of 50 pounds (23 kilograms) was expected to last the camel five days. The soldiers themselves also carried a five-gallon (23-litre) water carrier, among dry rations, and that, too, was expected to last five days. Additional items carried by the camels included rifles, 250 rounds of ammunition, blankets, a waterproof sheet, bivvy poles, firewood, spare clothing and other personal items. Once the rider was in the saddle, with his feet in a leather apron which hung from the saddle across the camel's shoulders, the average weight for the camel to carry could be as much as 150 kilograms. If a camel could not stand up once he was 'packed', the weight was considered too great and items would have to be discarded. But, once the rickety-looking legs of the camel pushed up and straightened out, the camel could walk for hours.

For Kiwis such as Algar, a relaxing game of football could quickly be mustered up, but just as quickly interrupted. 'We were going out to play a game of football at six o'clock one night and we got orders to saddle up and be ready to move in a quarter of an hour,' he recalled.

His time in active service finished at the end of November 1917, when he was part of a bombing raid that was sent to secure rations:

We were ready to go in, with a bomb in one hand with the pin out. I had a bomb in this hand with the pin out and another one in this hand and two in a tunic. Anyhow, the next thing I knew I was blown over. I don't know where it came from, but it couldn't have been anyone else but our shells ... another fellow and myself we threw our rifles away and threw our bombs away. And we took off. I could run; I was hit in the buttock and I was hit in the arm. He was shot through the calves in both legs. And we ran that far that we lost ourselves. We couldn't find a dressing station till about three o'clock in the morning. So we finally got to the dressing station and were evacuated.

I thought I'd broken my arm — but it had only broken the skin. When I got to the dressing station I had to have it in a sling. I couldn't move it and it was black and blue. I think I got the nosecap off a shell or something, a bomb. So I wasn't worried much about that one. Then I said, 'Oh, wait a minute; I've got another one here,' and I took my pants down and it was full of blood and skin. Blood was flowing down my leg.

Algar spent two-and-a-half months in the heavily populated 27th General Hospital, where the medical treatment was crude to say the least:

> There were no medicines in those days ... the only thing was iodine, and they used to bare all the wounds to the open sun and just heal naturally ... I had this piece of metal in my buttock ... my legs were swelling up and it was touch and go whether I was going to lose my leg. They never used to bother about anaesthetic or anything; they used to come along and roll me over and the doctor used to put his fingers in and work around in the wound, you know to try and find this foreign body that was causing the trouble. I had the narrow squeak of my life. It didn't fracture the sciatic nerve — if that had been touched I'd have been a cripple for life.

Perhaps unsurprisingly, the wound turned septic and formed an abscess. Two procedures were undertaken to lance the wound that left Algar with a two-inch (five-centimetre) scar on his backside. In March 1918 he was still complaining of stiffness and a sharp pain in his right hip upon flexing or bending, and sitting on anything hard for long periods of time caused further discomfort.

So his days in the saddle were over. He returned to New Zealand and was discharged from the army on account of the disability:

> I wasn't home any time and I was up before the board. Certainly I was alright and all the rest of it. I knew the doctor very well, and he knew I was a footballer of course. He came in and he just looked at me and laughed, you know. He said, 'Are you going to play football?' I said yes. And they stopped my pension right away!

After the war he was regarded as the best centre in Wellington football and, thanks to great form for Wellington, was chosen for the 1920 All Blacks who played three games against New Zealand provinces and seven matches across the Tasman. Algar only turned out twice in Australia, but did play the three home games and had the honour of captaining the team in the match against Manawatu–Horowhenua–Wanganui played at Palmerston North. He also scored a try in the 39–0 win.

He was close to final selection for the tests against the 1921 Springboks, and thus played for the 'seconds' against New South Wales who were also in the country. The visitors won 0–17.

Algar captained Poneke from 1919 to 1922, which included their championship win in 1921. Such was the strength of loyalties and spectator fervour surrounding Wellington club rugby at the time that well-known players such as Algar received a lot of sideline abuse. The cat-calls were at their most resounding in the 1922 Wellington club championship deciding game. It was the final club match of the season for the teams, both of whom had 25 points on the club table. The match of the day at Athletic Park, it was played in front of a then-record crowd of 16,000. The club rounds had been a test of attrition for both teams and their players, and both sides went into the game having to call in players or, in the case of Petone, move a back into the forwards. There had been some doubt about Algar playing, as he had reportedly had two shoulder dislocations during the season. With only a few minutes left to play, Petone were leading 7–5. As Petone mounted a threatening attack, a despairing Algar made a thoroughly reflexive action to halt the progress of an opponent and thrust out his foot. The referee, Mr Leith, immediately blew the whistle and had no hesitation in sending Algar from the field. The resulting penalty was kicked by Petone and the win was sealed 10–5.

Upon retiring as a player, Algar coached his club in 1925 and was made its patron in 1979.

ENLISTED: **Driver Alfred 'Alf' Hubert WEST (1893–1934)**
AGE AT ENLISTMENT: 22 years, 3 months, 17 days
ARMY NUMBER: 11/1995
EMBARKATION: Wellington, 13 November 1915; Wellington Mounted Rifles, 8th Reinforcements
LENGTH OF SERVICE: 4 years, 83 days

PLAYED FOR: Hawera; Taranaki 1920–25; North Island 1920–
   21; New Zealand Trials 1921, 1924
ALL BLACK NUMBER: 225
POSITION: Loose-forward
APPEARANCES: 1920–21, 1923–25; 24 matches, including 2
   tests; 20 points (6 tries, 1 conversion)

A Hawera clubmate of Richard Fogarty, West had played senior club rugby from the age of 18. George Nepia described his fellow Invincible, who wore something of a mischievous, toothy grin, as living 'under the slopes of Mt Egmont and there is a hard quality about his play which suggests the crags of the mountain'.

West's war service had begun with the Wellington Mounted Rifles in Moascar before being transferred to the New Zealand Divisional Ammunition Column in France where he worked as a driver. After only two months in Europe he was admitted to hospital suffering from swelling of lymphatic glands under his right arm. He spent two months recovering in the 2nd London General Hospital at Chelsea and the No. 2 New Zealand General Hospital in Walton, before a further two months at the Hornchurch convalescent camp.

Back in France he joined the New Zealand Field Artillery, from where he was chosen to play in the Divisional Football Team. He also spent time as a cook.

It was his time with the Services side that led to him, after only one game for Taranaki, being chosen to play for the North Island and then the All Black tour of Australia in 1920. To the amusement of his teammates he arrived in Wellington ready to sail with the sum of his luggage being wrapped up in a brown paper parcel. Obviously he had all he needed, as he missed only one of the tour games!

His two test-match appearances were against the 1921 Springboks in the second and third tests when he came into the side replacing 'Son' White.

One story has West preparing to play in the second match against New South Wales in 1923 when teammate and doctor Richard Sinclair (who also hailed from Taranaki and had a medical practice in Hawera) noticed a large boil on West's shin. It was, apparently, 'as big as a saucer'. West was asked what he was going to do about the carbuncle. He smiled and said he wasn't going to treat it at all. He was warned by his medical mate that he'd better have it lanced because if it burst inwardly, the bacteria could be life-threatening. Resigned to the better judgement of his colleague, he waited for Sinclair to collect his medical bag. Without so much as a grimace from West, the boil was treated in the hotel they were staying in, and he played the match a couple of days later.

Winston McCarthy considered West 'one of the hardest forwards to play for New Zealand', while he impressed a writer for *The Free Lance* when the Services team played Wellington in 1920, who wrote 'what a fine specimen of New Zealand manhood he is'.

West's best footballing was undoubtedly seen during his time with the Services side, but he was still good enough to make the tour to Britain in 1924. He was the oldest player in the touring party, listed in newspapers and rugby records as being 31 based on a birth year of 1893, but his service records put his birth as 6 May 1889. So he may in fact have been five years older than any other member of the team. Hence he was referred to with some frequency as an 'old-time footballer'.

Perhaps as a result of the way he carried his luggage in 1920, when being farewelled for England in 1924 his club presented him with a suitcase and a pocket-watch, and one speech in his honour stated that 'no more popular player ever went on to field than Alf West'.

On the Invincibles tour, an invitation was extended by a renowned public school for one of the team to appear at an assembly and talk about rugby football. By all accounts the 'Naki farmer proved highly entertaining. In fielding questions from the boys, West advised that for their own protection they should always wear shin pads.

West was often sought out by teammates for his sage advice on various aspects of their play, or tactics that should be employed, and he had a thunderous boot that saw him kick goals in club football from as far out as halfway.

Upon his return from the 1924–25 tour, West worked as a fencing contractor and was quick to return to club football, although a rib injury ended his season and slowed down his participation the following year. However, as club captain for Hawera from 1927 to 1929 he always had his kit with him in supporting his team home or away, and several times answered the last-minute call to get into his playing strip and join play on the field.

Sadly, just 10 years after sailing with the Invincibles, West died in hospital of cirrhosis of the liver and heart failure. He had always said that he played wholeheartedly but also for enjoyment, and the fact that the national selectors had seen him worthy of representing his country was very pleasing. He was buried in Hawera cemetery.

A year after his death, football friends were raising money for a memorial for Alf. It ultimately took the form of the Alf West Memorial Trophy, which, to this day, is awarded to the runners-up in the premier division of Taranaki club rugby.

1 October 1915

All New Zealand men aged 17–60 were required to register before 9 November 1915 as part of a 'civil register for the purposes of determining the resources of the Dominion in men. It was also noted that 'the registration does not involve enlistment'.

8 October 1915

ENLISTED: **Major William 'Billy' Spiers GLENN** MC **(1877–1953)**
AGE AT ENLISTMENT: Approximately 38 years
ARMY NUMBER: unknown
EMBARKATION: unknown; Royal Field Artillery, 1915–19
LENGTH OF SERVICE: unknown
PLAYED FOR: Waimate; Taranaki 1901–05, 1912; Taranaki–Wanganui–Manawatu 1904; North Island 1904–05
ALL BLACK NUMBER: 111
POSITION: Side- and back-row forward
APPEARANCES: 1904–06; 19 matches, including 2 tests

Glenn was born in Greymouth, the second of six children, but when he was a small boy his parents, George and Catherine, moved to Manaia in southern Taranaki to farm. In the centre of the main street stood a tall monument to members of the Armed Constabulary and Patea Field Force who were killed in the New Zealand Wars of 1868–69 (on which would be inscribed the names of those who died in later wars).

The Cyclopedia of New Zealand [Taranaki, Hawke's Bay & Wellington Provincial Districts], published in 1908, states that Glenn's first-class rugby career with Taranaki began in 1899. A 'W. Glenn' appeared as an emergency in an 1898 match against Manawatu, which would fit with him having just moved out of the junior grade. He was a constant presence in the team from 1901 to 1905.

In 1904, he married Linda Parsons at St Mary's Church in Parnell, Auckland, where the bride's widowed mother lived, and he began public service as a member of the Manaia Town Board while also holding committee positions or memberships with the Manaia Tennis Club, Egmont Racing Club and the Egmont Agricultural and Pastoral Association. He spent three years working as an auctioneer for the firm Steuart and Corrigan and began to develop his ownership of race horses.

Glenn was first chosen for the All Blacks in 1904, to face the British team in Wellington, and was the lightest of the home forwards and the only Taranaki representative in the team.

When the next All Black side was chosen in 1905 — to firstly undertake a three-match visit to Australia as well as four local games against Auckland, a combined Otago–Southland, Canterbury and Wellington prior to the larger expedition to Britain — he was joined by five other men from 'butterfat country': fellow forwards Jim O'Sullivan and Frank Glasgow, five-eighth Harry Mynott and speedsters Bunny Abbott and Jimmy Hunter.

Glenn played in 5 of the 7 preliminary games, but his participation in the 35-match Originals tour was constantly interrupted by injury or illness. He arrived in England suffering from a poisoned leg and wasn't fit to play until the sixth match, against Middlesex. In all, he played only 13 games on tour, and was so obviously fed up with the frustrations of injury and not playing that when games in North America were added to the itinerary shortly before the proposed conclusion of the tour, Glenn opted to return to New Zealand, via the Suez Canal and in the company of Eric Harper. Charlie Seeling and William 'Massa' Johnston also made their back but via direct steamer.

In August 1915, a decade after sailing from Wellington with the Originals, Glenn — a member of the Wanganui Mounted Rifles — was called up to go into camp with the 8th Reinforcements. For some unknown reason he instead travelled to London with his good friend Wellington lawyer Frank Newman, who was the son of a Member of Parliament, Dr A.K. Newman, and a partner in the firm Moorhouse, Hadfield and Newman. Both were granted commissions with the Royal Field Artillery. (Glenn's service record could not be obtained from archives in England so details such as his army number and length of service are not included above.) Glenn was gazetted as a second lieutenant on 15 October 1915. This put him in charge of a two-gun, horse-drawn unit of either 18-pounder field guns or 4.5-inch Howitzers. The *Athletic News* commented that Glenn 'coming to this country to offer his services as a soldier is only one more instance of the loyalty of the New Zealanders'.

In June 1916, while serving with the 73rd Battery, 5th Brigade, Royal Field Artillery (which at the time was under the command of the 3rd Canadian Division), he was awarded the Military Cross, 'for conspicuous gallantry and ability as Observing Officer. He was exposed to heavy shell fire for several hours, but with great coolness and judgement corrected the fire of his battery throughout, and sent back constant reports on the situation.'

At the same time, his friend Frank Newman was wounded and hospitalised in Boulogne. Newman's father sailed for France and toured hospitals and visited the commander of the New Zealand forces, General Russell, and New Zealand soldiers at Armentières. Upon his return he gave several public lectures recounting his observations of the war effort.

At one such event in Wanganui early in 1917, Newman mentioned Glenn's receipt of the Military Cross and spiritedly said that 'extraordinary precautions were taken against disease in this war, and this was the best fed, best clothed, best nursed, and best looked after army the world had ever seen'. He praised the efforts of the 'nation's womanhood', and proudly proclaimed that 'the New Zealanders were great athletes and their knowledge of football proved of the greatest service in making them quick and active'. Kiwi soldiers, he said, 'had the reputation of never having gone back from a position they had won until they were told', and he had been told 'by high authorities that the ultimate thing in this war was the bravery of the man with the bayonet who would "go into" the other man. The Maoris were splendid at bayonet fighting, and they enjoyed it.'

He concluded by urging the assembled 'to be prepared for greater hardships and further sacrifices, and to continually pray that the God of Battles might protect our boys and bring them safely home to us'.

Glenn's battery was attached to the 4th Canadian Division from September 1916 until July 1917. It reverted to being a British Army Brigade serving with the Second Army in October 1917, the Third Army in December 1917, the First Army in February 1918, the Fifth Army in July 1918 and finally returned to the Fourth Army in October 1918.

At war's end, Glenn held the rank of major and returned to New Zealand.

In 1919, he stood in the December general election (following the retirement due to poor health of the initially selected candidate), representing the Reform Party. They sat in the government benches under the leadership of Prime Minister William Massey.

Glenn became the first former All Black to enter parliament when he won the newly re-drawn seat of Rangitikei, securing 2,903 votes and a majority of 635. (An opposing candidate was Brigadier-General Meldrum, who had served with the Mounted Rifles.)

Glenn served on the NZRFU management committee as a selector in 1922–23 and in 1929, when shortly into his fourth term as an MP he announced that 'the pressure of private business made it imperative that he should retire'.

He was later a steward and trustee of the Wanganui Jockey Club. As a horse-breeder and owner he often caught up with old footballers and soldiers when attending race meetings around the country.

11 October 1915

ENLISTED: **Rifleman William August 'Jockey' FORD (1895–1959)**

AGE AT ENLISTMENT: 20 years, 1 month, 16 days

ARMY NUMBER: 26/173

EMBARKATION: Wellington, 5 February 1916; 4th Battalion, New Zealand Rifle Brigade

LENGTH OF SERVICE: 4 years, 36 days

PLAYED FOR: Merivale; Canterbury 1920–26; South Island 1921; New Zealand Trials 1921

ALL BLACK NUMBER: 241

POSITION: Wing

APPEARANCES: 1921–23; 9 matches; 21 points (7 tries)

Although diminutive in stature, hence his nickname 'Jockey', Ford was hugely popular in Canterbury rugby and was the top try-scorer for Canterbury in the 1922 (4), 1923 (6) and 1925 (9) seasons. His height in his service file varies from five feet six (168 centimetres) to five feet nine (175 centimetres). Undoubtedly the former is correct.

Ford, a drover born in Papanui, served with the New Zealand Rifle Brigade and came through the war physically unscathed, although he did see hospital time due to influenza and other illnesses.

He was a member of the Services side which won the King's Cup and then toured South Africa in 1919. Although it is hard to establish the playing XV for every game the army side played, Ford has been confirmed as playing in at least 30 of the team's matches. His try-scoring finishes thrilled spectators in Britain and South Africa.

Arguably his greatest try was the match-winning score when Canterbury beat the 1921 Springboks 6–5 at Lancaster Park. On the day before the game, the Springboks had been made honorary members of the Christchurch RSA. Torrential rain on the morning of the match saw a curtain-raiser between two primary-school teams moved to an outside field. When the players took to the field, the Springbok forwards — nicknamed the 'Big Bucks' by one reporter — were outweighing their home opponents by an average of 2 stone (13 kilograms) per man. According to the *The Sun* newspaper, the slippery conditions made the game one hard slog. The 15-stone (95-kilogram) J.J. van Rooyen was: 'commonly known as "The Tank", because of his playful habit of charging down field with several opponents hanging on to him — there is a legend that the tanks of the Western Front in the Great War were modelled after some "brass hat" had seen van Rooyen in action'.

The Springboks were utterly dominant at the scrum but struggled in the loose, and ultimately it was in that department that the home team won the match.

Shortly after the second half began, Ford (who had a bustling, busy game) made a run on the touchline just inside the Springboks' half and punted infield. The visitors' fullback, Gerhard Morkel, fielded the ball, but, as he tried to clear to touch, the Canterbury centre Colin Deans (younger brother of the famous but sadly deceased Bob) scragged him. The kick lobbed to Ford, who swerved past his opposite, deftly side-stepped two other defenders and crashed over the try-line in the tackle of two other Springboks.

Of his nine games for the All Blacks, five were against New South Wales. While regarded as tests by the media and public, the games were not accorded that status by the New Zealand Rugby Football Union. So, Ford finished his international career uncapped, when he could well have had five.

19 October 1915

ENLISTED: **Corporal Edmond RYAN (1891–1965)**
AGE AT ENLISTMENT: 24 years, 8 months, 2 days
ARMY NUMBER: 2/2715
EMBARKATION: Wellington, 8 January 1916; New Zealand
  Field Artillery, 9th Reinforcements
LENGTH OF SERVICE: 4 years, 21 days
PLAYED FOR: Petone; Wellington 1912–15, 1920–21, 1923

ALL BLACK NUMBER: 244
POSITION: Centre
APPEARANCES: 1921; 1 match

One of seven brothers to play for the Poneke seniors (with five of them making the Wellington representative side), Edmond Ryan worked as a boilermaker at the Petone railway workshops. He debuted for Wellington in 1912, and was twice in teams from the capital that lost Shield challenges in Auckland. It was a case of third time lucky for the hard-running outside back with a sharp side-step, who would tuck the ball tightly up under his arm before charging upfield, when he was part of the team that defeated Taranaki for the log in 1914. He continued to play representative football until entering Trentham at the end of the 1915 season.

A member of the 5th Garrison Artillery during peacetime, much of his time in service was spent working in France as a fitter with the New Zealand Field Artillery.

He was selected for the Divisional Football team in December 1916, and then the team to contest the King's Cup, which was captained by his younger brother, James.

Away from the football field he suffered from 'influenza of the larynx' and a range of infections, including a somewhat prolonged infection to his right ear.

Ryan returned to the Wellington team in 1920, and turned out against the Springboks the following year. The last of his 43 matches for Wellington was in 1923. Upon retirement, he lived out his days in what was then the relatively new suburb of Wainuiomata.

ENLISTED: **Bombardier John Alexander McNAB (1895–1979)**
AGE AT ENLISTMENT: 19 years, 10 months, 5 days
ARMY NUMBER: 11/2177
EMBARKATION: Wellington, 14 January 1916; Wellington Mounted Rifles, 9th Reinforcements
LENGTH OF SERVICE: 3 years, 252 days

PLAYED FOR: Celtic; Hawke's Bay 1920–24; Hawke's Bay–
   Poverty Bay 1921; North Island 1922, 1924; Hawke's
   Bay–Poverty Bay–East Coast 1923; New Zealand Trials
   1924
ALL BLACK NUMBER: 316
POSITION: Back-row forward
APPEARANCES: 1925; 1 match

Working as an engine-steerer, McNab was serving with the Territorial Army and living at Twyford, Hastings, when he enlisted. He arrived at Suez in time to join and train with the New Zealand Division before embarking for France, and was very fortunate that his time as a bombardier with the New Zealand Field Artillery was only broken by a bout of illness in October 1917. Then, exactly a year later, he was evacuated to hospital with trench fever.

As with a number of players who played only one match for the All Blacks in the years either side of the war, that statistic doesn't do justice to his overall first-class career. In the case of McNab, appendicitis rather than the dark lead of a selector's pencil saw the end of opportunity in black and ultimately his provincial rugby career.

The war and the vagaries of demobilisation meant he was 25 before he first played for Hawke's Bay, but he was part of the ascendant team that took the Shield from Wellington and he played in a dozen defences. Considering who selector Norm McKenzie had at his disposal (the likes of the Brownlie brothers and Sam Gemmell), it was saying something for McNab that he could be included in the side even if it meant he had to anchor the scrum at lock rather than slot in at his preferred position of back-row. He was another muscular, fit, laconic farmer-joker in the pack.

Heading back to the Bay after losing to Auckland in a match to raise money for the construction of the Auckland War Memorial Museum, McNab and the rest of the Bay side were aware of the less-than-favourable welcome they would get from 'Magpies' fans. 'You know, when I get home I think even the dog will bite me,' he was heard to jest.

Such was the selectors' interest in him as a utility-forward when they eyed the long tour to Britain in 1924–25 that he played in three of the trial games, but he did not make the final team list. His chance in the black jersey finally came in 1925 when he was a member of the All Black team that went to New South Wales. He played in only one game, the first 'test' against New South Wales, won 26–3, before being hospitalised with appendicitis. After an operation in Sydney, he returned to New Zealand and life on the farm.

20 October 1915

ENLISTED: **Private Eric McDonald 'Fritz' SNOW (1898–1974)**

AGE AT ENLISTMENT: 17 years, 6 months, 1 day

ARMY NUMBER: 6/3874

EMBARKATION: Wellington, 8 January 1916; Canterbury Infantry Battalion, 9th Reinforcements

LENGTH OF SERVICE: 2 years, 237 days

PLAYED FOR: Nelson club; Nelson 1919–24, 1926, 1927, 1929, 1930; Nelson–Marlborough–Golden Bay–Motueka 1921, 1930; South Island Country 1920; South Island 1923, 1927, 1929; New Zealand Trials 1921, 1924, 1927, 1929, 1930

ALL BLACK NUMBER: 341

POSITION: Back-row forward

APPEARANCES: 1928–29; 16 matches, including 3 tests; 3 points (1 try)

Such was the desire of Snow to serve with the NZEF, the Nelson plumber inflated his age by two-and-a-half years. He was one of three brothers to serve, and perhaps it was keenness to join the cause as his brothers Roy and Ashley had that led to Eric lying about his age when he first registered in June 1915.

Roy had departed with the 3rd Reinforcements and, having observed some of the Gallipoli landing operation, had stepped foot on the peninsula two days after the first wave of Anzac soldiers.

He spent four months in the hillside trenches before succumbing to dysentery and being removed to Alexandria. Ashley followed with the 5th Reinforcements, and met up with Eric at Gallipoli.

A member of the Nelson Volunteer Fire Brigade and the 12th Nelson Regiment, Eric served with the Canterbury Regiment before he was hospitalised with an infection of his middle ear. He then suffered a gunshot wound to the abdomen, which was classified as severe, towards the end of January 1918. Brother Ashley was also seriously wounded, and both men returned to New Zealand on the same hospital ship.

Snow had recovered enough by the winter of 1919 to resume playing for Nelson. At almost six feet two inches (188 centimetres) tall, he was a real asset for any side he played in when it came to the lineout. His knowledge of local players was highly regarded, so much so that he was installed as sole selector of the Nelson team in 1925 when the union's management committee sacked the previous selector following a vote of no confidence. (He would officially be appointed selector in 1934.)

In 1928, he became Nelson's third All Black (after George Harper, 1893, and Bill Smith, 1905) when chosen to tour South Africa. While in the Republic, he played a part in the return of a relic from the Boer War. Another Nelsonian, Lieutenant Colonel W.R. Pearson, of Wakefield, had returned from service in Africa in possession of a Mauser carbine rifle. It had been 'souvenired' from a Boer soldier taken prisoner by New Zealand soldiers. The brass plate on the butt of the rifle was inscribed with the initials 'P.J.P.'. On Pearson's passing the rifle was given to a Mr W.H. Bryant. A year before the All Blacks' trip, in an absolute fluke of circumstance, a South African newspaper also came into the possession of Bryant. One article caught his eye, that which covered the proceedings of a meeting in Cape Town at which a Mr P.J. Pienaar was a speaker. Bryant wondered whether Mr Pienaar was the 'P.J.P.' whose rifle had been in Nelson for nearly 30 years. So Bryant wrote to the editor of the newspaper, asking if he could forward a description of the rifle to Mr Pienaar.

Months later, when the All Blacks were in the Republic, Mr Pienaar made contact with Snow and called on the All

Blacks. The rifle had indeed been his, and, not only was he keen to be reunited with it, but the maker of the brass plate was, too. Pienaar, a 'well-to-do' man, showed his appreciation by showering hospitality on the touring footballers. Snow passed Pienaar's address on to Bryant, and Christmas 1928 saw the former Boer soldier celebrating the return of his prized possession.

Unfortunately for Snow, none of his nine games in South Africa were test matches, and when he did finally play test football, in Australia in 1929 at the age of 31, he was in the losing side three times as the Wallabies won 9–8, 17–9 and 15–13, their first clean sweep of the All Blacks.

23 October 1915

A unique football match took place between Australian and New Zealand representatives at Mudros West, Lemnos Island, at the end of October 1915. The match, which drew a 'large and enthusiastic crowd', was reported in the *Hawera & Normanby Star:*

> Following was the New Zealand team: Fullback, Murray (Auckland); three-quarters, Cuthill (Otago), Marks (Otago) and Bertrand (Taranaki); five-eighths, Cameron (Taranaki) and E. Roberts (Wellington); half, R. Wood (Taranaki); wing-forward, Taylor (Taranaki); forwards, Newell (Taranaki), Sullivan (Wellington), Smart (Canterbury), Richards (Canterbury), McNab (Auckland), Brownlee (Hawke's Bay) and Barber (Wellington). A strong wind was blowing, which interfered considerably with goal-kicking. New Zealand had the best of the matters throughout the game and in the first spell succeeded in compiling fifteen points, to their opponents' nil. The second half of the game was merely a walk over for the 'All Blacks,' who wore khaki, and another 18 points were added, the Australians only succeeding in obtaining one try. The following scored tries for New Zealand: 'Teddy' Roberts (3), Sullivan, Marks (2), Newell (2), Smart and Cuthill (2). Maber scored the only try for Australia.

Corporal J. Thorpe also wrote home about the match:

> The tide was out, and the match was played on the hard sand at the edge of the lagoon ... A strong wind was blowing and between poor posts and a soccer ball goalkicking was abandoned after several unsuccessful kicks had been made. The game was one-sided and apart from one or two flashes of brilliancy on the part of the Australian backs there was little in the game to raise excitement to a high pitch. The Maoriland forwards were far superior to their opponents ... Sergeant Syd. Paul (N.Z.) (a Taranaki rep) controlled the game in a satisfactory manner. It was played in two half hour spells.

15 November 1915

ENLISTED: **Rifleman Ernest Arthur 'Moke' BELLISS (1894–1974)**
AGE AT ENLISTMENT: 21 years, 7 months, 14 days
ARMY NUMBER: 23/1937
EMBARKATION: Wellington, 4 March 1916; New Zealand Rifle Brigade, 1st Battalion, E Company, 4th Reinforcements
LENGTH OF SERVICE: 4 years
PLAYED FOR: Moawhanga Huia and Hautapu clubs; Wanganui 1914, 1920–31; North Island 1920–22
ALL BLACK NUMBER: 226
POSITION: Wing-forward and loose-forward
APPEARANCES: 1920–23; 20 matches, including 3 tests, 6 games as captain; 27 points (9 tries)

A real Taihape identity, not just because he was a butcher in the town, Belliss was one of a raft of national sporting figures who came from the central North Island hamlet in the post-war years. New Zealand cricket captain Tom Lowry, Olympic athletics representative and national half-mile record holder Don Evans, and golfer J.P. Mortland were all Taihape residents at some time in their sporting careers.

Belliss's first taste of provincial rugby came in 1914 for Wanganui, but it was on the other side of the world towards the end of the war that he made a name for himself, in the King's Cup and Services football team in South Africa.

Apart from three bouts of what was probably trench fever, Belliss's time in active service with the 4th Battalion of the 3rd New Zealand Rifle Brigade was injury-free, and at the end of the war he was chosen to join the King's Cup–winning Services side for their trip to South Africa.

On the 1920 tour of New South Wales, there was a plethora of quality wing-forwards in the side, such as Harry Jacob, David Baird and Belliss, but Belliss quickly established his standing and played in 9 of the 10 games.

In the first 'test', it was Belliss's speed (having been an outside back in his younger days, as well as a middle-distance runner) that saw him selected at wing-forward. His performance in the match was not only eye-catching, but it also brought about a change in thinking regarding the role of the rover. Pre-war, the wing-forward had been a defender or attacker from the scrum, doing his best to unsettle the opposing half-back and then disrupt the plays of the inside backs. Being supremely fit and quick, Belliss also became a link man between his forwards and backs, quick onto loose ball or in support of his runners on attack. He scored five tries on tour, three of which were in two of the games against New South Wales.

When the 1921 Springboks played Wanganui, they literally wondered just what had hit them, as Belliss's dive-tackling (invoking the great days of the great Wanganui-born forward 'Bronco' Seeling) drew cheers from the crowd at Cooks Gardens every time he brought a man down. Rarely did he miss his target that day, and generally it was not uncommon for his tackling to be described as ferocious.

He scored a controversial try in the first test against the Springboks at Carisbrook, when he followed up a kick into the Springboks' in-goal that looked for all money as though it would be forced by winger A.J. van Heerden, a man of electric pace himself. Belliss kept up his pursuit and dived for the ball at the same time as van Heerden. The South African was adamant that he had been the first to get his hands on the ball, but local referee Ernie McKenzie (later selector-coach of the All Blacks and Hawke's Bay) awarded a try to Belliss. It was the first try scored by an All Black against the Springboks.

Then he became something of a national hero when it became known that he had played the third test match in Wellington while hindered by a broken thumb.

Belliss captained the All Blacks in Australia in 1922, leading from the front, and Winston McCarthy described him as being 'tireless and relentless, and threw himself into all phases of play with little regard for his own safety, let alone that of others. He was a feared opponent and a grand team man. Players of his era ranked him with the world's best.' Four of the tour games were played at the Sydney Cricket Ground, and one out at Manly. The side lost two of the three matches against New South Wales.

In 1923, the All Blacks played only three home games against New South Wales. Belliss appeared in two of the games, but, come the following year, as plans were being finalised for the tour of Great Britain, and the selectors whetted the nibs of their pencils, Belliss's name was eventually crossed out of contention.

But that was far from the end of his time on the field. He formally retired from Wanganui representative football in 1929 at the age of 34, after a match against Wellington, opposing Cliff Porter, who had been captain of the Invincibles, but his boots were always close at hand just in case Wanganui were struggling to field a fit team. That happened several times, and his ninety-eighth and last first-class appearance wasn't until two seasons later.

Newspapers paid credit to him as someone who had 'represented Wanganui on many occasions with credit to himself and the union, and his generalship many times has been the deciding factor. Belliss always played for the team rather than for himself, and his unselfishness was characteristic of the man.'

Belliss's grandson Peter was a three-time world champion at lawn bowls.

16 November 1915

ENLISTED: **Trooper Cyril James BROWNLIE (1895–1954)**

AGE AT ENLISTMENT: 20 years, 3 months, 10 days

ARMY NUMBER: 9/2256

EMBARKATION: Wellington, 4 March 1916; Otago Mounted Rifles, 10th Reinforcements

LENGTH OF SERVICE: 3 years, 188 days

PLAYED FOR: Hastings, Waiau and Wairoa Pirates clubs; Hawke's Bay 1922–26, 1927, 1930; Hawke's Bay–Poverty Bay–East Coast 1923; North Island 1924–25, 1927; New Zealand Trials 1924, 1927

ALL BLACK NUMBER: 291

POSITION: Back-row forward

APPEARANCES: 1924–26, 1928; 31 matches, including 3 tests; 33 points (11 tries)

Cyril Brownlie deserves to be regarded as one of the great All Black forwards, not just of the pre-World War II era but of all time. Not only was he was the biggest man in the 1924–25 touring party — which was saying something considering the company he was keeping — he was also one of the fastest in the side. He was possessed of great hands come lineout time, and was sure to make ground whenever he ran with ball in hand. Brownlie was a quiet giant, at six feet three inches (191 centimetres) and 15 stone (95 kilograms). Several All Black teammates nicknamed him 'Dummy', because he could appear to be as stiff and wooden as a ventriloquist's mannequin, but come game time he sprang to life.

Brownlie first gave notice that he was a player of great promise when he played two seasons for the Sacred Heart First XV. Initially, he was rejected as unfit to join the army due to slight varicose veins on his left leg. Once they had been treated, he finally enlisted nine months after his older brother Anthony, better known as 'Tony', and was assigned to the Otago Mounted Rifles, despite being from Napier. At the start of the war, soldiers had been included in their regional battalions and regiments, but as the war progressed and numbers had dwindled in various companies, men from outside the districts were added to them.

After a month at the school of instruction in Zeitoun, and a transfer to the Wellington Mounted Rifles at Tel el-Kebir, Brownlie was further transferred to the New Zealand Mounted Rifles Machine Gun Squadron at Bir et Malar in July 1916.

The role of the squadron members was described in *The Kia Ora Coo-ee: The official magazine of the Australian and New-Zealand forces in Egypt, Palestine, Salonica & Mesopotamia*, which was published monthly throughout 1918:

> Carrying a machine gun into action is no joke. The order has been given, 'Dismount. Guns off.' You leap off, hand your horse over to your pack leader, bundle the gun and tripod off the pack ... If you are No. 1, you shoulder the tripod, if No. 2 the gun; whilst Nos. 3 and 4 take two boxes of ammunition each from one of the ammunition packs; and off you start to the nearest vantage spot to get the gun into business ... Complete concealment of the gun position is highly desirable; but alas! not always practicable in an attack where, very often, a position has to be found in haste, and the gun put almost anywhere ... It is fine, once in action, to hear the old lady spitting out death; it gives you a great feeling of security, also the feeling that you are doing your duty in the Great War.

Eight months later, Brownlie had a run-in with a non-commissioned officer which resulted in him being 'awarded' eight days of Field Punishment No. 2 for 'failing to obey the order of an NCO' and 'insolence to an NCO'. Four months later, in July 1917, he again found himself in the detention compound at Moascar, only this time for 28 days. His indiscretions were listed as 'neglect of duty' and 'asleep on horse picquet line'. The sense of authority exhibited by many NCOs in the Middle East was notorious for being exacting and even extreme, and Brownlie was far from the only man punished for what was deemed to be insubordination.

In another issue of *The Kia Ora Coo-ee*, a contributor by the pen-name of 'Booligal Bob' wrote of how some soldiers would go to great efforts to lighten the punishment being endured by their mates:

Who said we couldn't get smokes sneaked into the Clink? I was doing twenty-eight days for telling a certain sergeant that he had no father. The Clink was a wire netting enclosure somewhere on the Canal. My cobber heard that I was without smokes, and immediately got to work. He approached the Clink from the rear, yarded up half-a-dozen of those beetles that old Pharaoh's missus used to call scared scarabs, squatted himself outside the wire, and pretended to be reading a book. After a while, he digs a straight line under the wire, fastens a smoke to one of the beetles, and puts him in the furrow. The insect marches straight ahead, and I got the cigarette. Others followed, and when one of the scarabs showed signs of going on strike, another one was detailed to do the job.

When it came to recreation, Brownlie represented the Mounted Rifles' football team, dwarfing not only his teammates but also most opponents.

In September 1917, he was treated in hospital for sores and abrasions on his left foot. Two months later, while qualifying as a first-class gunner at the school of instruction at Zeitoun, there came the tragic news that his brother Tony, by then a sergeant with the New Zealand Mounted Rifles, had been killed in Palestine on 14 November.

A year later, Cyril Brownlie's service came to an end as the result of contracting malaria. It has been said that Cyril and younger brother Maurice had little interest in football after the war until brother Lawrence made the All Blacks in 1920 and their father challenged the duo to match him. So, the two began making a 40-mile (64-kilometre) trip each winter Saturday from the family farm at Puketitiri to play football in Hastings, and two seasons later Cyril himself was an All Black.

Three times he appeared for the North Island in the company of Maurice, and joined him as one of the Invincibles, playing 20 of the 38 games. His tour was disrupted somewhat by injuries, but the great tragedy of Cyril's playing career was his infamy as the first man sent off in a rugby international.

On 3 January 1925, the unbeaten All Blacks played England at Twickenham in front of 60,000 spectators, among them the Prince of Wales. From the kick-off, both sets of forwards were involved in niggling. Following scrappy play from a lineout, with barely eight minutes gone, referee Albert Freethy of Wales blew the whistle with great gusto, pointed to Brownlie and ordered, 'You, go off.' For a few seconds, everyone was stunned. The All Black captain, Jock Richardson, appealed to the referee for him to change his mind and to the opposing captain, Wakefield, who said nothing.

Just what was Brownlie's alleged act of foul play has been debated almost as hotly as the Bob Deans non-try of 20 years earlier. The newspapers reported that Brownlie had kicked an Englishman on the ground, something no Englishman could testify to having seen or felt. Others claimed it was for a punch, but if there was one it was retaliatory and another offender was not punished.

So, in chilling silence, with his head bowed, Cyril Brownlie walked from the field. Metres away, watching him depart, was the resolute Maurice.

Cyril played the next three games on tour and five in Australia in 1926, as well as continuing to be a mainstay of the Hawke's Bay side until 1927, but his punishment at Twickenham was something that haunted his All Black and Hawke's Bay teammate George Nepia for many years afterwards (as no doubt it did Cyril). Nepia wrote in his autobiography of Cyril's dismissal from the field and the team rejoining him under the stands at halftime:

He is sitting upon a bench, still in his togs. Brownlie has been a soldier and a farmer, as both he has become inured to the cycle of life and death that governs our lives. He is a big, powerful, mature man. Yet the tears are rolling down his cheeks. You carry the lump in your throat for the rest of your life when you think of him sitting there in his loneliness. Poor Cyril! We did our best to comfort him then, later and for the rest of the life that was cut off far short of his time.

Brownlie was convinced by Hawke's Bay selector-coach Norman McKenzie to turn out for the province again in the 1930 Shield challenge against Southland. Having been playing club football, Brownlie agreed and was a valued mentor for some of the younger players who were new to the side. Although he scored a try in the challenge, the match was won by Southland, 9–6. A few days after returning home, he walked into the local post office where McKenzie worked. According to McKenzie:

> He had a parcel under his arm which he handed to me and said, 'Here you are, Mac. I have finished with these. They may be handy for someone else.' After he departed I opened the parcel and in it were Cyril's football boots. That was an action typical of Cyril. He was a man of few words, but a man of undoubted integrity, a man whom I admired very much indeed.

ENLISTED: Corporal Albert Robert 'Mick' LOMAS (1894–1975)

AGE AT ENLISTMENT: 21 years, 1 day
ARMY NUMBER: 13/3045
EMBARKATION: Wellington, 29 February 1916; Auckland
  Mounted Rifles, A Squadron
LENGTH OF SERVICE: 3 years, 279 days
PLAYED FOR: Thames RSA and Thames City clubs; Auckland
  1920, 1924–25, 1928; Auckland–North Auckland 1921;
  New Zealand Trials 1924; North Island 1926
ALL BLACK NUMBER: 310
POSITION: Front-row forward
APPEARANCES: 1925–26; 15 matches; 9 points (3 tries)

Serving with the New Zealand Mounted Rifles in the Middle East, Lomas was wounded in action in Rafa in January 1917. In what sounds like a very lucky escape, he suffered a 'slight' gunshot wound to the thorax, the injury not serious enough to remove him from duty. Three months later, while fighting in Gaza, he was wounded again, suffering a gunshot wound to his left thigh. In

July of the following year, he was hospitalised due to swelling of his left hand.

A curious aspect to his service record is that he was selected to try out for the army football team in England and sailed for Britain from Port Said to join the team, but, despite arriving in March 1919, he didn't join the team and returned to New Zealand from England three months later.

Returning to Thames after the war, he made five appearances for Auckland in his debut season of 1920, then played for the combined Auckland–North Auckland team which faced the 1921 Springboks at Eden Park.

It was 1924 before Lomas appeared for the blue-and-white hoops again, unavailability caused by work as a fisherman, plus travelling the distance from Thames to Auckland. However, when he appeared on the scene again in 1924, he showed tremendous form for a 30-year-old and, having shone in trials games to select the touring party for Britain, France and North America, many considered him a likely inclusion. He wasn't selected, but when he appeared for Auckland against the All Blacks prior to their departure he helped dish out a lesson in front-row play. Auckland triumphed, 14–5, and the All Blacks won only 6 of the 23 scrums contested in the match. This led to George Tyler, who had been one of the stars of the 1905 tour to Britain, lambasting the All Blacks as the worst team to ever leave New Zealand. While his words came back to haunt him, perhaps the lessons learnt from Lomas and his fellow front-rower Lintott were important ones for the team that a few months later would be known as 'The Invincibles'.

In 1925, Lomas played in all six June–July matches in Australia, as well as the games that book-ended the tour against Wellington and Wellington–Horowhenua. None of the Invincibles were considered for that tour, but they were for the one-off match against New South Wales at Eden Park in September. Lomas was selected for that team, which included 13 of those who had returned unbeaten from the Northern Hemisphere, and the side won comfortably, 36–10.

He was also part of the North Island side that crushed the South 41–9 in 1926. The All Blacks' itinerary for that year saw them play Wellington, then six matches in Australia and a game against Auckland before dispersing. Lomas, now very much a first-choice hooker, made six appearances, including the three 'tests' against New South Wales in Sydney. His final match for the All Blacks was the 11–6 win over Auckland, but that was not his final first-class match.

Two years later, with the All Blacks in South Africa, in a season when Auckland played 13 matches and undertook a southern tour (which began in Wairarapa before matches against Canterbury, South Canterbury, Otago and Southland), the union fielded a B side twice on the same day that the A side was playing. Lomas turned out for Auckland for the last time as part of a scratch team in their 13–17 loss to Wellington at Athletic Park, and gave a great account of himself on a day when the Auckland forwards weren't expected to dominate, but did. According to one newspaper report, were it not for 'one or two inexplicable blunders' on the part of the referee, they could have stolen the game.

Through his later role as chief fire officer of the Thames fire brigade, Lomas was a well-known character in the town and surrounds.

18 November 1915

ENLISTED: **Private Robert 'Bobby' Stanley BLACK (1893–1916)**
AGE AT ENLISTMENT: 22 years, 2 months, 26 days
ARMY NUMBER: 9/2048
EMBARKATION: Wellington, 4 March 1916; Otago Mounted Rifles, 10th Reinforcements
LENGTH OF SERVICE: 303 days
PLAYED FOR: Pirates, University and White Star clubs; Otago 1911, 1913; Buller 1914; South Island 1912, 1914
ALL BLACK NUMBER: 211
POSITION: First five-eighth
APPEARANCES: 1914; 6 matches, including 1 test; 9 points (3 tries)

The great rugby commentator Winston McCarthy wrote of Black as 'nimble and fast with terrific speed off the mark — a dashing, straight-running and clever five-eighth, one of the most brilliant players Otago Boys' High School produced'.

He appeared for the South Island in 1912 and 1914. Although rugby historian Arthur Swan has listed Black as being an Otago representative in the 1914 side, he was by that time representing Buller, having left Dunedin to take up a job with the Bank of New South Wales in Westport.

Misfortune followed him to both inter-island games. An injury sustained in the 1912 match kept him out of representative football in 1913, while he limped out of the 1914 match. Fortunately, that didn't prevent him being chosen for the 1914 tour of Australia, where he played at first five-eighth in 6 of the 10 matches, including the first test against Australia, won 5–0.

He began his service with the Otago Mounted Rifles, in the same squadron as Cyril Brownlie, but once in camp at Tel el-Kabir, where the New Zealand forces were preparing to sail to France, he was transferred to the 2nd Battalion of the Canterbury Regiment.

Shortly after his arrival in France, he was absent without leave for nearly five hours one evening. The indiscretion cost him two days' pay.

The next written entry on his Casualty Form–Active Service record recorded him as missing in the field. (See page 162.)

11 December 1915

ENLISTED: **Lieutenant Eric Arthur Percy COCKROFT (1890–1973)**

AGE AT ENLISTMENT: 25 years, 3 months, 1 day

ARMY NUMBER: 24096

EMBARKATION: Wellington, 27 May 1916; Canterbury Infantry Battalion, 13th Reinforcements

LENGTH OF SERVICE: 3 years, 194 days

24683839383565539578583539

PLAYED FOR: University, Pirates and Timaru High School Old Boys clubs; Otago 1911–12; South Canterbury 1913–15, 1919–20; South Island 1914

ALL BLACK NUMBER: 203

POSITION: Wing and fullback

APPEARANCES: 1913–14; 7 matches, including 3 tests; 7 points (1 penalty, 1 dropped goal)

A nephew of 1893–94 All Black and Permanent Artillery Force member Samuel Cockroft, Eric Cockroft made his debut for Otago in 1911. He was called into the All Blacks in 1913 to play the third test against the visiting Australians.

As his club and provincial form had been outstanding in 1914, there was some outcry from southern quarters when he was not included in the team list to tour Australia. However, due to George Loveridge suffering an ankle injury in the first game, Cockroft was cabled and joined the team as a replacement, playing at fullback in the final six matches.

Cockroft was teaching at Timaru Boys' High School in 1913 when he was appointed to the position of territorial officer for the school's cadet corp. His own cadet training included time as a sergeant while a pupil at Invercargill High School, as a lieutenant with the Mataura Defence Cadets, and as a captain with the Officer Training Corps when undertaking teacher training in Dunedin.

During the war he served with the 3rd New Zealand Machine Gun Company in France, having spent a couple of months after arriving in England at the Machine Gun School in Grantham. In France, he was hospitalised in November 1916, suffering from trench fever, but rejoined his unit a month later.

The official history of the 'Machine Gunners' mentions Cockroft during the German offensive of March to August 1918:

An instance of the sterling fighting qualities of the machine gunners was furnished during the heavy minenwerfer bombardment that took place on 17th July. When Lieut. E. A. Cockroft was visiting one of his subsections in Faith Trench, in front of Hébuterne, he noticed the heavy minenwerfer bombardment directed on the locality where his other subsection was—in Sonia Avenue. Being anxious about the fate of this subsection, Cockroft went round to investigate, with his O.C., who happened to be with him. They reached Sonia Trench just as the bombardment ceased, and found it completely blown in for thirty or forty yards before the gun positions were reached. They met Sergt. Sherwood, who was in charge of the subsection, going methodically about clearing up the mess around the mouth of an occupied dugout that had been blown in. The severity of the bombardment was apparent from the fact that the whole ground round the emplacements was torn up with still reeking craters. By a miracle the two emplacements were intact, although the lips of the huge bomb craters were almost touching them.

As Sherwood feared an enemy raid would accompany the bombardment, he kept both guns manned, and distributed his men to avoid casualties. He remained with his leading gun numbers (Privates Blacklock and M. A. Churton), standing to their guns, which were kept mounted and laid throughout the bombardment.

In July 1918, Cockroft injured his chin and upper lip when he fell from a horse while on a recreation ride one evening. When Cockroft stopped to speak to a friend, the horse side-stepped into some wire on the roadside. The startled horse threw Cockroft, who was then attended to by a medical orderly.

For the last four months of the war he was a training officer and then quartermaster at Grantham Camp.

After playing for the Reserve or Depot 'All Blacks', alongside his brother Les, he played for the New Zealand army's United Kingdom XV in their match against the Divisional XV, from which were then chosen the Services side to South Africa, but he was not included in that team.

He resumed teaching at Timaru Boys' High School, played cricket for South Canterbury in 1920–21, and in 1924 published a 40-page coaching manual titled *Rugby Football: Some Present Day New Zealand Methods*.

Headmaster of Ashburton High School until 1949, he became a dual international when he represented New Zealand on the bowling green in 1953.

TRENCH HUMOUR

A well-known soldier's rhyme from World War I went as follows:

Little puffs of powder,
Little squirts of lead,
Make a man remember
He must keep down his head.

---

14 December 1915

ENLISTED: **Corporal Leslie 'Les' Frank CUPPLES** MM **(1898–1972)**

AGE AT ENLISTMENT: 17 years, 10 months, 18 days

ARMY NUMBER: 3/2011

EMBARKATION: Wellington, 4 March 1916; New Zealand Medical Corps

LENGTH OF SERVICE: 3 years, 236 days

PLAYED FOR: Tokaanu; Bay of Plenty 1920–23; North Island 1922; New Zealand Trials 1924

ALL BLACK NUMBER: 252

POSITION: Back-row forward

APPEARANCES: 1922–25; 29 matches, including 2 tests; 18 points (6 tries)

At the outbreak of war, the Southland-born Cupples was a fit, tall and strong young man working as a telegraphist's cadet in Foxton. This job may have been secured for him by his uncle, Mr F.O.V. Acheson, who worked in a government department in Wellington. Like many young men, Cupples elevated his age to enlist in December 1915.

In Cupples's case, he claimed to be three years older than he was. His older brother, Errol, who was still living at Otautau, had enlisted a month earlier on turning 20 years of age, and one wonders whether that played some part in Leslie signing up. In the days long before computerised records which allow for cross-checking, and with the brothers signing up on different islands, the fact that Leslie put his birth date as 8 February 1895 meant nothing to officialdom. But we can now see that on paper he had become Errol's 'older' brother. Not only that, he was barely nine months the elder.

Errol joined the Wellington Artillery Division of the 10th Reinforcements while Leslie trained with the Field Ambulance section of the Medical Corps. They both travelled home to Otautau in February 1916, to spend their final leave with their widowed mother, Jane, before heading overseas.

In October 1917, Cupples was awarded the Military Medal for 'distinguished and heroic conduct', an award that brought great delight to the township of Otautau. Both brothers returned home safely after the war, although Errol had been wounded in France, and they lived in Tokaanu in the Bay of Plenty, where Leslie farmed.

Cupples made his provincial debut for the Bay in 1920, and turned out for the team against the 1921 Springboks, a match played midweek in Rotorua and lost 9–17. He was in the thick of the forward play, seeming to delight in the contest with his big Springbok opponents.

The following year he was chosen for the All Blacks' eight games in Australia and New Zealand, starting in five of them as a side- or back-row forward. His next appearance was in September the following year, when the third test against the visiting New South Welshman was used by the national selectors as something of a trial ahead of the much-anticipated tour to Britain the next year. There were 14 changes to the side for the match against the Waratahs, but despite that the All Blacks won, 38–11.

In a squad where as many as eight of the men could play as a side- or back-row forward, Cupples proved to be a dependable member of the 1924–25 All Blacks on their short tour to Australia, and then in Britain, Ireland, France and Canada. The second-tallest man in the side (after Cyril Brownlie), he played in 23 of the 38 matches, including the Ireland and Wales test matches.

While on tour, his penchant for wearing butterfly-wing collars was of some amusement to his Invincibles teammates, but there probably weren't many opportunities for him to wear them around the farm at Tokaanu.

15 December 1915

ENLISTED: **Sergeant Bernard Francis 'Frank' SMYTH (1891–1972)**

AGE AT ENLISTMENT: 24 years, 10 months, 4 days

ARMY NUMBER: 4/2138

EMBARKATION: Wellington, 1 April 1916; New Zealand Field Engineers, 11th Reinforcements

LENGTH OF SERVICE: 3 years, 181 days

PLAYED FOR: Marist; Canterbury 1915; South Island 1922

ALL BLACK NUMBER: 257

POSITION: Front-row forward

APPEARANCES: 1922; 3 matches; 3 points (1 try)

Smyth had made only one appearance for Canterbury (against Otago) when inter-provincial rugby was suspended due to the war. At the time of his enlistment he was working as a bricklayer for the Christchurch Drainage Board, and his place of birth was recorded as Capleston, just outside Reefton on the West Coast. He had registered for compulsory military training in Greymouth, but a move east across the ranges to Christchurch saw him serve with the Territorials in that city.

In February 1917, his name came up in a conscription ballot for the Christchurch Military District, by which stage he was already overseas, having left with the 11th Reinforcements 10 months earlier, and had already experienced the Battle of the Somme.

In April 1918, he was mentioned in despatches 'for distinguished and gallant service and devotion to duty during the period Sept. 25, 1917 to Feb 24th, 25th 1918'.

On embarking for home aboard the SS *Arawa* from Tilbury in April 1919, he was admitted to the ship's hospital suffering from an abscess on his face, which may have been the result of his having been active in the boxing ring while part of the army of occupation in Germany, winning an Allied Forces title.

In 1922, seven years after his sole first-class game of football, the stalwart of the Christchurch Marist club was somehow included in the 1922 South Island team. Thanks to a good showing in the match held in Auckland, he was included in the All Black tour of Australia and associated matches against New Zealand teams. Smyth took the field on only three occasions (once across the Tasman), meaning his final tally of first-class matches stood at a meagre five when he turned down playing for Canterbury upon his return.

An insurance company manager, in 1926 he was a member of the executive committee organising Christchurch celebrations marking the fiftieth anniversary of the arrival of Marist Brothers in New Zealand.

1916

10 January 1916

ENLISTED: **Sapper George 'Bear' LOVERIDGE (1890–1970)**

AGE AT ENLISTMENT: 25 years, 2 months, 26 days

ARMY NUMBER: 10498

EMBARKATION: Wellington, 1 May 1916; New Zealand Field Engineers, Divisional Signallers Corps, 12th Reinforcements

LENGTH OF SERVICE: 3 years, 208 days

PLAYED FOR: Tukapa; Taranaki 1912–15; North Island 1913

ALL BLACK NUMBER: 206

POSITION: Wing

APPEARANCES: 1913–14; 11 matches; 20 points (6 tries, 1 conversion)

One of five Taranaki players (along with Stohr, Dewar, Cain and Roberts) who caught the mail train to Wellington to join the rest of the All Black party bound for North America in 1913, Loveridge only came into the side — after great showings for Taranaki in their Ranfurly Shield win over Auckland and the inter-island game — when the Auckland fullback O'Leary announced he would not be available. Loveridge, principally a wing with a great burst of speed, could play anywhere in the back line. On tour the only position he didn't occupy in his eight games was first five-eighths, somewhere he frequently played when turning out for his Tukapa club and the Taranaki provincial side.

The following year he ricked his ankle in the muddy ground during the first match of the 1914 tour to Australia, the 27–6 win over New South Wales, and although a replacement was sent (Eric Cockroft, who many thought should have been in the squad originally) he stayed on with the team, but made only one more appearance three weeks later, against Queensland.

The last of his 29 first-class games was in the 1915 season, and at the beginning of 1916 he enlisted. A telegraphist with the Post and Telegraph (whose territorial unit he was a member of), Loveridge was assigned to the Divisional Signallers Corps and served with them in France.

At the end of 1916 he was sent to England suffering from what was known as 'trench mouth': ulcers, swollen gums and loose teeth. While waiting to have his treatment, he turned out for the New Zealand Base Depot football team, in whose ranks were fellow pre-war All Black teammates Teddy Roberts, George Sellars and John O'Brien.

Loveridge spent time with the 2nd Taranaki Home Guard during World War II, and served as President of the Tukapa club in 1958–59.

17 January 1916

ENLISTED: **Private William Robert HARDCASTLE (1874–1944)**

AGE AT ENLISTMENT: 41 years, 4 months, 18 days

AUSTRALIAN IMPERIAL FORCE NUMBER: 5680

EMBARKATION: Sydney, 3 June 1916; 3rd Infantry Battalion, 18th Reinforcements, Australian Imperial Force

LENGTH OF SERVICE: 2 years, 41 days

PLAYED FOR: Petone, Melrose and Glebe (Sydney) clubs; Wellington 1895–97; North Island 1897; New South Wales 1898; Australia 1899, 1903

ALL BLACK NUMBER: 71

Position: Forward
Appearances: 1897; 7 matches; 3 points (1 try)

A product of Petone High School who had spent three years with the Wellington Rifles, Hardcastle was added to the 20-man All Black touring party to Australia in 1897 when four of the original selections withdrew. He ended up playing in 7 of the 11 matches, including the 2 losses: 8–22 in the second of 3 games against New South Wales and 10–11 in the final match against Auckland once back in New Zealand.

Hardcastle returned to Australia several months later, and the following year, having been part of the Glebe team that won the first Sydney club competition, appeared for New South Wales before being chosen in the Australian team for their first-ever international series, against Great Britain in 1899.

Four years later he was in the Australian side (along with two other New Zealand-born players, Sid Riley and Charlie Redwood) which played the All Blacks in the first-ever clash between the two countries.

With the growth of rugby league in Sydney, Hardcastle was attracted to the new game and represented Australia in 1908 at home and in England. In doing so, he created something of a record for himself in having represented two countries in international rugby football and one of those countries in two rugby codes.

In 1910, to the amusement of newspaper gossip columnists, Hardcastle had to be treated at St Vincent's Hospital in Sydney after playing a match in boots that were a size too small. The cramp became intolerable and slow to relieve, so medical treatment was sought.

He was 42 when he sailed from Sydney with the 3rd Infantry Battalion of the Australian Imperial Force (AIF), and his listed occupation was 'labourer'. Once in England, he transferred to the Machine Gun Battalion and served at the Western Front for about six months before poor health began to dog him. He spent time in Australian army hospitals in France before complaining of pain in his lower back and legs. He was diagnosed as suffering from myalgia and rheumatism before being sent across the Channel to the Berrington War Hospital. His wife, Mary, was informed that he was suffering from sub-acute nephritis. He worked for a time as a waiter in an officers' mess, but his health deteriorated as problems with his heart and kidneys increased. While his own playing days were well behind him, he reportedly helped organise some matches between army teams.

Hardcastle sailed from England nine days after the Armistice, and was discharged from the army on medical grounds in February 1919. In 1931, perhaps demonstrating how little some servicemen treasured their medals, he wrote to the records officer of the AIF asking if he had been issued with two of his war medals and was told that he had actually collected and signed for the medals in person in 1921 and 1924.

23 January 1916

Featherston military camp was opened, and was used as a base for advanced training by the Mounted Rifles, Signallers, Artillery, machine-gun specialists and the Army Service Corps.

14 February 1916

ENLISTED: **Lieutenant Colin MacDonald GILRAY** MC, OBE **(London) (1885–1974)**

AGE AT ENLISTMENT: 30 years, 10 months, 28 days

ARMY NUMBER: unknown. Initially posted to the Rifle Brigade, 6th (Special Reserve of Officers) Battalion

LENGTH OF SERVICE: 3 years, 71 days

PLAYED FOR: University and London Scottish clubs; Otago 1904–06; South Island 1904; Oxford University (Blue 1908–09); London Scottish

ALL BLACK NUMBER: 135

POSITION: Wing

APPEARANCES: 1905, 1 test; represented Scotland 1908–09, 1912, 4 tests

The first All Black to become a dual rugby international, Scotland-born Gilray had moved to New Zealand with his family when his father was appointed chair of English language and literature at Otago University.

Perhaps unsurprisingly, young Colin was a gifted scholar and was seemingly able to excel at anything he turned his attention to. His great form for the University football club and Otago provincial side just a year after having been part of the Otago Boys' High School First XV saw him selected in 1904 as part of the combined Otago–Southland team that gave a fine account of itself in an 8–14 loss (with the back-play of the home side drawing good mentions) against the visiting Great Britain team.

Regrettably he had to decline touring with the 1905 team to Britain on account of his university studies. He did, however, play for the All Blacks a few weeks later against the touring Australians at Tahuna Park (won 14–3). His academic dedication resulted in first-class honours in English and German, and a second in Classics.

Besides football, Gilray also found time while at university to indulge in debating, acting and athletics, winning the national university long-jump title three times. His popularity and standing on the campus saw him elected president of the student union.

His academic results saw him awarded the fourth New Zealand Rhodes Scholarship in 1907 (the third awarded to a student from Otago University) to study at London's Middle Temple for admission to the bar. He quickly settled into life at one of the great seats of learning (as well as teaching at the Mill Hill School) and continued to excel at football, for which he later won two Oxford Blues, and turned out against the touring Australians in 1908.

As a wing he had been known for his strong running and try-scoring ability. At Oxford he also played at centre, and his ability to set up tries for the men outside him had no better demonstration than when Oxford won their clash with Cambridge in December 1909, by an astounding record score of 35–3. Ronald Poulton scored five tries while Scottish rep Hugh Martin bagged four. Poulton and Martin and eight other players in the side were or would go on to achieve test caps for England or Scotland, with Poulton captaining the side in the season before the war. (He was killed in action by a sniper's bullet early in 1915.) The ball used in the game remains on display in the Oxford University rugby club rooms to this day.

That same year, Gilray made the first of his four test appearances over four seasons for the Scottish rugby team, twice against England and once against Ireland and Wales. In one of the matches against England, he came up against another former Otago University clubmate, A.C. Palmer. In 1911, he was captain of the London Scottish club.

Upon admission to the bar in 1913, Gilray returned to New Zealand and worked for Reid and Rutherford Barristers and Solicitors in Milton. He had even been persuaded, after exhibiting great reluctance, to take to the field once more for University when an injury occurred at a match at which he was a spectator.

As political tensions rose in Europe and the outbreak of war looked imminent, Gilray was quite forthright in his view that the best way to peace was through compromise, rather than conflict. When the war was not over by Christmas 1914 nor 1915, Gilray returned to London and enlisted for the Rifle Brigade in February 1916. Several weeks later he reported for duty at Oxford. He became a second lieutenant with the 6th (Special Reserve) Battalion in July of the same year, before beginning active service in France with the 13th Battalion the following month.

One soldier's account of his time in the 13th Battalion describes one of Gilray's experiences at the Western Front:

On November 12th, 1916, we moved on to Hedauville, and spent the night there in bivouacs. Next morning we continued our march to the trenches, and after resting a while near Englebelmer we pushed on to Mesnil and Hamel; then, late the same night, we trudged our way to the Green Line, our appointed place of assembly for the pending Battle of the Ancre. During the last stage of this dreary journey in the rain and the sleet, our route was heavily shelled and we lost many splendid fellows … At 4.15 on the morning of November 14th the Battalion had warning to launch an attack on the German trenches in two hours' time. The objective was Beaucourt Trench … The assault was held up by heavy rifle and machine gun fire for close on an hour, but the Battalion went forward at 7.15 under cover of a protecting barrage from our Artillery, and after a terrific struggle gained a firm footing in the enemies' defences some three hundred yards north west of Railway Alley, capturing large batches of prisoners and huge quantities of material. Our left flank had now become exposed and enemy snipers were giving a lot of trouble, but after a time the newly won position was finally consolidated and our bombers then started blasting their way up Beaucourt Trench toward Leave Avenue. By midnight more ground had been wrested from the Germans, and on the following day the men of 'D' Company rounded off the Battalion's success by taking Muck Trench. The Battle of the Ancre, fought in wintry conditions of the worst kind, was proclaimed a military success, yet our rejoicing was on a muted note for once again our losses were appalling. Included in the 93 dead were 2nd Lt. W.D.M. Wilkinson, Coy. Sergt.-Majors Williams, James and Squires, and Sergts. Dean, Green, Harris, Martyr, Tomkinson and Wally, while there were eleven officers on the wounded list, among them Capt. T.G. Skyrne, a South African, Lieut. R. Colville-Jones from Buenos Aires, and Capt. Colin Gilray, a New Zealander once famous on the Rugby fields.

Gilray had reportedly suffered gunshot wounds to the head and one side of his body.

Promotion to captain of his company came at the end of April 1917, and the awarding of a Military Cross to him was gazetted in August 1917. A short time later he was invalided back to England suffering 'PUO' (pyrexia — or fever — of unknown origin).

Upon his recovery he was attached to the 21st Officer Cadet Battalion as an instructor from the beginning of December 1917 until the end of the war. During the latter half of that time he was in command of a unit of company cadets.

Gilray returned to New Zealand from Glasgow with wife and child, and a year after the end of the war he was back working for Reid and Rutherford. There, he received advice that his Military Cross had been received and plans were afoot for a ceremony for him to be formally and publicly awarded it. On 23 February 1920, Gilray wrote to Defence Headquarters:

> I beg to acknowledge the receipt of your memo of the 17th re my Military Cross, and wish to state that I shall be greatly obliged if you will make no arrangements for the presentation of the same. I purposely avoided a presentation in England, & with all respect be it said, have no intention of attending one here. If the Cross cannot be forwarded me through the post I [would] rather not have it.

The medal was duly sent to him.

He became the second principal of John McGlashan College in Dunedin in 1922, and 12 years later was appointed principal of Scotch College in Melbourne, which at that time had a roll six times larger than that of John McGlashan College.

The move to Australia meant that Gilray had to retire from the New Zealand Territorials list of officers to retain his rank. Another matter that came to light was that Gilray had never received his service medals from the British Army, and so further flurries of letter-writing sought them.

Although Gilray was an effective administrator of Scotch College, he found the size somewhat impersonal and his leadership of the school became one with an increasing air of military command. The outbreak of World War II brought personal sadness to him as he watched and read of college old boys having to answer the call to arms as he had when a young man.

On retiring as principal in 1953 he became deputy chancellor of Melbourne University, a post he held until 1961. He was awarded an OBE and died in Melbourne in 1974.

NEW ZEALAND SCOTS

Other New Zealand-born footballers who won international caps overseas and who served during World War I include the following:

Andrew Lindsay Representing Scotland in the 1910–11 seasons (two caps v Ireland) seasons, Lindsay was a former pupil of Southland Boys' High School and a Dunedin University club player who had gone to London to study medicine. After briefly returning to New Zealand to work at Timaru Hospital, he was in England at the outbreak of war and served as a major with the Royal Army Medical Corps, winning the Military Cross.

Nolan Fell Nelson-born Fell was living in Edinburgh studying medicine at Guy's Hospital when selected to play against the 1905 tourists, but he stood down, preferring not to oppose his fellow New Zealanders. He was capped seven times for Scotland in 1901 and 1903. During World War I, he was a captain with the Royal Army Medical Corps.

William Traill Ritchie Ritchie (army number 50246) played for Scotland against England and Ireland in 1905 while studying mechanical science at the University of Cambridge. Back in New Zealand, he was working as a lieutenant in the Motor Service Corps when he asked to be transferred to the 8th (South Canterbury) Mounted Rifles. He had 2 years, 19 days service as a gunner and battery sergeant major with the New Zealand Field Artillery, arriving in England with the 40th Reinforcements in September 1918. Ritchie was awarded the Meritorious Service Medal in 1919 'in recognition of valuable services rendered in connection with the war'.

1 March 1916

After the withdrawal from Gallipoli, the New Zealand (Infantry) Division came into being at Moascar, following the separation from Australian forces. At this time, the Maori Contingent was renamed the Pioneer Battalion. Under the command of Major General Andrew Russell, the division was deployed for service in France and Belgium — the Western Front.

In England, the main New Zealand reserve and reinforcement training base was officially established at Sling Camp (the 4th New Zealand Infantry Brigade Reserve Camp) on the Salisbury Plain in Wiltshire. It was there that new reinforcements were trained before being sent to France, along with those who had recovered from illness or injury and were deemed fit for further service. A number of other service depots were later established throughout the southern counties, such as: Codford convalescent camp; Brocton training camp, which accommodated the New Zealand Rifle Brigade when Sling became overpopulated; Christchurch (Hampshire), home to the New Zealand Engineers; Ewshot, which accommodated the New Zealand Field Artillery; Grantham (Lincolnshire), base for the machine gunners; and Hornchurch, the command depot. The No. 1 General Hospital was at Brockenhurst, Hampshire.

Across the English Channel, the major base depot closest to the fighting was that at Étaples on the French coast. It was a vast expanse of tents, cabins, stables, horse-yards, garages and storehouses. Camps and hospitals were also set up outside the city of Rouen.

15 March 1916

A sense of life in camp — and the role played by rugby — is captured in published letters the soldiers wrote to family and friends back at home, such as this one by Sergeant Frank R. Wilson:

> In spite of the warm Egyptian weather, football is carried on, and some excellent games have been witnessed. A divisional tournament was arranged, each battalion entering a team, and the Australians, Engineers, Artillery, Maoris and Rifle Brigade one each … On Sunday last the eventful match was decided on the hard Ismaïlia ground. Leave was granted to all desiring to view the game, and thousands willingly trudged the five miles. The day was brilliant and the gentle breeze along the canal could not affect the play owing to

the thick grove of tall pines encircling the flat ground. On all sides the arena was densely thronged with New Zealand, Australian, Indian and English soldiers, French and English sailors and Egyptian natives. General Birdwood and General Russell looked on from a point of vantage and [Lieutenant] Colonel Plugge was an interested spectator. Through the trees on one side lay the beautiful gardens of Ismaïlia, while alongside lay Lake Timpsah, with its battleships and monitors, and above all poised and throbbed the ubiquitous 'plane … The Maoris filed out at 3pm a motley team in red, green striped and khaki jerseys … Soon after Teddy Roberts led on the Wellington fifteen with uniform jerseys (green, with red band) with one odd Taranaki yellow and black.

Another glimpse is given in a letter from Private George Hall of Birkenhead, 1st Battalion, Auckland Regiment. He was to die from wounds in France, on 4 July 1916.

While in camp at Ismaïlia we had some first-class Rugby football matches — games between platoons, companies and battalions. Wellington won the championship beating the Maoris, who were runners-up, by three to nil, after a magnificent though somewhat dirty, game. The Maoris had such well-known men as Jack Hall, Kaipara and [Tom] French playing for them, too, but Wellington were too 'hot'. They had five New Zealand reps. in their team including Teddy Roberts and Billy Wilson (Rangi's brother).

27 March 1916

The Dominion newspaper reported a highly unusual rugby encounter in Wellington:

Hobble-skirted Football: A Gala Postponed
As the troops from the Trentham Camp are to parade through Wellington on Saturday next afternoon, and races are to be held on the Trentham course on Saturday week, the New Zealand Natives' Association has decided to postpone its unique football gala until

Saturday, April 15. On that occasion a football team of young ladies, to be selected by Mrs. McVicar, will be pitted against a team of soldiers from the Trentham Camp, who are to be handicapped by having to wear hobble-skirts. Rugby rules are to be observed (more or less) during the game. Another event will be the hobble-skirted military running championship of New Zealand. The gala, which is in aid of the fund for entertaining and caring for soldiers, will be held on the Athletic Park, by the kind permission of the Rugby Union.

12 April 1916

ENLISTED: **Sergeant Nathaniel Arthur 'Ranji' WILSON (1886–1953)**
AGE AT ENLISTMENT: 29 years, 10 months, 25 days
ARMY NUMBER: 18936
EMBARKATION: Wellington, 26 July 1916; New Zealand Rifle Brigade, 6th Reinforcements
LENGTH OF SERVICE: 3 years, 201 days
PLAYED FOR: Athletic; Wellington 1907–15, 1920; Wellington Province 1907; North Island 1907–08, 1911–14
ALL BLACK NUMBER: 151
POSITION: Loose-forward
APPEARANCES: 1908, 1910, 1913–14; 21 matches, including 10 tests; 18 points (6 tries)

Wilson was a key member of the Athletic club's five-season domination of Wellington club football, which began in 1910, although with the outbreak of war the title was shared with the Wellington club in 1914. (That record of success stood for over 50 years.) He made 121 first-class appearances, 75 of which were for Wellington. He also played in a remarkable six inter-island matches, the first of those appearances occurring before he had even played for the senior Wellington side. Following the retirement of Dave Gallaher and the switch to Northern Union by 'Bronco' Seeling, Wilson established himself as *the* provincial loose-forward in the years immediately preceding the war.

Although his given names were Nathaniel Arthur, everybody knew him as 'Ranji' (although sometimes newspaper editorial and printing staff erred and the copy was printed as 'Rangi'). The nickname came from Wilson's Anglo-West Indian heritage and his likeness to the famous Anglo-Indian cricketer Ranjitsinhji.

Wilson's test debut came as a 22-year-old against the Anglo-Welsh in 1908. He missed only one of the All Blacks eight games in 1910, playing all but one as a back-row forward. Although he played two tests against the visiting Australians in 1913, he was curiously overlooked for the tour to North America. He returned to the side in 1914 and played in 10 of the team's matches that year, missing only the fourth match in Australia against New England at Armidale.

As captain of Wellington, he had the joy of accepting the Ranfurly Shield from Taranaki's Dick Roberts when his side won the final Shield game played before the war.

Known as Arthur Wilson on his service record, he began active service in France in December 1916, before being briefly hospitalised with an undiagnosed illness in April 1917, and scabies a year later. While recuperating in England he played for the United Kingdom XV. Upon returning to the field of war, he played for the Divisional XV in France before being wounded in action in September 1918, suffering a chest wound. Three months later he was turning out for the Divisional XV in the King's Cup. He was chosen to tour South Africa with the side, but was then omitted from the team due to being 'coloured'.

Once back in New Zealand, and with the resumption of Ranfurly Shield fixtures, he captained Wellington in their generous season of putting the log on the line in every game they played, whether home or away. When Wellington lost the Shield in the final match of the season, against Southland in Invercargill, he promptly retired from provincial rugby but continued to be a presence in the Wellington club competition.

Wilson's brother Billy, who had also served overseas and played football for army teams, had converted to Northern Union (and played for New Zealand shortly before the war) after being banned from playing by the Wellington union. In a club game,

Petone player Dave (Duilio) Calcinai and Billy came to blows. Ranji stepped in and broke Calcinai's jaw. Billy took the fall for his brother and was sent off, leaving the field and the game of rugby union. Calcinai took Ranji to court, knowing it was Ranji who had clobbered him, but after more than two hours of deliberation the jury gave a verdict of 'not guilty' on account of insufficient evidence having been placed before the court.

A Wellington selector from 1922 until 1926, and one of the seven All Black selectors when a series of trials were held to choose the team to make the 1924–25 tour to the Northern Hemisphere, Wilson is credited by some with 'discovering' George Nepia.

He was president of the Athletic club, 1945–46.

13 April 1916

The much-anticipated fund-raising rugby match at Trentham was gathering momentum, as recorded in *The Dominion*:

> Burlesque Football
>
> The ladies engaged in the burlesque football match put in another good practice last night, though it is of course difficult to pack the scrum without rumpling their hair. The ball that is to be used on this occasion has been autographed by members of the team, and is to be presented to Lieut.-Colonel Potter, Camp Commandant, on behalf of the men at Trentham. The Challenge Cup, which was presented by Mr. R. Turnbull, is now on view in Messrs. George and George's window in Cuba-street. Mr. H.A. McKenzie has presented a trophy to the lady who brings the first soldier down. The soldiers at Trentham are taking a keen interest in the match. Mrs. Annie McVicar has been elected captain of the ladies team.

At the same time as funny football was being played in New Zealand, the first stirrings of more serious competition were happening wherever the army boys were stationed. Competitions were played throughout the division by soldiers in camps in France and Britain, and one of the 'hot' teams was a Wellington selection that had in its

midst Teddy Roberts, Ranji Wilson and Reginald Taylor. A team
chosen from the trench troops, described by one soldier writing home
as 'almost an All Black team', was to play a South African selection,
but movements by the German Army required the footballers to go
back to the front.

A team of Kiwi soldiers from Hornchurch played unbeaten
matches against Australians, Artists' Rifles, 2nd Life Guards,
Public Schools and Guards Depot. Then they came up against a
similarly unbeaten team from the South African Heavy Artillery
at the Queen's Club. (They were heavy in name and nature, as
they boasted a typically big forward pack, averaging an estimated
14 stone, or 89 kilograms, per man.) The South Africans won
7–0, the match being described in *The Sportsman* newspaper as
being played 'as if their national Rugby reputation were at stake
… in many respects it was old fashioned Rugby, very lofty, very
robust with heaps of fierce tackling and doughty feats of saving'.
The New Zealanders got their revenge several weeks later at
Richmond, winning 5–3. The match, raising money for the Sailors
and Soldiers Tobacco Fund, was reported by the *Morning Post* as
being 'the type of colonial play which the New Zealanders, above
all others, have made so efficacious by the attention they paid to
systematic forward work'.

A short piece of British Pathé film footage exists of the encounter,
beginning with both sides posing for the camera before shots of
the crowd and the match. The play is far from gentle, with every
conceivable sin-binning offence of the modern game taking place in a
forward mêlée lasting only a few seconds.

As a measure of how physical the games could be, one New
Zealander suffered two broken ribs and a cracked collar-bone in one
match.

2 May 1916

ENLISTED: **Driver Edward 'Ned' HUGHES (1881–1928)**
AGE AT ENLISTMENT: 35 years, 6 days
ARMY NUMBER: 20156

EMBARKATION: Wellington, 19 August 1916; New Zealand
    Rifle Brigade, 10th Reinforcements
LENGTH OF SERVICE: 2 years, 232 days
PLAYED FOR: Britannia and Poneke clubs; Southland 1903–08;
    Southland–Otago 1904; South Island 1907; Wellington
    1920–21; North Island 1921
ALL BLACK NUMBER: 144
POSITION: Front-row and wing-forward
APPEARANCES: 1907–08, 1921; 9 matches, including 6 tests;
    3 points (1 try)

Given that there were 14 years between Hughes's first and last
appearances for the All Blacks, one would have assumed that he
played more than a mere nine games for his country. His provincial
debut for Southland was in 1903, although there are claims that
he debuted as early as 1898, aged just 17.

He appeared at wing-forward for Otago–Southland in their
8–14 loss to the 1904 'Great Britishers', and his name was on
one of the early lists of players being considered for selection on
the 1905 tour to Britain. For some unknown reason he did not
even make the Otago–Southland team that played the All Black
tourists before their departure, nor the New Zealand side that
played Australia while the Originals were sailing for Britain.
National honours finally came in 1907 when he was chosen for
the All Black tour to Australia, albeit as a replacement for George
Tyler, who had to withdraw due to business commitments.
Although not a tall man, even for a front-ranker, at only five feet
seven inches (170 centimetres), Hughes was a canny scrummager
and fearless spoiler of opposition dribbling rushes. Such was
his speed and strength that his wing-forward forward play was
also top-notch, and he turned out for the South Island in that
position.

He played in the 1908 Southland side, captained by the
Originals' vice-captain, Billy Stead, that lost to the Anglo-Welsh,
8–14 (the identical score to the 1904 game), in a very hard-fought
match. Also in the Southland side were future All Black soldiers

Jimmy Ridland and Donald Hamilton. (In the hours before the match, Prime Minister Sir Joseph Ward had unveiled a Boer War memorial in the presence of the teams.)

Hughes had signed the controversial 'affidavit of loyalty' to the NZRFU so as to be eligible to play in the 1908 inter-island match, at a time when the first professional Northern Union team was being assembled by Albert Baskerville. The following year the Britannia and Pirates clubs were suspended from the Southland Rugby Union competition on account of the refusal, by both sides, to play a midweek game in atrocious weather. So, the clubs decided to stage a benefit game under Northern Union rules. A big crowd watched the teams play under the rules of the other code at Bluff in July 1908. As a result of their rebellion, all of the players were individually suspended from rugby union, so a month later Hughes turned out for the Southland Northern Union team against Wellington in Petone.

The following season, Hughes tried another winter code, chasing the round ball as part of the Celtic soccer team in Invercargill, although he quickly developed a reputation as someone who manhandled other players too much. (So adept was Ned at sport in general that there are even claims that he won a national wrestling championship.) Union's loss was league's gain, as Hughes stayed with the mushrooming code and played for New Zealand against Great Britain in 1910.

Hughes moved to Wellington with his wife, Clara, and the couple lived in Vivian Street, with Ned working as a self-employed cooper.

His service in France as a driver with the Army Service Corps was ended in June 1918, when he was hospitalised suffering from ametropia, an eye condition wherein the refraction of light to the retina causes problems with focus on objects near or far. The cause of his condition was blamed on being gassed several times at the front. Due to his defective vision, he was classified as unfit for duty in June 1918, and sailed for New Zealand two months later.

Several birth dates appear on documents in his army files, but that which appears most consistently is 26 April 1881. So, when he made his final appearance for the All Blacks in the second test against the 1921 Springboks, he was 40 years and 123 days old, and his debut season of first-class football had been 18 years earlier. (To this day Hughes continues to be accorded the title of the oldest man to have played test match rugby.) Mischievously, in later years Hughes was even known to tell newspaper men that he had in fact been 46 when he took to the field against the 'Boks in Auckland.

Hughes moved to Australia in 1923, which initially did prove to be the 'lucky country' for him. He joined the YMCA football club in Sydney and captained the fifth-grade team, before undertaking regular work on federal construction projects in Canberra. He won £5,000 in a racing sweepstake when a horse called Star Stranger won the Metropolitan Handicap in 1926. Despite the windfall, he assured all who asked that he intended to continue working and hoped to also begin some rugby coaching.

A veteran who proudly wore the badge of the New Zealand Returned Services Association when not in his work clothes, he lost his life in 1928 as the result of an industrial accident.

3 May 1916

ENLISTED: **Gunner Edward William 'Nut' (or 'Nuts') HASELL (1889–1966)**

AGE AT ENLISTMENT: 27 years, 2 months, 7 days

ARMY NUMBER: 17602

EMBARKATION: Wellington, 2 January 1917; New Zealand
Field Artillery, 20th Reinforcements

LENGTH OF SERVICE: 3 years, 187 days

PLAYED FOR: Merivale; Canterbury 1909–14, 1920; South
Island 1911, 1920

ALL BLACK NUMBER: 197

POSITION: Front-row forward

APPEARANCES: 1913, 1920; 7 matches, including 2 tests;
21 points (3 tries, 6 conversions)

'Nut' Hasell was a popular member of 1912 Christchurch club champions Merivale, who had an unbeaten season, and the Canterbury side that beat Otago in Christchurch for the first time in 19 years. The red-and-blacks beat their southern rivals again at Tahuna Park in Dunedin the following year, thanks to two goals from marks kicked by Hasell.

His impressive front-row play, as well as an ability to kick goals, saw him win a place in the All Blacks for the final two tests against the visiting Australians in 1913, and he became one of the few players to have scored a try on test debut.

'Nut', whose nickname came about because his surname was pronounced 'Hazel' rather than 'Hassle', worked as an accountant for G. Harper Son & Pascoe, the law firm in which former All Black Eric Harper was a partner.

Once in England with the troops, while stationed at Chadderton Camp with the New Zealand Field Artillery, Hasell captained a South Island football team against a selection of North Island artillerymen. The match was played at Watersheddings in Oldham, with the South winning 10–0. All proceeds from the gate-takings went to the Oldham Infirmary, with an estimated £500 being raised.

Hasell was hospitalised with a kidney infection in June 1918, and joined the Reserve football team while recuperating, and from there the side for the King's Cup tournament. He then made the Services team that travelled to South Africa, proving invaluable as a goal-kicker once more.

In 1920, he played five games on the tour of Australia, including in the third 'test' against New South Wales as a side-row forward. Five of the six conversions he kicked for the All Blacks were in the match against a New South Wales XV at Sydney, won 31–18.

'Nut' coached Canterbury to their famous 6–4 win against the 1921 Springboks and, seven weeks later, unofficially undertook the same role with the All Blacks before their game in Christchurch against New South Wales, which was lost 0–17.

In his later years he was an accountant for Crown and then New Zealand Breweries in Christchurch.

WORLD WAR I HONOURS

The Military Medal (MM) was first awarded in 1916. It was a decoration recognising bravery of non-commissioned officers (NCOs) and other ranks. The ribbon was of vertical blue, white and red stripes, and the back of the medal carried the head of King George V and bore the words 'For bravery in the field'. (Later, it would bear the image of the reigning monarch, until it was discontinued in 1993.)

The Military Cross (MC) — a silver cross with a crown at each apex and a ribbon of two silver bands separated by a dark blue or black band — was instituted at the end of 1914 and was awarded for acts of bravery by junior officers and senior NCOs.

The Distinguished Conduct Medal (DCM) had been in existence for 60 years by the time World War I broke out. It bears the words 'For distinguished conduct in the field' and was awarded to NCOs and other ranks.

The Distinguished Service Order (DSO) had been awarded to officers recognising acts of gallantry (for which the Victoria Cross was not deemed appropriate) since 1886.

ENLISTED: **Second Lieutenant Cyril Edward 'Scrum' EVANS (1896–1975)**
AGE AT ENLISTMENT: 20 years, 3 months, 23 days
ARMY NUMBER: 17258
EMBARKATION: Wellington, 23 September 1916; New Zealand Field Artillery, 17th Reinforcements
LENGTH OF SERVICE: 3 years, 42 days
PLAYED FOR: Christchurch High School Old Boys; Canterbury 1920–21; South Island 1920
ALL BLACK NUMBER: 239
POSITION: Full-back
APPEARANCES: 1921; 1 match

Evans had 10 years as a Canterbury cricket representative, whereas his first-class rugby appearances totalled only 10 matches. He was an accounting clerk with Pyne and Co., and his father worked at Canterbury College. Evans had unbroken service with the New Zealand Field Artillery in France from February 1917 through until September 1918. At that point he was detached to England to train for a commission. By the time he was promoted to second lieutenant, in February 1919, the war was over, and two months later he sailed home to New Zealand.

Evans made the Canterbury cricket side at the end of that year, and then represented his province in football in 1920. Despite having had little first-class football, he was deemed good enough to be included in the South Island team. Delight at being part of the Canterbury team that beat the Springboks in 1921 would have been dampened somewhat by being in the All Black side that lost 0–17 to New South Wales. So ended his rugby career.

30 May 1916

ENLISTED: **Sapper John Gerald 'Jack' O'BRIEN (1889–1958)**

AGE AT ENLISTMENT: 30 years, 5 months, 21 days

ARMY NUMBER: 26899

EMBARKATION: Wellington, 25 September 1916; Auckland Infantry Battalion, 17th Reinforcements

LENGTH OF SERVICE: 3 years, 166 days

PLAYED FOR: Marist; Auckland 1911–13, 1920; North Island 1920

ALL BLACK NUMBER: 210

POSITION: Fullback

APPEARANCES: 1914, 1920; 12 matches, including 1 test; 7 points (1 try, 2 conversions)

O'Brien was part of the first senior side fielded by Auckland Marist, and made his way into the Auckland team in 1911. His appearances would be sporadic due to the fact that he wasn't the first-choice fullback at the time. That was a shame for the fans who would make their way to Alexandra Park to watch the Auckland side, as O'Brien was one of those fullbacks who had an innate feeling for positional play, which proved a huge frustration for teams trying to carve off territory with kicks.

Across three seasons he played in only 8 of Auckland's 21 matches. More often than not the position was filled by Joe O'Leary, who had been the top points-scorer for the All Blacks in 1910 and had captained the side from that position in two of the 1913 home tests against Australia.

Selected for the 1914 All Black tour of Australia, O'Brien had the misfortune to break a bone in his leg while making a tackle. It was during his fifth consecutive appearance on the tour (which began with a match against Wellington), and his form had been superb. The initial diagnosis was that he might only have been off the paddock for a fortnight and could be available for later matches on the tour, but that was not to be.

A telegraphist living in Richmond Road, he had been a Territorial Force member with the Ranfurly Rifles in Napier and the A Battery in Auckland.

He qualified as a first-class signaller at Sling Camp in February 1917, and played for the Base Depot XV. He finally left for service in France as a sapper in October that year. A series of hospitalisations for pneumonia and scabies saw him back in England, from where he was chosen for the army team to contest the King's Cup.

His skills as a fullback received no greater compliment than when the Prince of Wales admiringly commented on his play that, 'If I dropped my kit bag from the dome of St. Paul's, O'Brien would catch it.'

Part of the Services side in South Africa and against Auckland in October 1919, he had two final representative matches for the blue-and-white hoops in 1920, the last of which was a dramatic and unsuccessful Ranfurly Shield challenge against Wellington, lost 20–23. Chosen for the All Black tour of Australia, in which he made seven appearances including the drawn match with Auckland on their return, he became one of only a handful of All Blacks to have played for the side before and after the war.

His parents had farmed at Morrinsville, and O'Brien resigned from the Post and Telegraph Department to run the farm in 1928, and lived out his days there.

ENLISTED: **Private George Maurice Victor SELLARS (1886–1917)**

AGE AT ENLISTMENT: 30 years, 1 month, 14 days

ARMY NUMBER: 26923

EMBARKATION: Wellington, 25 September 1916; Auckland Infantry Battalion, 17th Reinforcements

LENGTH OF SERVICE: 1 year, 10 days

PLAYED FOR: Ponsonby; Auckland 1909–15; North Island 1912; New Zealand Maoris 1910, 1912, 1914

ALL BLACK NUMBER: 182

POSITION: Front-row forward

APPEARANCES: 1913; 15 matches, including 2 tests; 6 points (2 tries)

Ponsonby stalwart and then Auckland selector-coach Dave Gallaher brought Sellars into the provincial team in 1909. The following year he was chosen for the first ever New Zealand Maoris side, which played 19 matches in Australia and New Zealand, winning 12 and drawing 2.

George's brother Percy, better known by his second name Roy, also played for the Maoris in 1912. Many have wondered just how it was that Sellars, who looked very much a white European, could be included in the Maoris team. The manager of the Maoris side, Wiremu 'Ned' Parata, knew the whakapapa of players eligible for the side, and he knew that George's great-grandfather, who had immigrated to the Bay of Plenty in the middle of the 1800s, had taken a Maori bride.

Sellars had begun playing rugby when at Napier Street School and joined Ponsonby as a junior, but was quickly promoted into the senior ranks. He captained the club and was a dynamic roaming forward for Auckland at a time when they held the Ranfurly Shield. There were further appearances for the Maoris side in 1912 and 1914.

Sellars's debut for the All Blacks came in 1913 when he played in the match against Australia in Wellington (won 30–5), then in all but 2 of the 16 games on the North American tour. He declared himself unavailable for the 1914 All Black tour of Australia, but continued to turn out in the blue-and-white hoops of Auckland. By the time of enlistment, the 30-year-old Roman Catholic shipwright had played 29 times for his province.

Sellars sailed for England as part of the 17th Reinforcements and joined active service in France at the start of March 1917, as part of the Auckland Regiment's 1st Battalion. By the end of the month he was in a segregation camp, where he spent four weeks being treated. He rejoined his battalion on 2 June 1917, five days before the attack on Messines, when he was killed in action.

1 June 1916

ENLISTED: **Private James 'Jim' McNEECE (1885–1917)**
AGE AT ENLISTMENT: 30 years, 5 months, 8 days
ARMY NUMBER: 27561
EMBARKATION: Wellington, 23 September 1916; Otago
    Infantry Battalion, 17th Reinforcements
LENGTH OF SERVICE: 1 year, 21 days
PLAYED FOR: Waikiwi; Southland 1905, 1907–08, 1912–14;
    South Island 1913, 1914
ALL BLACK NUMBER: 199
POSITION: Utility forward
APPEARANCES: 1913–14; 11 matches, including 5 tests;
    6 points (2 tries)

An all-round sportsman who also represented Southland at cricket, McNeece was a big man for his day, standing six feet two inches (188 centimetres) tall and weighing over 14 stone (89 kilograms). He could comfortably slot into any position in the forward pack and occasionally on a wing. (His brother A.M. McNeece joined him in the Southland side as an outside back, making notable appearances against the 1908 Anglo-Welsh and 1913 Australian sides.)

Goal-kicking was another string to the big man's bow, but his appearances for Southland over seven seasons were infrequent. One of the funny things about rugby representation is shown in McNeece playing more games for the All Blacks than he did for Southland. By contrast, his brother had three times as many appearances for their province but never achieved higher honours in a South Island or All Black side.

There was something of an outcry, particularly in Southland, when McNeece and his provincial teammate Jimmy Ridland were not selected for the 1913 tour to North America. However, he did make the touring group to Australia the following year and scored, 20 minutes from time, the only try in the first test 5–0 victory in Sydney.

Another brother, John, had fought in the last weeks of the Gallipoli campaign and been wounded. He was on his way home by the time Jim enlisted.

Like hundreds of soldiers who entered Trentham, McNeece's dental health was not good. There were no school dental nurses or the like back in those days, so one of the first stops for new soldiers was the dentist's hut. Extractions were the common cure for tooth decay. McNeece also occasionally had epileptic seizures, and he suffered at least one while in camp.

He was posted to the 8th Company of the Otago Regiment in France in the first week of January 1917. Five months later he suffered wounds to his back and shoulder and was admitted to the No. 9 Australian Field Ambulance. (See page 223.)

26 June 1916

ENLISTED: **Private Michael 'Mick' Joseph CAIN (1885–1951)**
AGE AT ENLISTMENT: 30 years, 11 months, 19 days
ARMY NUMBER: 27852
EMBARKATION: Wellington, 16 October 1916; 2nd Battalion, 12th Reinforcements

LENGTH OF SERVICE: 3 years, 141 days
PLAYED FOR: Clifton; Taranaki 1908–14, 1920–21; North
    Island 1913, 1914, 1920
ALL BLACK NUMBER: 187
POSITION: Front-row forward
APPEARANCES: 1913–14; 24 matches, including 4 tests;
    17 points (5 tries, 1 conversion)

By the time Cain played his last pre-war match for Taranaki in the losing defence of the Ranfurly Shield against Wellington at the Stratford Showgrounds, he had chalked up 53 matches for his province, plus 2 All Black tours (to Australia and North America). Considering he had not played football until he was 21, and had made the Taranaki side only two seasons later, he had quickly proven himself to be one of the most consistent and natural front-rowers in the country.

In his first season of first-class rugby in 1908, he was part of the Taranaki team that beat the touring Anglo-Welsh 5–0. On tour with the All Blacks in 1913, his day job as a labourer no doubt accounted for the fact that he was always fit and willing to take his part in the team. He played in 14 of the 16 tour matches, and the following year in Australia missed only 2 of the 11 games. When he underwent his medical examination at the beginning of June 1916, the doctor examining him wrote that Cain 'had never been ill'.

He sailed for England in October 1916, on the *Willochra*, the same ship that he had travelled to North America on with the All Blacks four years earlier.

In September 1917, Cain wrote to his brother John in Waitara, telling him that he was in such good fettle that he had been chosen to play for the Divisional football team in Blighty. He also wrote that he had seen a good amount of fighting and, while uninjured, the thing that had hurt him was seeing his 'old football pals "go West"'.

A member of the Services side in the King's Cup and then South Africa, James Ryan (who had captained the side in the King's Cup), later said that Cain, along with fellow front-ranker 'Nuts' Hasell, 'were champions. They thought, talked and practised hooking as if it was a religion.'

Cain's All Black appearances would have straddled the war years if he had not withdrawn from the 1920 tour to Australia. When he played his final season for Taranaki — with the highlight no doubt being the clash with the 1921 Springboks — he had just turned 36.

THE NUMBER 9 PILL

This medication was dispensed as a cure-all for every ill, such as the ubiquitous scabies and even venereal disease. Lance Corporal F.Q. Symes, of 2nd Wellington Infantry Division, wrote in the soldiers' newspaper *Shell Shocks* of one occasion when it was hilariously prescribed:

Long ago, when sweating under the strain of squad drill at Trentham, we came to regard it as a panacea for all ills, but the latest use to which this notorious, solidified medical concoction has been put to use is, to use a mild term, the dizzy limit. A private in one of the regiments, somewhere in France, attended Sick-Parade the other morning suffering from a sprained ankle. The MO, adjusting his pince-nez, fingered and scrutinised the affected limb for some time, and hinted significantly about plaster of Paris, poultices etc. Presumably, the supply of this valuable commodity was exhausted, but a substitute was soon forth-coming, and the docile patient almost collapsed when the MO handed him No. Nines with the following instructions: 'Crush these up to the consistency of a powder, then mix to a stiff paste with warm water and apply to the affected part, completing the treatment by tying a stiff bandage around it.' Truly we live and learn. What next?

27 June 1916

ENLISTED: **Private Richard John 'Jock' McKENZIE (1892–1968)**

AGE AT ENLISTMENT: 24 years, 3 months, 12 days

ARMY NUMBER: 28594

EMBARKATION: Wellington, 7 December 1916; Auckland Infantry Battalion, 20th Reinforcements

LENGTH OF SERVICE: 1 year, 337 days

PLAYED FOR: Petone and Marist clubs; Wellington 1909–13; Auckland 1914; North Island 1912–14

ALL BLACK NUMBER: 179

POSITION: Five-eighth

APPEARANCES: 1913–14; 20 games, including 4 tests; 57 points (17 tries, 1 conversion, 1 dropped goal)

Lyttelton-born McKenzie had established himself as a regular for the All Blacks in the two seasons prior to the outbreak of war, having made his debut for Wellington aged only 17. He was just 20 when he represented the North in his first inter-island match, but of course by then he was a seasoned provincial player renowned for his accurate passing and creativity with ball in hand.

He played 12 games on the 1913 tour of North America, split between playing at first five- and second five-eighths, showing off his skills as an elusive runner and scoring 13 tries. On the 1914 tour of Australia he played seven games and, after the tour, having moved from Wellington to Auckland, he played two games for his new province.

After two months' active service in France, McKenzie suffered a slightly sprained ankle during training operations in May 1917, but worse was to come in August when he suffered a severe gunshot wound to his chest during the Battle of Pilckem Ridge in what has become known as the Third Battle of Ypres. Dangerously ill, he was admitted to the General Hospital at Étaples and then evacuated to England.

Major F.M. Twistleton (who was killed in Palestine in November 1917) wrote about the impact of bullets in a letter home:

> To my mind bursting bullets are the worst. One, the pointed German bullet[,] the nickelling is so thin that the friction of the air wears it through and it bursts with a very sharp snap. That is what many men call explosive bullets; the nickelling mushrooms back and if it gets home it makes an ugly wound.

In November 1917, McKenzie was classed as unfit for active service, and after two further months of convalescence he was discharged and returned to New Zealand, arriving back in March 1918.

McKenzie's army days were over, and sadly so were his footballing days. He was just 25. Once back in New Zealand, he moved to the Waikato, where his mother lived, and became licensee of the Hamilton Hotel before moving to Matangi to farm. He was a Waikato selector in 1930.

29 June 1916

ENLISTED: **Private James Alexander Steenson BAIRD (1893–1917)**
AGE AT ENLISTMENT: 22 years, 6 months, 12 days
ARMY NUMBER: 29720
EMBARKATION: Wellington, 16 October 1916; Otago Infantry Battalion, 18th Reinforcements
LENGTH OF SERVICE: 342 days
PLAYED FOR: Zingari–Richmond; Otago 1913
ALL BLACK NUMBER: 190
POSITION: Centre
APPEARANCES: 1913; 1 test

Amazingly, Baird played only three first-class matches, and one of those was the second test against the touring Australians in 1913.

He had played senior football for Zingari–Richmond, where the former All Black captain Jimmy Duncan was coach, before being selected for Otago. He appears to have shown such promise as a three-quarter that newspapers reported he was considered for the touring squad to North America. Baird wasn't named in that group, but after only two matches for his province, and little more than a season of senior club football, he found himself called into the All Black team for the first test against the touring Australians in Dunedin. His selection came about after Eric Cockroft had to withdraw due to injury, although several newspaper pundits wondered whether, even as a substitute, he really was up to the All Black standard. On match day, those concerns seemed well-founded, as nerves seemed to plague young Baird, whose passing was somewhat timid, although he did give a good account of himself as a defender.

A crowd of 9,000 enjoying a nice afternoon with a light breeze saw the All Blacks win 25–13. Despite the heavy ground conditions, eight tries were scored in the match, but it was a scrappy encounter.

Baird remains the eighth-youngest man to represent his country, at 19 years 270 days. Incidentally, a teammate in that All Black side, who would also serve in World War I — William Francis — was younger still, at 19 years 221 days. Rarely has international football seen two teenagers make their debuts in the same match.

The following week's test was in Christchurch, the first time the All Blacks had played an international at Lancaster Park, although they had played against Canterbury in 1905, prior to leaving for Britain. An injured hand kept Baird out of contention for that test.

Serious illness in 1914 kept him from the rugby field altogether. He suffered a bad case of pneumonia and pleurisy, but by the time of enlistment the medical officer noted that he had made a complete recovery and that both lungs were functioning normally. He was passed fit to serve.

Baird had been only three months in France with the 4th Company of the Otago Infantry Regiment's 1st Battalion when the 'big stunt', the Battle of Messines, was staged. (See page 220.)

25 July 1916

ENLISTED: **Sergeant David 'Dave' GALLAHER (1873–1917)**

AGE AT ENLISTMENT: 42 years, 8 months, 24 days

ARMY NUMBER: SA 3229/1st NZEF 32513

EMBARKATION: Wellington, 16 February 1917; Auckland
Infantry Regiment, 22nd Reinforcements

LENGTH OF SERVICE: 1 year, 70 days

PLAYED FOR: Ponsonby; Auckland 1896–97, 1899, 1900,
1903–05, 1909; North Island 1903, 1905; Auckland
selector and coach 1906–15; New Zealand selector
1907–14

ALL BLACK NUMBER: 97

POSITION: Front-row and wing-forward

APPEARANCES: 1903–06; 36 matches, including 6 tests, 27 as
captain; 14 points (4 tries, 1 conversion)

One of the myths that has surrounded the story of Gallaher joining the war effort was that he did it as a result of hearing the news that a younger brother had been killed while fighting in the Australian forces. Closer examination of his service record shows that Gallaher had actually undergone the pre-enlistment medical examination before his brother's death.

Another myth some writers persist with is that Gallaher changed his name from Gallagher around the time of his Boer War service. An extraordinary number of documents, such as travel papers, property titles, bereavement cards, wedding invitations and so on, in national archives, libraries and family collections, show the family name without the second 'g' on their arrival in New Zealand and that spelling was clearly in use well before Dave was an adult.

Army service was nothing new to the man born in Ramelton, in the northwest corner of Donegal, Ireland, who had travelled with his family to New Zealand when aged four. He had served during the Boer War with the 'Silent' Sixth Contingent, registering for service stating that he was a couple of years younger than he actually was. After his time with the Sixth ended, he stayed in South Africa and joined the Tenth Contingent, but the war ended shortly after.

A FELLOW KIWI-BORN PLAYER

Another footballing member of the 10th Contingent in South Africa was Arthur Corfe. Born and raised in Christchurch, he attended Christ's College, until his family moved to Australia when his father was appointed headmaster of Toowomba Grammar. A forward, he played in the second test for Australia against Great Britain in 1899, the first international series involving the Australians. The match was lost 0–11, but three weeks earlier he had scored two tries in Queensland's upset 11–3 win over the visitors. His Boer War experience had begun with the 3rd Queensland Contingent. By the time of World War I, Corfe was living in England. He served as a lieutenant colonel with the Royal West Kent Regiment. Twice wounded and taken prisoner, he was decorated with the DSO and two bars and the Croix de Guerre.

By the time Gallaher went to Africa, he had already established himself in the Auckland rugby team, and as a well-known member of the Ponsonby rugby club. On his return from fighting on the veldt, where conditions were harsh — hot by day, cold by night, and with difficulties supplying moving contingents with food and clothing — Gallaher missed the 1902 season as he recovered from the effects of the war.

Once back to full health, he returned to the rugby field and was included in the All Black team to travel to Australia. He played in their first-ever test, against Australia at the Sydney Cricket Ground.

Opposing Gallaher in the front row was a man who, despite that being his only test appearance, was also to have a distinguished and influential career on and off the rugby field: Ted Larkin. The New South Welshman was a key figure in the establishment of rugby league in the state, being the first full-time secretary. From 1913 to 1915 he was a member of the state's legislative assembly.

Answering the call to war, he was killed at Gallipoli on 25 April 1915. Also in the Australian side was Auckland-born Sid Riley, who returned to New Zealand, settling in Ponsonby and playing league for Auckland in 1912. He served with the Auckland Infantry Regiment in the 17th Reinforcements.

In 1904, when the team from Great Britain visited New Zealand and played one test, in Wellington — the first rugby international held on New Zealand soil — Gallaher played in the position of wing-forward. Captain of the tourists, Scotsman Dr David 'Darkie' Bedell-Sivright, and fearsome forward Englishman Blair Swannell (who shortly after settled in Australia and toured New Zealand with the 1905 Australian side) would both lose their lives at Gallipoli.

While selections were being made for the 1905–06 tour to Britain and Ireland, Gallaher was suspended by the New Zealand Rugby Football Union, which alleged that he had over-claimed on expenses incurred getting to and from the Wellington test. After something of a stand-off, Gallaher settled the dispute by refunding some of the money. He was then chosen as captain for the tour, which rankled with some southern members of the touring party. Aboard ship, and in the best interests of the team, Gallaher offered to resign. A vote was taken, and he was retained as captain. One of the keys to Gallaher's handling of that situation, and his preparation of his teammates for their arrival in England, was undoubtedly his experience as a soldier aboard ship on the way to the Boer War. He knew how important it was to get all the elements of fitness, food and hygiene right, so that the players arrived in England in great shape and excited about the games ahead.

Due to an injury Gallaher missed playing against Ireland in Dublin, and Munster in Limerick. The opposing captain for those matches was Basil Maclear, a captain with the Royal Dublin Fusiliers, who died in France after being shot in the throat in 1915.

Gallaher retired from playing when he returned from the tour, but became Auckland selector (and coach) overseeing their Ranfurly Shield reign from 1906 to 1913. He was also an All Black selector.

With the outbreak of war, Gallaher saw many of the young men he had coached sailing away to fight overseas. His younger brothers, Charles and Douglas, had taken up arms as Australian troops with the 11th Infantry Battalion. Both fought and were wounded on the bloody slopes of Gallipoli. Charles, the more serious casualty, with shrapnel lodged dangerously close to his spinal cord, was sent back to Australia, taking no further part in the war. Douglas spent time in Egypt recovering from a series of wounds before being sent to the Western Front. Promoted to the rank of company sergeant major, he was killed in action on 3 June 1916, amidst the horror that was the Battle of the Somme.

When Gallaher was farewelled before departing in February 1917, the *Evening Post* reported that he 'received a presentation of a purse of sovereigns from his business friends in that city last week, and Capt. Beck D.S.O. handed him the pair of binoculars which he had used at Gallipoli'. Beck had been awarded his DSO in November 1915 for 'distinguished service in the field during the operations in the Dardanelles'. Shortly after, he was invalided back to New Zealand.

After time in Sling Camp in May 1917, where he caught up with a lot of footballers, Gallaher arrived in France and spent nearly three weeks at Étaples.

Ormond Burton, soldier and war historian, later wrote of meeting Gallaher at a gas training school: 'The man who had been something of a Field Marshal in the realm of international sport was now a Sergeant in 3/Company. We became very friendly. He was a very pleasant, modest and likeable chap ... I liked him very much.'

On 26 June 1917, Gallaher joined the 2nd Battalion of the Auckland Regiment in the field. (See page 235.)

27 July 1916

ENLISTED: **Sergeant Percival 'Percy' Wright STOREY (1897–1975)**

AGE AT ENLISTMENT: 19 years, 5 months, 16 days
ARMY NUMBER: 32739
EMBARKATION: Wellington, 15 November 1916; Otago Infantry Battalion, 19th Reinforcements

Of the 1913 All Black team that played Australia at Athletic Park, Wellington, on 6 September, eleven would serve in the war. Three – 'Norkey' Dewar (front left), 'Doolan' Downing (centre, middle row) and George Sellars (third from right, back row) – would die on foreign fields. Five of the Australians would lose their lives in the war, too. *(Private collection)*

On 5 September, 1914, before sailing with the Main Body of the New Zealand Expeditionary Force, Auckland volunteers were acknowledged and entertained at Eden Park, with a match between Auckland and Wellington. *(Sir George Grey Special Collections, Auckland Libraries)*

The 1924–25 All Blacks, the 'Invincibles'. Thick white borders around the portraits above indicate forwards who were veterans of World War I. *(Sir George Grey Special Collections, Auckland Libraries)*

LENGTH OF SERVICE: 3 years, 112 days

PLAYED FOR: Waimate, Excelsior and Zingari clubs; South
 Canterbury 1920–23; South Island 1920; New Zealand
 Trials 1924

ALL BLACK NUMBER: 224

POSITION: Wing

APPEARANCES: 1920–21; 12 matches, including 2 tests;
 50 points (16 tries, 1 conversion)

As a teenager playing club football, Storey had established himself as frustrating prey for those trying to tackle him. He was very quick off the mark, light on his feet even on boggy grounds, and able to maintain his speed even when dancing around or between his opponents.

He enlisted for service six-and-a-half months shy of his twentieth birthday by putting his birth date back a year, to 1896. At the time he was working as a traveller for the Oamaru company Darling and McDowell, well-known South Canterbury grain and produce merchants and stock and station agents.

Storey had six months' active service under his belt by the time he suffered a shrapnel wound to his right arm on 12 October 1917, the dark day at Passchendaele. He was removed to England for treatment, and after two months in hospital and recuperating he was mostly stationed at Sling Camp, apart from undertaking training and courses of instruction at Tidworth and Larkhill camps.

From Sling he joined the King's Cup army football team and was chosen to tour South Africa with the Services side in 1919. In 12 matches for those teams he scored 13 tries.

Prior to his departure with the 1920 All Blacks to Australia, the *Auckland Star* wrote that Storey was 'one of the "discoveries" of war Rugby. He gave a taste of his quality in the New Zealand Army team's match with Wellington and satisfied the critics that the good opinions formed of him abroad were deserved.'

What a discovery he was: top try-scorer on tour, including enjoying one of those afternoons that became so familiar to touring All Black wings against lesser opposition, when he bagged four tries against Manning River District.

Storey captained South Canterbury against the Springboks in 1921, and scored a try in the All Blacks' first test win at Carisbrook in 1921, crossing the line after the All Blacks ran a blindside move from a scrum near to the Springboks' line. He played in the second test loss, but injured his shoulder and missed the third test. He was approached to tour Australia in 1922, but declared himself unavailable.

During World War II he enlisted again and was a sports officer at Burnham Military Camp, but ill health began to plague him in the form of varicose veins and breathlessness (an examining medical officer in 1944 noted he had put on two stone, or 13 kilograms, while in camp!). He was also suffering from deteriorating vision, a very common complaint from veterans who had been exposed to gas on the Western Front.

Storey served as an All Black selector in 1944.

1 August 1916

The Military Service Act 1916 brought into force the conscription of Pakeha men.

No first-class rugby matches were played in 1916, and Lancaster Park was planted out in potatoes, which were sold to raise funds for both the war effort and the local rugby union. They, like their associates around the country, were facing financial hardship due to the fact that had little or no income from gate-takings.

Policemen were regularly sighted at junior football games, which led to a number of letters being written to newspaper editors arguing that the last place a shirker would try to hide would be among spectators at rugby matches.

21 August 1916

ENLISTED: **Corporal Maurice John BROWNLIE (1897–1957)**
AGE AT ENLISTMENT: 20 years, 11 days
ARMY NUMBER: 30422

EMBARKATION: Wellington, 8 February 1917; Mounted Rifles
   Brigade, 21st Reinforcements
LENGTH OF SERVICE: 3 years, 18 days
PLAYED FOR: Hastings; Hawke's Bay–Poverty Bay 1921;
   Hawke's Bay 1921–27, 1929, 1930; Hawke's Bay–Poverty
   Bay–East Coast 1923; North Island 1922–25, 1927; New
   Zealand Trials 1924, 1927
ALL BLACK NUMBER: 261
POSITION: Loose-forward
APPEARANCES: 1922–28; 61 matches, including 8 tests, 19
   games as captain; 63 points (21 tries)

Enlisting nine months after older brother Cyril (see page 100),
Brownlie had á run-in with authority when he was absent without
leave from Featherston Camp and forfeited two days' pay. He left
New Zealand with the Wellington Mounted Rifles and, like Cyril,
joined the Machine Gun Squadron once at Moascar.

Football featured in his down-time in the desert, when he
played in the striped jerseys of the Mounted Rifles alongside Cyril
and Robin Harper, brother of All Black Eric. In October 1918, he
contracted malaria while serving in Gaza, spending a month in
hospital, and then he had to wait until June 1919 before sailing for
New Zealand from Suez.

Upon his return he farmed the family land at Puketapu and
had no real interest in organised football. But, with the selection
of brother Jack (who went by his second name Lawrence) for the
All Blacks to meet New South Wales in 1920, a challenge was
thrown down to Cyril and Maurice by their father, who felt that
they, too, could make the national team.

Dominating appearances in club football saw Maurice chosen
in the Hawke's Bay–Poverty Bay side to play the 1921 Springboks.
Also in the forward pack was his good friend Tom Heeney, who
would move from the dark, cramped conditions of scrums and
forward play to the bright lights and open rings of professional
boxing when he challenged for the World Heavyweight Title
against Gene Tunney in New York in 1928.

George Nepia (who also played in the combined team against the 'Boks) first encountered the Brownlie brothers in a club game in 1920, when they turned out for the Hastings club. Poor young Nepia was playing on the side of the scrum when he had his first sighting of Maurice:

> He weighed only fourteen stone [89 kilograms], but he gave the impression of being at least half as big again as that. He had a great, square face, a chest like a barrel and legs that reminded you, with their sinews, of the vines of the rata ... [He] was fast and he was strong — strong like a lion, quite unhurtable ... They were hard men, like rocks.

Brownlie quickly became the dominant forward of New Zealand and All Black rugby in the 1920s. His first match for the All Blacks was against New South Wales at the Sydney Cricket Ground in 1922.

He was unemotional around his teammates off the field, so quiet that some considered such a champion player to be somewhat aloof in the way he wouldn't fraternise with opposing teams after a match. So relaxed before big matches was he that it was not unusual for him to have to be woken just before his team made its way to a ground by bus. On the field, he was without peer in the period between the two wars: influential, bright-eyed, determined and aggressive.

Maurice watched as Cyril was sent from the field in the 1925 test against England, and it inspired him to one of his, and the All Blacks', finest-ever performances. He scored an extraordinary solo try, helping the 14-man All Blacks defeat England 17–11. The try-line was 20 metres ahead of Maurice, but so too were four English defenders. He carried all of them with him as he plunged over the line. The English captain that day, W.W. Wakefield, described Brownlie's determination to get to the line thus:

> Somehow he went on, giving me the impression of a moving tree-trunk, so solid did he appear to be and so little effect did various attempted tackles have upon him. He crashed through without swerving to the right or left.

His Hawke's Bay coach and close friend, Norman McKenzie, wrote of Maurice in 1961 that he was

> the greatest man I have ever seen as a siderow forward: great because he was great in every aspect of forward play. He could handle the ball like a back, he could take the ball in the lineout and burst clear, he could stimulate movements, and, greatest of all, he had the ability to lead his forwards out of a tight corner, yard by yard, along the touchline. For sheer tenacity I have seen no one equal to Maurice Brownlie. His outstanding qualities were strength and resolution. He was in every respect a remarkable man and one of the finest physical specimens of manhood I have ever seen … He was a hard, but never a tough, player, and though he was often a marked man and set upon, he never complained, but got on with the game.

So revered (and feared) was Maurice in provincial rugby, particularly as captain of Hawke's Bay during their great Shield reign of the 1920s, that a referee once famously told an opposing player who, like a young enthusiastic bull deer taking on the old stag, was giving the Hawke's Bay legend a bit of niggle, to 'leave Mr. Brownlie alone'. (A famous poem, titled with the same phrase, was published by the *Truth* newspaper.)

Brownlie captained the All Blacks in South Africa where they tied the four-test series, 2–2. Just what an achievement that was became more and more obvious as the decades passed and series after series was lost in the Republic. It was 1996 before the All Blacks finally won a series in South Africa, earning the side led by Sean Fitzpatrick the moniker 'The Incomparables'.

Teammate Jack Hore marvelled at Brownlie's physicality when taking on the typically big South Africans in the test matches. 'Maurice grasped a Springbok forward about his waist, lifted him high and dashed him to the ground. It was the most amazing demonstration of strength I have ever seen; but then, Morrie was the strongest man I ever saw.'

Brownlie's stature continued to grow, even when he had hung up his rugby boots. The *Herald*'s famous rugby writer Terry

McLean was known to describe Brownlie with phrases likening his physique and play to that of Greek gods at rest or at war.

It is interesting to see that for a man of such standing he had no interest in the administration of the game, unlike a number of his peers who went on to hold selectorial or management positions with the national union. He was quite content living the life of a back-country farmer, quietly involved in his rural community and its activities, such as pony clubs and so on.

Maurice Brownlie should be acknowledged as one of the greatest forwards the game has seen, and a forerunner to modern players of longevity and dominance such as Colin Meads, Sean Fitzpatrick and Richie McCaw. His record of 61 appearances for the All Blacks (19 as captain) stood for nearly 30 years until surpassed by Kevin Skinner in 1956. A remarkable feature of the total number of 119 first-class games he played was that just over half of them were for the All Blacks. The only other centurion of the pre-World War II period to have a percentage approaching anything like Brownlie's was the great Originals fullback Billy Wallace, who played 51 times for New Zealand out of 112 overall appearances.

22 August 1916

ENLISTED: **Corporal Harold Vivian 'Toby' MURRAY (1888–1971)**

AGE AT ENLISTMENT: 28 years, 6 months, 13 days

ARMY NUMBER: 31025

EMBARKATION: Wellington, 19 January 1917; Machine Gun Section, 21st Reinforcements Specialist Section

LENGTH OF SERVICE: 2 years, 203 days

PLAYED FOR: Ellesmere, Irwell and Springfield clubs; Canterbury 1909–14; South Island 1910, 1911, 1913, 1914

ALL BLACK NUMBER: 180

POSITION: Wing-forward

APPEARANCES: 1913–14; 22 matches, including 4 tests; 36 points (12 tries)

In the 1909 and 1910 representative seasons, Murray was the top try-scorer for Canterbury, scoring five times in the latter season. The bulk of those tries were scored when he was playing on the wing, but the next season he moved permanently to wing-forward.

His All Black debut, in which he scored a try, was the 30–5 win over Australia in Wellington, but of the remaining 21 games he played in black, 19 were overseas. When it came to touchdowns, he had completely contrasting All Black tours. In North America he scored 11 tries from his 12 appearances, but in Australia in 1914 he failed to dot down once in his 7 games.

Murray was one of the many soldiers who had an operation to repair varicose veins prior to being classed as fit for service. Shortly before leaving New Zealand, the farmer from Lincoln turned out for the 19th Reinforcement Specials football team at Athletic Park against a Wellington side (all under the age of 20) in their final match of the season.

After a month's final training with the Machine Gun Section at Grantham Camp in May 1917, he left for France. At the start of April 1918, after eight months at the Western Front, he was evacuated to hospital in England suffering a shrapnel wound to his right thigh.

Upon recovery and transfer back to the Machine Gun Depot at Grantham, Murray turned out for the depot's football team, which also had in its ranks Eric Cockroft. The side had comprehensive wins over the Harrowby Officers, Northumberland Fusiliers, Uppingham College and the Royal Air Force at Hucknall. The team of airmen was described in one match report as being 'composed mainly of South Africans and they were sportsmen of the first order'.

Murray was selected for the United Kingdom XV, but there is some contention as to whether he did actually appear in the King's Cup tournament.

During World War II Murray served as a platoon commander with the Waipara Battalion.

24 August 1916

ENLISTED: **Lance Corporal Johnstone 'Jock' RICHARDSON (1899–1994)**
AGE AT ENLISTMENT: 17 years, 4 months, 22 days
ARMY NUMBER: 34988
EMBARKATION: Wellington, 14 December 1916; 20th
Reinforcements, New Zealand Mounted Rifles
LENGTH OF SERVICE: 3 years, 17 days
PLAYED FOR: Alhambra, Waikiwi and Pirates clubs; Otago
1920–22; Southland 1923, 1925–26; South Island
1921–22, 1924–25; New Zealand Trials 1921, 1924
ALL BLACK NUMBER: 234
POSITION: Loose-forward
APPEARANCES: 1921–25; 42 matches, including 7 tests;
16 games as captain; 58 points (18 tries, 2 conversions)

Richardson's desire to serve saw him put his age up by four years, registering as John. ('Johnstone' would only be used by him when he signed an army will form in 1918.) Physically, the big lad with hazel hair, who stood nearly six feet (183 centimetres) tall and would be an Otago shot-put champion after the war, more than convinced the recruiters that he was old enough to fight.

The teenager's time as a machine gunner in the Middle East was blighted by ill health. He suffered painful swelling to veins in his legs, cysts and eventually the all-too-common malaria. He finally saw good health and unbroken service in the last months of the war, and embarked for a return home in June 1919.

His provincial debut was for Otago in 1920, and the next year he made the South Island side. After impressing for his province against the visiting Springboks, he was elevated to the All Blacks and played all three tests against the visitors. He looked completely unfazed, tussling with the big South African forwards as though he was a seasoned veteran of international football.

Although he had made his All Black debut the year before, it was in the 1922 North versus South match on a sodden

Eden Park that Richardson really started to show his class. He dominated the lineouts, made several imposing tackles and, with conditions under boot favouring a dribbling game, was in great command of the ball when it was on the toe. Many left the ground of the opinion that he was the best forward on the park that afternoon.

Richardson was part of the 1924 South Island side that were walloped by the North 39–8 in Wellington. Long before phrases such as 'player welfare' and 'concussion tests' entered the rugby parlance, Richardson suffered a boot to the head early in the game which noticeably affected his cognisance of play. In one instance he fielded the ball and then stood still, allowing the chasing North Island winger to make an easy albeit bemused tackle. After the match, Richardson told a member of the press that he could remember his captain, Arnold Perry, who happened to be a doctor, giving him a quick check. 'From then on till the bell rang out at halftime my mind was a blank. The bell brought me back to life, and when I looked and saw the score was twenty-five to nil against us I was the most surprised man on the field.'

Richardson first captained the All Blacks against New South Wales in 1923, and again in 1924. So, having been captain for two series, and being a certainty for selection, many considered he would be appointed captain of the team to tour Britain. But the captaincy of the side that would come to be known as the Invincibles was a tangled web of provincial politics and playing form. Eventually Cliff Porter was chosen as the team leader, but when he couldn't hold his place in the side, Richardson captained the team in the internationals against Ireland, Wales and England.

As the Invincibles tour drew to a close, Richardson had the misfortune to break his fibula during practice in Vancouver. Playing on the wing and trying to beat the speedy Jim Parker, just as he went to pass the ball he was trapped awkwardly in a tackle and, according to one report, 'a snap was heard all over the field'.

Fortunately the injury was not as bad as first feared, but he never again donned the black jersey. He had captained the All Blacks 16 times and never lost a match.

Upon his appointment as secretary of the Southland Rugby Union at the beginning of 1927, Richardson retired from rugby and oversaw the development of Rugby Park in Invercargill. In 1929, he married Ella Hutchinson and the couple moved to Australia.

CONDITIONS UNDERFOOT

If rugby players thought some of the grounds they had played on were in a bad state in the middle of winter, they were nothing compared to what they might face on a battlefield. The troop newspaper *Chronicles of the NZEF* (which was a mix of news, hospital admissions, sports results and light-hearted items) carried a piece of black humour about conditions on the Somme:

> Somme Mud
> To form an idea of what one feels like after a few days' wet weather fighting on the Somme, just think of a Taranaki cowyard at its worst after, say, six weeks' rain. Multiply the result eleven times, then roll in it, taking special care to rub it well into your hair, eyes, ears, mouth and rifle. Take a day's rations and stamp them well into the mixture also, and use a newly emptied benzene tin for drinking purposes. Carry a nice hefty load — for instance, a bag of potatoes — through it all day, being sure to fall down every minute and a half and consider yourself buried several times by shells that are too close for comfort. Continue treatment for some days, being careful not to shave or wash during this period. You can then realise what the cablegram means when it is reported that 'the weather interfered with operations'.
> L.M.G.

The New Zealand Division suffered a heavy toll at the Somme in a month's dreadful fighting from mid-September 1916. More than 6,000 men were wounded and 2,000 killed. The bodies of the majority of those fatalities were never recovered.

29 August 1916

ENLISTED: **Trooper James Hislop PARKER** MM, CBE
(1897–1980)
AGE AT ENLISTMENT: 19 years, 6 months, 28 days
ARMY NUMBER: 35304
EMBARKATION: Wellington, 5 December 1916; Machine
   Gun Section, New Zealand Mounted Rifles, 19th
   Reinforcements
LENGTH OF SERVICE: 3 years, 9 days
PLAYED FOR: Christchurch High School Old Boys; Canterbury
   1920, 1923; South Island 1924; New Zealand Trials
   1924
ALL BLACK NUMBER: 299
POSITION: Wing-forward
APPEARANCES: 1924–25; 21 games, including 3 tests;
   56 points (18 tries, 1 conversion)

Hailing from Lyttelton where he worked as a clerk for the
New Zealand Shipping Company, Parker was ruled unfit for
enlistment in July 1916, due to 'slight' varicose veins on his right
leg, but following an operation which left him with a small scar
(noted when he had his next medical test) he was then passed
fit. It was also observed that he had 'slight' stiffness of the left
elbow. At the second medical examination Parker was asked
whether he had ever been off work due to illness and injury.
When he replied that he hadn't, the medical examiner wrote, 'a
most suitable man'.

That suitable man served with the Mounted Machine Gun
Section in the Middle East and was awarded the Military Medal
for bravery in the field in October 1918. He suffered what was
recorded as a slight dose of malaria, but a recurrence of the illness
kept him out of top-level football for two seasons.

He was initially chosen for the final test against the 1923 New
South Wales side, but work commitments prevented him from
joining the team.

The following year he became an Invincibles member, and was rated the fastest man in the side after winger Jack Steel, no doubt thanks to his training and successes as a sprinter when a teenager. He was the only All Black to play as both a back and a forward during the tour, making one appearance on the wing against Cumberland.

Such was his form and (less controversial) style of play at wing-forward that he kept tour captain Cliff Porter out of the team for the internationals against Ireland, Wales and England. He scored three tries against Cornwall and five against North Midlands.

Parker stepped away from football to concentrate on his orchards, but also to again recuperate from malaria, and later became chairman of the New Zealand Apple and Pear Board. His service to the fruit industry was acknowledged with a CBE in 1964. He was a member of the New Zealand Rugby Union executive from 1939 to 1956, and managed the 1949 All Blacks in South Africa. His service to the national union saw him elected a life member in 1959.

19 September 1916

† DIED: **Second Lieutenant Frank Reginald Wilson** †

Frank Wilson (see page 55) was the first former All Black to lose his life at the Western Front. He died as the result of wounds suffered at the Somme, in the Battle of Flers-Courcelette. Under the orders of Brigadier-General Earl Johnston, the 1st Canterbury, 1st Auckland and 1st Otago battalions were to advance on the village of Flers, which was a scene of utter ruin and devastation following days of shelling from both sides. The three battalions had to approach through a series of trenches and then approximately half a mile (800 metres) of open ground. The Canterbury men left Firstly, followed by the Aucklanders an hour later, and a short time after that, Otago. Once there, they were to attack German positions.

Private Baverstock of the 1st Canterbury Battalion wrote of the advance of 17 September:

> When we were roughly half-way to the Switch, a big high-explosive shell burst shatteringly at the head of our platoon and wiped out about a third of us. We passed their bunched up dead bodies in a deep shell-hole a second later ... Rifle fire cracked past us from our left flank ... The din was just terrific and the barrage seemed to have converged on our point of entry into the Switch which was being heavily shelled just then for all that high ground was under close observation ... The whole locality was being plastered with high explosive and a deal of rifle fire came from Goose Alley and High Wood ... We came in for a lot of sniping as we clambered over places where the trench had been blown in ... Before long we ran into open ground with Flers village about 500 yards [460 metres] away ... The tall trees to the right of the track into the village were collapsing under heavy shell-fire.

The three battalions reached the position where they were to prepare to attack the German lines by about 1 p.m. Once they had assembled, word came through that plans had changed and their next move had been called off.

Wilson was seriously wounded during the disastrous advance, but it was two days before he was treated at the 2nd Field Ambulance. He was moved the same day to the 45th Casualty Clearing Station, but passed away after a short time there.

His family — mother Elizabeth, sister Rose and brother Albert — were first notified that he had been wounded, then within hours received a telegram bearing the tragic news that he had in fact died. In his will, Wilson had bequeathed all of his property and possessions to his mother.

His final resting place is the Dernancourt Communal Cemetery Extension.

On the first anniversary of Wilson's death, Bert Hayson (who besides being a chum of his, a fellow teacher, rugby enthusiast and member of a well-known Herne Bay family was for a time headmaster of Wellesley Street School) placed an In Memoriam item in the *New Zealand Herald*, which simply read: 'He was indeed, a man.'

21 September 1916

† DIED: **Private Robert 'Bobby' Stanley Black** †

Two days after Wilson's death, 1914 All Black Robert Black (see page 106) disappeared in the dirt and dark of a night-time raid on the Somme. The 2nd Battalion of the Canterbury Regiment made a silent night-time advance in an attempt to capture a spur of the Goose Alley trench. Black and his men made their move across a road and then on the uphill incline at 8.30 p.m. A supporting barrage helped their advance, but then the Germans counterattacked. Thanks to the arrival of two platoons from the Nelson Company, the 2nd Canterburies were able to hold their position during a horrendous four hours of hand-to-hand combat, exploding grenades and bullet hails. At 4 a.m. the 2nd Canterburies were still holding their objective, but Bobby Black had become one of the many casualties.

In Casualty List No. 434, released to the Press Association by the Defence Department four weeks later, Black was among more than 110 men listed as missing, and that did not include the nearly 20 more missing presumed killed.

Black was declared 'Killed in Action' at a court of inquiry held two months after he was declared missing in action. A Corporal O'Connor told the court that, 'On the night of 21 September, 1916, Private Black was acting platoon sergeant. He was on [the] extreme left of the line. During the advance I was with him for a few yards. Then we were separated. Since that night I have never seen him. We searched for him that night and could find nothing of him. He was with Private Eagle, also now missing. I am of the opinion that he went too far and was probably captured.'

At the Caterpillar Valley Cemetery, Black is among the 1,205 New Zealanders listed as having been lost in the fighting with no known grave. (Amazingly, over the passage of time the remains of eight of the men listed on the memorial have been identified and buried.) When the body of a New Zealand soldier — unnamed but known to be from the New Zealand Rifle Brigade — was repatriated in 2004 to lie as the 'Unknown Warrior' at the National Cenotaph, his remains were lifted from the Caterpillar Valley Cemetery.

The grief of a mother for the loss of her only child is palpable in three words that were part of an In Memoriam notice placed in the *Evening Star* and the *Otago Daily Times* by Mrs Black two years after Bobby disappeared on the Somme: 'Still hoping on.'

1 October 1916

To break up the monotony of time in the trenches, behind the lines, under instruction or in physical training, a variety of light-hearted games were devised by training staff. The exercises were to complement the physical requirements of fighting, keep the men keen, alert and competitive, and at the same time assist with relaxation and maintaining good spirits. One such manual of sports, *Games for Use with Physical Training Tables and Training in Bombing*, 1916, was issued to officers along with Army Orders on 1 October. It included instructions for relays using 'indian clubs' and between-the-legs ball-passing relays, which were to be familiar to primary-school children for decades to come. Another, with elements of rugby football and association football, was called bomb ball:

Bomb Ball
A game for bringing into play the muscles used in bombing, and for
the development of quick and accurate throwing.

Ground — Any football ground or open space, marked out as
under; the size of the rectangle may be varied to suit the amount of
ground available.

The goal should be marked out on the ground, no goal-posts
being necessary.

Teams — The players should be disposed as in Association
Football, but a lesser number than eleven a side should take part if the
ground is small.

Apparatus — Some object approximating to the weight, size and
shape of a grenade, care being taken that it is not such as to be likely to
injure the players. The following is suggested: a small oval-shaped bag
of canvas or thick calico, filled with sand or small shot to the required
weight and securely sewn up.

Referee — A referee should control the game, as in football.

Method of Playing — The ball is passed from player to player
by hand, the object being to land it in the goal. It may be passed
backward or forward as in Association Football, and the 'off-side' rule
will apply in the same way. The passes are taken on the run, and the
ball must be picked up and similarly passed on at once.

The ball may be caught with both hands, but must only be
thrown by one. Only two methods of throwing are allowed: (1) For
long distances, a full over-hand throw, as shown in the diagrams
in 'Training and Employment of Bombers,' March, 1916; (2) For
short distances, a 'put', made in the same manner as 'putting-the-
shot'.

In order to exercise equally both sides of the body and to develop
skill and accuracy with both hands, the throwing-hand may be
changed every 10 minutes or so, as the discretion of the Referee.

To start the game, Captains toss, and the winner has the first
throw and the right to select the goal he wishes to defend. The teams
are then drawn up, the forwards [teams also had a line of half-backs
and backs] along their respective starting-lines. The referee blows his
whistle and the game commences by the centre-forward taking the
first throw or 'put.'

In the course of the game, if the ball lands in the goal, or is caught in the goal, and subsequently dropped within it by any player, a goal is scored.

If the ball is caught in the goal before touching the ground and thrown out at once no goal is scored.

If the ball goes 'behind' or into 'touch', it is thrown in similarly as in Association Football, but with one hand, and this also applies to a 'corner.'

After a goal has been scored, the game is started again as at the commencement.

Charging — No charging or rough play is admissible. Passes may be intercepted, or throws frustrated, with the open hand.

Fouls — Fouls may be given for (1) Running with the ball, instead of passing it at once as soon as caught or picked up; (2) Throwing the ball in any way but the two methods allowed; (3) Catching hold of a player; (4) Any form of rough play; (5) Being 'off-side'; (6) Using the wrong hand for throwing.

Penalties — A penalty for a foul will take the form of a free throw against the offending side from the place where the foul occurred. In the case of rough play, a goal may be allowed against the offending team for each similar offence after the first caution.

Duration of Game — From 20 to 30 minutes each way, according to the condition of the men.

4 October 1916

ENLISTED: **Trooper 'Dean' Eric Tristram HARPER (1877–1918)**
AGE AT ENLISTMENT: 38 years, 10 months, 3 days
ARMY NUMBER: 35694
EMBARKATION: Wellington, 31 May 1917; New Zealand Mounted Rifles, 26th Reinforcements
LENGTH OF SERVICE: 1 year, 207 days
PLAYED FOR: Christchurch; Canterbury 1900–02, 1904–05; South Island 1902, 1905; Canterbury–South Canterbury–West Coast 1904

ALL BLACK NUMBER: 112

POSITION: Wing and centre

APPEARANCES: 1904–06; 11 matches, including 2 tests;
24 points (6 tries, 3 conversions)

As mentioned earlier, one of the myths surrounding the enlistment of Dave Gallaher is that he joined up spurred on by the death of a brother. While that is incorrect, the circumstance does actually apply to his teammate from the first All Black home test in 1904 and the trip made by the Originals in 1905–06, Eric Harper.

One of 10 children of whom 8 were boys, and a grandson of the first Anglican bishop of Christchurch (which played a part in his nickname, 'Dean Eric'), he underwent the preliminary medical examination in July 1916 but was deemed unfit for service due to having varicose veins. When news reached the family in mid-August that a younger brother, George, who was serving with the New Zealand Mounted Rifles Machine Gun Squadron (and had been decorated with the DCM for actions at Gallipoli, where he had been wounded) had been killed during a battle with Ottoman forces at Bir el Abd, Eric had surgery on the troublesome veins and was then able to enlist. Another brother, Robin, was also serving in the Middle East and sent George's possessions back to Eric.

Harper entered camp five weeks before his wife, Beatrice — who had been a widow prior to the couple marrying in the Roman Catholic Westminster Cathedral in London in July 1913 — gave birth to their second child, Anne. A son, Frederick, had been born in March 1914.

A man of extraordinary talents, Harper followed his well-known father George into the legal profession, after schooling at St Patrick's College, Silverstream, and Christchurch Boys' High School and tertiary studies at Canterbury College.

His provincial rugby debut came for Canterbury in 1900, after he had become known for his power and speed as an outside back playing for the Christchurch football club. Such was his athletic ability that he won national titles in 1901 and 1902 in the 440-yards (400-metre) hurdles and then the 880-yards (800 metres) events.

THE ARMY 'ALL BLACKS'

A team of footballers from the Reserve Group at Sling Camp, recuperating after suffering wounds at the front, played several matches in late October and throughout November 1916. Although they could be best described as the New Zealand Reserve Group team, most reports of their matches called them the 'All Blacks'. The team did wear black jerseys, shorts and socks with white bands, but, apart from Ned Hughes, Teddy Roberts and Ranji Wilson, these were men who had only played provincial rugby in New Zealand.

Among the games they played were matches against Plymouth (won 11–6), 'Wales' (9–7), London Rifle Brigade (59–0) and Public Schools (16–5).

The match against 'Wales' in Swansea drew a crowd of close to 5,000 and raised funds for the *Daily Post* Swansea Prisoners of War Fund.

In 1904, having completed his legal studies and final examination, he was admitted as a solicitor of the Supreme Court. Through his work in the Christchurch Magistrates' Court he became known as a keen litigator and a forceful defender of his clients.

He was part of the Canterbury–South Canterbury–West Coast side that faced the 1904 Great Britain side at Lancaster Park, and a week later he debuted for the All Blacks in the one-off test at Athletic Park. He was something of a late addition to the 1905 touring party, but his time away with the team was noted for his lack of availability due to injury. While fellow speedster Jimmy Hunter was setting all sorts of try-scoring records, Harper was consigned to being a spectator, making only one test appearance in the New Year's Day 1906 encounter with France, in which he scored two tries. With the unexpected addendum of a series of games in North America, Billy Glenn and Harper took the option of returning to New Zealand ahead of their teammates.

Harper retired from rugby on his return to New Zealand, having become a partner with his father and a Mr G.D. Pascoe in the legal firm George Harper, Son and Pascoe. (The family name lives on in the firm of Anthony Harper.) The following year he represented Canterbury at cricket, playing out of the United and later West Christchurch cricket clubs.

Harper's uncle, Leonard, had apparently been the first Pakeha to cross the Southern Alps, and his son Arthur inherited a love of mountaineering. He founded the New Zealand Alpine Club in 1891. With no further sporting commitments, Eric joined him and club members in exploring the ranges west of Christchurch. It is believed that in 1908 Harper was the first to scale the heights of the Denniston Pass, and the nearby Eric's Stream is named after him. In 1913, in the company of cousin Arthur and George Denniston, he scaled the difficult Mt Davie.

Harper and his family lived in a large house at 8 Kilmore Street. It was demolished in 1998 as part of an expansion of Cathedral Grammar School.

After he was accepted for the Mounted Rifles, Harper (who had undertaken three years' service with the Territorial Force prior to the war) sailed with the 26th Reinforcements as a regimental sergeant major (RSM). He was appointed Acting RSM while on the *Moeraki*, and then Acting Ship's SM on the *Port Lincoln*. Once at Moascar, in November 1916, according to a letter sent to *The Press* newspaper by a colleague from the legal fraternity, Oscar Alpers: 'he begged to be relieved of his stripes; he wished to get into the firing-line at once, and he refused to be set over men who had been in action till he himself had been tried in the ordeal of battle'.

Three weeks later he was serving in the field with the New Zealand Mounted Rifles. (See page 257.)

9 November 1916

ENLISTED: **Lieutenant Stanley Keith SIDDELLS (1897–1979)**
AGE AT ENLISTMENT: 19 years, 3 months, 24 days
ARMY NUMBER: 44561
EMBARKATION: Wellington, 31 December 1917; Wellington
    Infantry Battalion, 33rd Reinforcements

Length of service: 2 years, 355 days
Played for: Wanganui & College Old Boys, University and
    Pahiatua clubs; Wanganui 1914–15; Wellington 1920–
    22; New Zealand Universities 1921; North Island 1922;
    Wellington–Manawatu 1922; Wairarapa–Bush 1923;
    Bush 1923, 1927
All Black number: 250
Position: Wing
Appearances: 1921; 1 test

At the end of January 1916, 18-year-old Siddells wrote from his home in Guyton Street, Wanganui, to the Minister of Defence, the Honourable J. Allen:

Dear Sir,
I hope my intrusion upon your valuable time will be pardonable, but my eagerness to help my country is my only excuse. I am not yet 19 years of age and my people do not want me to go to the war till I am 20 years old. The war may be over then or it may not. I saw your statement in the Dominion concerning those desirous of joining the aviation corp and I thought perhaps I could find out about it. Sir what I should like to know is this, whether there is any pay attached to the position and how long does the course long [sic]. I am sitting for a commission in February and perhaps if I am successful, I shall put in an application about July for the aviation corp. Sir, if you would oblige me by answering those two questions then I shall be extremely grateful.
    I have the honour to be sir your obedient servant, S.K. Siddells

Colonel C.M. Gibbon, Chief of the General Staff, replied on behalf of the minister, advising that:

I am directed to inform you that only those who have gained a Pilot's Certificate at Messrs. Walsh Brothers' School of Flying, Auckland, can be considered for commissions and recommended to the Royal Flying Corp as suitable candidates. No assistance can be granted by the New Zealand or Imperial Governments until such time as a person has received his Pilot's Certificate from Messrs. Walsh Brothers' School.

I enclose a copy of the conditions for your information. If you will communicate with Messrs. Walsh Bros', Auckland, they will give you full information regarding their school and fees charged.

The Walsh Brothers, Leo and Vivian, flew a seaplane they had built themselves, the first in the Southern Hemisphere. The instructor was George Bolt (later memorialised by having the main road to Auckland Airport named after him). Their flying school was at Mission Bay, with makeshift hangars sitting roughly where the iconic fountain is today. Students paid £100 for a course that, if they passed it, would see them gain a Royal Aero Club certificate, which would then admit them to the Royal Flying Corps in England. (In the South Island, the aviation school was at Sockburn, later renamed Wigram.)

The next correspondence regarding Siddells's prospective service was from his parents, who wrote to a family friend, George Hunter MP, for assistance in lobbying the Minister of Defence to delay Siddells's call-up to camp so that he could finish his exams to qualify as a teacher. According to Siddells's father, Siddells had become more eager to join the army after his older brother was rejected due to a weak heart and rheumatism. His parents allowed him to give up his position as a house master at Napier Boys' High School on the condition that he finish his studies. They were worried that if he didn't and 'was spared to return' from the war, he might not quickly settle back into work.

There was a to-ing and fro-ing of correspondence and telegrams between Wellington and Wanganui, initially rejecting the family plea, until it was discovered that Siddells was in fact listed on a later draft. So he could finish his exams, and would also be an NCO once in camp.

While in Trentham, he fractured a bone in his hand, which delayed his departure overseas. Once away to war Siddells was assigned to the New Zealand Rifle Brigade, serving with the 4th Battalion at the Western Front for four months, until suffering a gunshot wound to the knee in August 1918. That ended his war but not his letter-writing, for, like many veterans, he found that obtaining medical treatment for conditions he believed to have been caused by active service was not easy to do once a soldier had been discharged. In January 1920, he wrote to the Assistant Director of Medical Services:

Sir,

I have just received your Form B.R.170 in which you inform me that my application for treatment is not approved, because the disability is not considered to be due to or aggravated by War Service. But I submit to you the following personal facts, which would not be included in the official application made out by the Medical Officer, and contend that the disability, though not caused on active service, was aggravated and brought about by active service. I returned to New Zealand on Oct. 1 1918 and ever since leaving England my health has been failing. On the boat I was always getting medicine. Since arriving back in N.Z. I have done no work and have tried to bring my body into good working order by salts fruit and regular exercise. But it seems to be of no avail. Scratches on my hand poisoned and for over a month I have been annoyed with suppurated fingers. My reason for not applying for treatment sooner was that two of my sisters who are both Army nurses came home on leave and they attended to my external needs. But I began to suffer from headaches and to feel anyhow [sic], especially inactive. Just after Christmas I got a bad throat, I suffered with septic throats on active service and was feeling so bad that I resolved to seek medical aid and so I went to the Defence office and got an order on the Medical Officer. I was taken so bad on the afternoon of that day that I was sent into the Wanganui Hospital immediately by my people, thus I did not see the Medical Officer. The Medical Superintendent placed me in the Diphtheria Ward and a swab taken **some hours** after my being placed there showed a positive result.

The Medical Superintendent during a conversation said that anyone so 'run down' as I was would be likely to contract any disease germs floating around.

The contention then is that being so run down my body in such a condition doubtless due to Active service, would receive such germs, and thus the disability was aggravated by Military Service. I might mention I have lost 20lbs in weight since returning, also I am not receiving any pension.

Trusting that with these additional facts placed before you, you will reconsider your decision.

I have the honour to be sir, yours obediently ...

Defence Headquarters then re-considered the matter. An internal memo to the Director-General Medical Services included the handwritten comment that 'treatment should be offered to him as an act of grace'.

Siddells studied law at Victoria University, turning out for their football team and for Wellington. He was described as a very orthodox fullback, but won selection for the All Blacks in the final test against the 1921 Springboks.

Having completed his studies, he moved to Pahiatua to practise law, and he played for Bush. In 1927, they had the first challenge after Wairarapa were controversially awarded the Ranfurly Shield after it was ruled that Hawke's Bay had fielded an ineligible player. Bush were soundly beaten 53–3 in a match that was very much an exhibition of star back Bert Cooke's talent. He scored 19 points for the holders. One newspaper report stated that Siddells 'the ex-All Black played a deplorable game at fullback, being too bulky, too slow and too uncertain'.

Siddells served as secretary and sole selector of the Bush Union. He was elected mayor of Pahiatua, and appointed acting commandant of the internment camp at Pahiatua in May 1943, until troubled by sciatica in April 1944. His discharge was delayed while he was temporarily posted to a Polish refugee camp 'to cover the entry of the Polish children' in October 1944. After that he was discharged from the army with the rank of captain.

15 November 1916

Future parliamentarian and author John A. Lee had been working as a barman at the Anchor Hotel in Auckland when he enlisted at Trentham in March 1916 (falsely declaring that he was married). While in camp in England he wrote somewhat disparagingly of the game of rugby and its culture in the *Chronicles of the NZEF* published on 15 November:

About Football

The other day a few of our boys secured leave. Ah me! Those men in misguided moments must buy footballs. A soccer and a Rugby ball they brought home on Saturday night, and on Sunday morning we girded up our loins for the slaughter. Church over, we commenced the morning's play, the soccer players playing the Rugby men [at] soccer in the morning, and the Rugby men the soccer team Rugby in the afternoon. It is after the Donnybrook I write this, a fact which Mr. Editor will tumble to when he hears of the shaky hand and runs foul of the more shaky composition. I said 'about football,' at the start. I pass football over in one sentence, and talk of the afternoon. We, the soccer team, easily astonished the Rugby men at our game, but when their game took place in the afternoon, we found that our opponents of the morning were champion wrestlers. The way they put half-nelsons on to us, stood us urgently on our heads, and tangled us up in some sort of a beehive called a scrum, fair gets me. A man needs to be a centipede to play Rugby decently, and have every leg shod with a pair of tens. Our treatment at the hands of the Rugby men was responsible for a dream I had last night, and also for the stiffest legs ever. I dreamt that I visited the British Museum Year 3,000 and there beside a rack saw a rugby football. It had beside it a placard bearing the following: — 'Instrument of torture; period 20th century. Football was a method of punishment to which over bumptious soccer players were condemned. In it men were compelled to play on a place called a gridiron. Here they threw somersaults, used strange language, hung on to other players' boots with their chins, did tangos called scrums and became so stiff that for days after they had to externally apply large quantities of whiskey to gain free use of their limbs. One of the main attractions of the game was the play of a man termed the half-back, who linked up the backs to the forwards. He was generally a missing link, and was discovered by everyone in the world at the time except Darwin. The winners were those who scored the greatest number of points awarded by a referee, for some unknown reason. It has been said that the main reason was intimidation by rough-looking men, who walked up and down the side-line, tearing up packs of cards and displaying their biceps. They also asked the referee to annihilate space at the rate of 100 yards per 10 sec., and on such occasions the referee generally obliged. Even so, it is even then doubtful as to how they reckon up the points. After matches they adjourned into public houses and there proceeded to buy ten-gallon kegs, and they sat around them and talked about it. What "it" was is also rather vague. Anyway, it can safely be stated that this football was some punishment. Men after playing it generally climbed about the landscape like square-gaited trotters. They were stiff, it seems. Also the beer consumed resulted in another sort of stiffness, sometimes termed stoney broke. Where the difference existed between the different stiffnesses has not yet been discovered, but' — Reveille. Damn it all, we had a good Sunday's sport anyway, but should anyone in the future ask me to play footer, I'm going to sing them the words of an old song;— 'Let me alone I'm married, married,' it goes, and before I play this somersaulting, tearing, swearing game of Rugby again, I'll vamoose to the comparative safety and quiet of the trenches. 'When in Rome' says some chump! Well they play soccer here, and it's soccer for me. Wish the fashion would set toward ping-pong or counter lunch. That's sport.

Lee was awarded the DCM in August 1917, for

conspicuous gallantry and devotion to duty. During our offensive he showed great dash and coolness in attacking and capturing a machine gun with its team. Later when the advance was held up by an enemy post, he skilfully rushed it with two of his comrades capturing two machine guns and forty men.

Nine months later while fighting at Mailly-Maillet a bomb blast caused a grievous wound to his left hand which saw him undergo a series of operations in England and the amputation of his left forearm four months later. After the war he was an active member of the Returned Services Association and entered parliament as a Labour politician. He fell foul of his colleagues and was expelled from the party in 1940. He established the Democratic Labour Party, later renamed the Democratic Soldier Labour Party, and was a prolific author of books and articles. He died in 1982.

16 November 1916

The first conscription ballot — to bolster the 23rd and 24th Reinforcements by 1,300 men — was held in Wellington in the presence of the Government Statistician, Malcolm Fraser, a magistrate, departmental workers and a number of invited guests and reporters. Young female employees of the Statistics Department spun two barrels of marbles with one marble drawn from each. Their numbers were then combined and matched with boxes of cards containing the names of single men whose names were on the National Register. At the end of the process, all present sang 'God Save the King'.

17 November 1916

ENLISTED: **Private Eric Leslie WATKINS (1880–1949)**
AGE AT ENLISTMENT: 36 years, 7 months, 30 days
ARMY NUMBER: 45442
EMBARKATION: Wellington, 13 November 1917; Auckland Infantry Regiment, 30th Reinforcements
LENGTH OF SERVICE: 2 years, 302 days
PLAYED FOR: Wellington College Old Boys and Raetihi clubs; Wellington 1901–06; Wanganui 1907; North Island 1904, 1906
ALL BLACK NUMBER: 140
POSITION: Front-row forward
APPEARANCES: 1905; 1 test

Watkins played 40 games for Wellington as a hooker, in many of them binding with his Wellington College Old Boys' teammate, Ernie Dodd. We can only imagine the shenanigans the two mates must have got up to in their intertwined footballing years, which reached a peak in 1905 when, both having missed selection for the tour to Britain, they played their only test against the visiting Australians in Dunedin.

While Dodd's playing days ended due to work commitments and relocations, Watkins quit the amateur game for a year to have cartilage from his right knee removed following an accident, and then, once restored to full health, he signed up to take part in the All Golds Northern Union tour.

Working as a surveying contractor at Kakatahi, south of Raetihi in the central North Island, he was initially rejected as unfit for service, but after an operation he was accepted. Unfortunately for Watkins, the condition flared again in camp at Larkhill and he was shifted to the catering department. Once back in New Zealand, he was discharged at the end of November 1919.

11 December 1916

ENLISTED: **Gunner Charlie Edward 'Bronco' SEELING (1883–1956)**
AGE AT ENLISTMENT: 33 years, 6 months, 27 days
ARMY NUMBER: 37172
ATTESTED IN ENGLAND
LENGTH OF SERVICE: 2 years, 56 days
PLAYED FOR: Pirates and City clubs; Wanganui 1903; Auckland 1904, 1906–09; North Island 1906, 1908
ALL BLACK NUMBER: 115
POSITION: Loose-forward
APPEARANCES: 1904–08; 39 games, including 11 tests; 33 points (11 tries)

On the All Black tour 'Home' in 1905–06 and in matches played by Auckland in the first half of their great Ranfurly Shield era of

1906–13, there was no more fearsome sight for a ball-carrier than the looming figure of 'Bronco' Seeling. The man with the ball had a choice: accept the tackle and the pain that might come with it, or try to evade Seeling. The problem with trying to move out of range of the big Wanganui-born forward was that Seeling was the best exponent of the flying tackle the game had seen. He would launch himself towards an opponent and bring him crashing to the ground. But Seeling's game wasn't just one of brute force. Author W.J.T. Collins said of him that there was 'in one man the characteristics of the six forwards you have most admired — physique, fire, skill, endurance, judgement — and you have Charles Seeling, second to none in the variety of his gifts'. His muscular play, combined with his movie-star looks, had fans flocking to catch a glimpse of him on the Originals tour.

Seeling signed for Wigan in 1910 and played more than 200 games for the famous league club, initially as a back but then he moved into the forwards. He took part in three successive English rugby league finals (1910–12) plus the 1911 Challenge Cup final, and some still speak of him as the best forward to play the 13-man game.

He enlisted in the New Zealand Expeditionary Force in England, and he spent a year in camps training as a gunner with the New Zealand Field Artillery. His arrival was a real talking-point for his fellow soldiers, and was noted in a number of newspaper columns. He was quickly included in the Depot football team, and when they undertook matches in Wales, 'Bronco' was their tour guide, regaling the team with tales from the Originals' visit a decade earlier and the famous match against Wales at Cardiff.

Football was a break from camp boredom, which clearly affected Seeling — he went absent without leave from the Field Artillery reserve depot in Aldershot for two weeks at the beginning of January 1918. A month later he finally saw action in France.

After the war he returned to playing league for another two years, and upon retirement from the game became proprietor of the Roebuck Hotel, at Standish Gate in Wigan.

In 1956, and soon to return to New Zealand to visit old friends and his hometown of Wanganui, 'Bronco', wife Bessie and daughter Mary Lowe were killed in a horrific car accident. His 18-month-old granddaughter Margaret survived the crash.

13 December 1916

ENLISTED: **Staff Sergeant Major James RYAN (1887–1957)**

AGE AT ENLISTMENT: 29 years, 10 months, 5 days

ARMY NUMBER: 62753

EMBARKATION: Wellington, 16 November 1917; Wellington Infantry Regiment, 31st Reinforcements

LENGTH OF SERVICE: 2 years, 336 days

PLAYED FOR: Petone and Feilding Technical College Old Boys clubs; Wellington 1905–15, 1920; Manawatu 1920; North Island 1914

ALL BLACK NUMBER: 169

POSITION: Utility back

APPEARANCES: 1910, 1914; 15 matches, including 4 tests, 2 games as captain; 20 points (6 tries, 1 conversion)

Perhaps the greatest proof of the fact that the Services rugby team was an army initiative, and not something the rugby union instigated, is that little remains of the service record of the man who captained the army team to win the King's Cup competition — a mere five pages with three abbreviated mentions of his being part of the Divisional XV and then the post-war Services football team to South Africa.

Ryan had been a constant in the Wellington backline since debuting at the age of 18. Great versatility saw him able to play everywhere except halfback, and his All Black representation initially followed in the same vein in 1910, with him standing in matches at fullback, centre and first five-eighth. However, when chosen again in 1914 for another tour of Australia, he regularly took his place at centre.

The first year of Ryan's service had been spent as an instructor with the New Zealand Permanent Staff in England before spending three months on active service in France. As a regimental sergeant major, with a decade of first-class football under his belt, and having the captained the All Blacks in two matches (against Wellington and Central–Western Districts in Australia), he was deemed the ideal man to lead the Divisional XV and he did so with aplomb. A keen but fair-minded competitor on the field, he was a genuine and humble speech- and toast-maker off it.

Ryan remained with the army after the war, retiring with the rank of captain.

22 December 1916

ENLISTED: **Sergeant John Victor MACKY (1887–1951)**
AGE AT ENLISTMENT: 29 years, 3 months, 19 days
ARMY NUMBER: 46239
EMBARKATION: Wellington, 13 August 1917; Auckland
   Infantry Regiment, 29th Reinforcements
LENGTH OF SERVICE: 2 years, 358 days
PLAYED FOR: University; Auckland 1911–14
ALL BLACK NUMBER: 198
POSITION: Wing
APPEARANCES: 1913; 1 test

Macky played only 17 matches on the wing for Auckland between 1911 and 1914, the latter stages of their eight-year Ranfurly Shield era, but scored a phenomenal 22 tries.

His form year was 1912, and it is a shame that there were no matches for the All Blacks that season, as he undoubtedly would have been selected and thus had more than one match to his name. His season wasn't just good, it remains one of the best in the history of the Ranfurly Shield. Although Auckland had only three challengers for the Shield that year, Macky set some incredible records: he scored every one of Auckland's tries in their three defences, with one against Taranaki (game won 6–5), four against Wellington (12–0) and one against Otago (5–5). To this day, no other player has scored six consecutive tries for their team or had their four tries be the total points for their side in a match. Jokes abounded among Auckland supporters that it was a good thing Macky worked as an accountant, because if he kept scoring the way he was he'd be the only person able to keep a tally!

In scoring he displayed all the attributes of a good wing, finishing backline passing movements, swerving past defenders, kicking and chasing and returning speculative kicks in rain, wind and sun.

He finally won a call-up to the All Blacks for the second test against the 1913 Australians, and, although five tries were scored by the All Blacks in winning 25–13, none were to Macky, who observers felt had not played well generally.

His name was drawn from a conscription ballot in January 1917, but he had already volunteered. Between enlistment and departing with the 29th Reinforcements Auckland Infantry Regiment A Company six months later, Macky was promoted to the rank of sergeant. On arrival in France, and on joining the 4th Reserve Battalion of the Auckland Regiment, he reverted to corporal. By March 1918, having attended NCO instruction and passed 'very Good', he had joined the 1st Battalion of the Auckland Regiment and — at his own request — reverted to lance corporal.

In 1938 he contributed a six-page chapter entitled 'Rugby and How to Play It' to R.A. Stone's book of football profiles, *Rugby Players Who Have Made New Zealand Famous*. As befits a man who had spent time in the army's Education Department, the concise chapter of instruction and example concluded on a more philosophical note: 'Rugby is a glorious game, but it should not become other than the means to an end — the promotion of virile health and strength and the building of character — to better fit players for the more serious responsibilities of life.'

26 December 1916

The New Zealand Reserve Group team played another War Prisoners Fund benefit match against 'Wales' in Swansea. Despite the fact the match only went ahead at the last minute — camp sickness, obtaining leave for the players, and general army bureaucracy proving a series of obstacles to finalising the event — this time the estimated crowd number was 20,000! At halftime the score was 3–3. Teddy Roberts goaled shortly after halftime for a 6–3 lead, and minutes later the New Zealanders thought they had taken the lead when one of their wingers crossed the line following a backline move from a scrum, but for some reason the try was disallowed. (Shades of 1905!) Wales equalised with a try, but the conversion hit the posts. New Zealand had the best of the play for the last quarter of the game, but could not convert their dominance to points. The match ended 6–6. After the game the players enjoyed the generous hospitality of the proprietor of the Park Hotel, Swansea, Mr Jack Goode, who himself had played rugby for Ireland.

1917

4 January 1917

ENLISTED: **Private Robert Graham TUNNICLIFF (1894–1973)**
AGE AT ENLISTMENT: 22 years, 6 months, 30 days
ARMY NUMBER: 46901
EMBARKATION: Wellington, 26 April 1917; J Company, 25th Reinforcements
LENGTH OF SERVICE: 2 years, 172 days
PLAYED FOR: Nelson College Old Boys and Umere clubs; Nelson 1919; Buller 1922–28; New Zealand Trials 1924, 1927; West Coast–Buller 1925; Seddon Shield Districts 1926; South Island Minor Unions 1928
ALL BLACK NUMBER: 289
POSITION: Front-row forward
APPEARANCES: 1923; 1 match; 3 points (1 try)

Another of the one-test All Blacks, Tunnicliff had his only match against the 1923 New South Wales team.

A schoolteacher, whose father's name was Ivanhoe, Tunnicliff was the sixth of only eight Buller players to make the All Blacks (the last being Bill Mumm in 1949), and the only All Black to come from the Umere Rugby Club (which in 1958 joined with the Karamea and Little Wanganui clubs to form the Karamea club). There was no real question about the validity of his selection given that he appeared in the national trials the following year, and then three years after that, but he was fortunate that the selectors spread national honours around during the 1923 series.

As a front-row forward, he was quick off the mark, which, combined with being most adept at keeping the ball on the toe, meant he was something of a weapon when it came to dribbling rushes.

A product of Nelson College, where he had three years of cadet training, he was employed by the Nelson Education Board and was teaching at Karamea when he enlisted.

On the troopship to Devonport he became ill, and he was immediately admitted to hospital when the ship docked in July 1917, where he stayed for three weeks. He joined the 2nd Canterbury Infantry Battalion in France in October 1917, and five months later was wounded in action, suffering a gunshot wound to his right thigh. This of course meant more hospital time, convalescing at Hornchurch, and then retraining at Sling, Codford and Larkhill camps. He returned to New Zealand on the *Waimana* in May 1919.

Tunnicliff retired from teaching to farm at Karamea, and during World War II was in the Home Guard, serving as a platoon commander with the Westport Battalion's C Company. As late as 1958 he obtained a distinguished pass in Administration and Military Law exams and was consequently promoted from lieutenant to captain with the Royal New Zealand Army Service Corps.

10 January 1917

ENLISTED: **Corporal Cecil 'Ces' Edward Oliver BADELEY (1896–1986)**
AGE AT ENLISTMENT: 20 years, 2 months, 3 days
ARMY NUMBER: 43665
EMBARKATION: Wellington, 12 June 1917; Signal Section, 27th Reinforcements Specialists Company
LENGTH OF SERVICE: 2 years, 134 days

PLAYED FOR: Grammar and Whangarei High School Old Boys
    clubs; Auckland 1916–17, 1919–21, 1924, 1927, 1938;
    North Auckland 1926; North Island 1919–21; South
    Island 1922; New Zealand Trials 1921, 1924, 1927
ALL BLACK NUMBER: 215
POSITION: Five-eighth
APPEARANCES: 1920–21; 15 matches, including 2 tests,
    3 games as captain; 27 points (9 tries)

Although originally from Oamaru, the Badeleys were a well-known family in the Auckland suburb of Remuera. A law clerk for the firm of Gittos and Uren, who had offices in central Auckland's Shortland Street, Badeley had been a stand-out player in Auckland Grammar's First XV of 1915.

The first of his 19 games for Auckland was at Eden Park the following year against an army team from Trentham. He joined the 27th Reinforcements Specialists Company as a signaller and sailed from New Zealand on the troopship *Maunganui* at the start of June 1917. (His older brother William had a mere five months of service in 1915, getting only as far as Albany in Western Australia, before being hospitalised in Melbourne and then discharged due to 'epileptiform attacks'.) Although he qualified as a first-class signaller in November 1917, Badeley's time overseas was mostly spent carrying out administrative duties for the records department.

Badeley was first chosen for the All Blacks in 1920, and showed during the matches in Australia just what an electric player he could be, whether at first or second five-eighth or centre. In 1921 he played as first five-eighth in the first two tests against the Springboks, and the following year played in a fourth inter-island match, coming on as a replacement for the South Island team. This meant he was one of the few players to have represented both islands in the annual fixture. In that match, his brother Vic was a replacement for the North Island and won inclusion in the tour to Australia. Ces did not.

Tragically, Vic's career was cut short when he suffered a serious head injury in an All Black trial in Auckland in May 1924. An exciting centre, very much one of the best players in that position in the country at the time and considered something of a certainty for the upcoming tour to Britain, he was knocked unconscious while making a tackle and rushed to hospital. He didn't regain consciousness until later that evening. He spent nine weeks in hospital, during which there was little physical recovery, before it was discovered that there was likely to have been a fracture to his skull, which was putting pressure on his brain.

Four months later another, younger brother, Bert, suffered serious concussion in a club match between Grammar Old Boys and Ponsonby. The following year, the Auckland and Wellington club champions — Ponsonby and Poneke — played a benefit game for Vic which raised over £300.

Ces captained the All Blacks on their brief trip to New South Wales prior to the lengthy visit to Britain, and all money was on him being captain of the All Blacks for that tour. After all, when an official team photo was taken in Wellington, he was the man in the captain's position. However, the dark world of captaincy appointments, and a niggling knee injury, saw the job handed to Cliff Porter. As it happened, Badeley didn't make an appearance until the eighth match of the tour, against North Midlands, and turned out for only one other match. His playing days were over.

There are suggestions that Badeley felt there were times when he could have played for the 'Invincibles' again on tour, but the selection committee thought otherwise. Although confined to the sidelines, he was a respected member of the side and undertook an unofficial role as coach of the backs.

Having been a publican in Taupo for many years, Badeley lived out his final years in Auckland's Ranfurly War Veterans' Home.

13 January 1917

The New Zealand Reserve Group team lost by one point to the unbeaten Army Service Corps team at Old Deer Park. The backline had three changes from the side that had played on Boxing Day, but into the pack came the legendary Charlie Seeling. His presence seemed to be as exciting for his fellow players as it was for the 3,000 spectators, which included New Zealand Prime Minister William Massey, New Zealand High Commissioner Sir Thomas Mackenzie and Brigadier-General Richardson, Commander of the New Zealand Expeditionary Force.

Inter-unit matches were played in Sling Camp every Wednesday afternoon, with rumours that a team from the trenches was soon to make its way to England for a series of games.

24 January 1917

ENLISTED: **Second Lieutenant John 'Jack' ORMOND/ Tiaka OMANA (1891–1970)**

AGE AT ENLISTMENT: 25 years, 1 month, 23 days

ARMY NUMBER: 45638

EMBARKATION: 8 February 1918; Maori Contingent, 26th Reinforcements

LENGTH OF SERVICE: 2 years, 100 days

PLAYED FOR: Mahia; Wairoa; Hawke's Bay 1923–25; Northern Maori 1923–25

ALL BLACK NUMBER: 284

POSITION: Side-row forward

APPEARANCES: 1923; 1 match

There were high hopes for the competitiveness of the New South Wales team that visited New Zealand in 1923, given that the previous year the All Blacks had suffered a 1–2 series loss in the test matches in Sydney. However, they managed to win only 2 of their 10 games in New Zealand (against South Canterbury and Waikato–Thames Valley–Bay of Plenty), scoring 119 points and conceding 245.

The All Black selectors were already beginning to formulate their touring party to Britain the next year, and so the matches against the Waratahs became trials games, with 37 players used in the three-test series. Ormond was one of 14 changes in personnel for the third and final 'test'. Also making their debuts were fellow Hawke's Bay players 'Bull' Irvine and Lui Paewai, who at little more than a month past his seventeenth birthday remains the youngest player to have represented the All Blacks. (Had test caps been awarded, Paewai would have been, to this day, the youngest man to play an international for the All Blacks, exactly two years younger than current record-holder, the late Jonah Lomu.)

Ormond had fashioned a good record for himself as a member of the Pioneer Battalion side and the Ranfurly Shield–holding Hawke's Bay team, for whom he played 10 games during their famous reign. He captained Wairoa and represented Northern Maori before hanging up his boots at the end of 1925.

He had finished his secondary education at Christ's College and played for the First XV in 1908, but illness saw him return home the following year.

At the time of attestation he was farming at Apoutama Bay on the East Coast. He spent four months at Trentham before a further five months at the Narrow Neck Military Camp on Auckland's North Shore, which was the base for the Maori Contingent and the 'South Seas' volunteers.

A year after beginning his service he sailed for England. He then spent time in Brocton, Sling and Rouen camps, often attached to the gas schools, from where he first played for the Pioneer Battalion football team.

A well-known sheep-farmer at Mahia, during World War II he was a second lieutenant with the Wairoa Battalion Home Guard.

He twice stood as the Ratana candidate in the seat of Eastern Maori before winning it for Labour in the general election of 1943, deposing Apirana Ngata, who had held the electorate for a remarkable 38 years. As a new Member of Parliament, Ormond spoke in the House about the frustrations felt by Maori ex-servicemen when dealing with the Rehabilitation Department. He expressed his sadness that he couldn't speak Maori in the debating chamber, and suggested that all parliamentary papers be published in Maori as well as English. On his retirement from politics in 1963, his farewell address to the House concluded with his singing a waiata and playing harmonica.

31 January 1917

The official New Zealand Divisional Rugby team was announced in the *Chronicles of the NZEF*. The army 'All Blacks' chosen from footballers serving in France were selected to travel to England for four matches against the Army Service Corps at Richmond, New Zealand Command Team (Sling) at Queen's Club, Public Schools Service Team again at Richmond, and finally Wales in Cardiff. The squad (with their rugby representation and army units as published) was:

Backs: G. Scott (2nd Otago), Taieri, Kaitara, Otago; D. Miller (2nd Auckland), North Shore Albions, Auckland (N.U.); W. Wilson (1st Wellington), Athletic, Wellington, New Zealand (N.U.); T.A. Gibson (Artillery), Pirates, Wanganui; H.W. Adams (Artillery), Athletic, Wellington; G. Owles (Artillery), Christchurch HSOB and Oriental; G. Murray — *Captain* (1st Auckland), Ponsonby, Auckland, Oriental, Wellington; E. Ryan (Artillery), Petone, Wellington; Rua Rogers (Pioneers), City Rovers, Auckland (N.U.); J.C. McIntyre (Artillery), South Auckland; S. Cameron (1st Wellington), Warwick, Taranaki; N.F. Stead (2nd Batt., NZRB), Star, Southland; F.A. Ross (1st Auckland), University, Auckland; C. Brown (Engineers), Tukapa, Taranaki.
    Forwards: R. Taylor — *Vice-captain* (1st Wellington), Clifton, Warwick, Taranaki, North Island, N.Z.; R.J. Casey, Marist Bros, Auckland; H.D. Whittington (2nd NZRB), Hawera, Taranaki, North Island; J. Moffat, Oriental, Wellington and South Canterbury, South Island; C.H. King (2nd Canterbury), St. James's, Wellington; T. French (1st Auckland), City, Auckland, County Union (S.I.); P. Fogarty (1st NZRB), Union, Otago; J. Pine (Pioneers), Waimate, Taranaki; W. Ball (1st Wellington), Athletic, Wellington; D. Sullivan (3rd NZRB), Melrose, Wellington, North Island; E.L. Cockroft (Artillery), Star; W.G. Bright (1st Auckland), Parnell, City Rovers.

Lieutenant Colonel Arthur Plugge, then Director of Physical Training for the New Zealand Division, was quoted as saying,

'You can assure everybody that when the team gets to England they will be thoroughly fit, and they will be straight from the trenches — they will spend the day previous to leaving, in the front line.'

Points of interest today are the inclusion of Northern Union players, indicated in the list with '(N.U.)'. Being an army team, it was one free of the politics that had divided players, unions and their loyalties for almost a decade in New Zealand.

Sadly, as war had interrupted the domestic competition in New Zealand, so it intruded on the planned two-week trip and the games were cancelled.

1 February 1917

ENLISTED: **Private Henry Gordon 'Abe' MUNRO (1896–1974)**
AGE AT ENLISTMENT: 20 years, 1 month, 24 days
ARMY NUMBER: 49303
EMBARKATION: Wellington, 16 November 1917; Specialist Company, New Zealand Machine Gun Battalion, 31st Reinforcements
LENGTH OF SERVICE: 2 years, 273 days
PLAYED FOR: University; Canterbury 1920–21; Otago 1922–23; New Zealand Universities 1921, 1923; South Island 1924; New Zealand Trials 1924
ALL BLACK NUMBER: 294
POSITION: Front-row forward
APPEARANCES: 1924–25; 9 matches; 9 points (3 tries)

A fitter who had been employed by the Invercargill firm of J. Johnston and Sons, Munro was in a specialist company as part of the New Zealand Machine Gun Battalion in the 31st Reinforcements. He was promoted to sergeant in June of 1917, but in the early months of 1918 he suffered from rubella and influenza, so his time was mainly spent undertaking courses of instruction in the reserve camps in England.

After the war he studied at Canterbury and Otago universities, representing both provinces and the New Zealand students' team on the football field.

In 1924, having played all three 'tests' in Australia against New South Wales, he left New Zealand with the tourists to Britain, very much viewed as a first-choice front-rower. On board the ship to Britain, Munro appeared as part of the team's 'jazz band'. He featured on drums, Freddie Lucas played banjo and mandolin, and Maurice Brownlie and Jock Richardson played kazoos!

Unfortunately for Munro, in the fourth match he played and the seventh of the tour, which was against Leicester, he badly damaged ligaments around his knee, which essentially saw the end of him as a playing member of the side. However, he proved invaluable to the touring party as someone with a refreshingly positive demeanour. He did take to the field in the final game of the tour against Victoria in British Columbia, Canada, and even scored a try, but it was his last appearance for the All Blacks. Later in the year, further injury saw him retire from the game altogether.

Munro remained involved with the sport, particularly with club coaching and the management of universities rugby, and he also worked on the new stands that were built at Carisbrook in 1958. He was president of the Otago union in 1949–50.

2 February 1917

ENLISTED: **Driver Brian Verdon McCLEARY (1897–1978)**

AGE AT ENLISTMENT: 20 years, 16 days

ARMY NUMBER: 50589

EMBARKATION: Wellington, 22 November 1917; Army Service Corps, 32nd Reinforcements

LENGTH OF SERVICE: 2 years, 273 days

PLAYED FOR: Marist; Canterbury 1920, 1923; South Island 1923–24; New Zealand Trials 1924

ALL BLACK NUMBER: 297

POSITION: Hooker

APPEARANCES: 1924–25; 12 matches

Time in reserve depots in England during the war proved highly frustrating for Dunedin-born McCleary. He suffered an injury to his left elbow which restricted the duties he could undertake, and the interminable wait to return to New Zealand (he eventually boarded the *Cordoba* in the middle of July 1919) saw him frequently punished for failing to parade or being insolent when he was on parade.

In 1920, McCleary became the New Zealand Amateur Heavyweight Boxing Champion when he defeated Maurice Brownlie in front of a packed house in Napier. Brownlie was several inches taller than McCleary and a stone (six kilograms) heavier, but McCleary was an accurate puncher with both hands and quick of foot. A newspaper report of the bout described it as

> the greatest bout of the evening. McCleary, with a knowledge of his opponent's disastrous punch, presented an elusive front, his foot-work being splendid. Brownlie was plainly seeking a knock-out. He delivered swings which beat the air or were half spent before they met their objective. The Ashburton man's condition began to tell at the end of the second round, and though he got some ugly-looking hits, he took them smiling, and sent back rattling connections which counted. In the final round McCleary made the pace. The Hastings' man's punch was palpably weak and McCleary held command, winning the championship amid loud applause. McCleary was carried shoulder-high from the ring.

From there he went on to represent New Zealand at the Australian amateur championships.

In the ring in 1923 he encountered Tom Heeney (who had been part of the Poverty Bay forward pack with Maurice Brownlie that faced the 1921 Springboks). Heeney had just fought Cyril Whittaker over 15 feisty rounds, at which point the referee stopped the fight and awarded it to Heeney. Immediately afterwards, Whittaker collapsed in his seat, and was rushed to hospital and operated on in the early hours of the morning. After spending a day in a coma, he died. Devastated by the death of his opponent, Heeney had some hesitation getting back into the ring, despite the fact that Whittaker should not perhaps have had the fight after suffering bad headaches which resulted from copping a boot to the head in a football game.

Heeney's management lined him up against McCleary two months later in a fight for the New Zealand heavyweight title and a purse of £200. Heeney was a stone-and-a-half (10 kilograms) heavier, taller and with a longer reach than McCleary, and was ahead on points (having won 9 of the 14 rounds) when, with a left and two rights, he sent McCleary to the canvas for a nine-count. On regaining his feet, McCleary was knocked down again and, on rising for the third time, very groggily, he was knocked out cold. Unable to be revived, he was taken to a private hospital. It was three o'clock the following morning before he regained consciousness.

The *Truth*'s report of the bout described it as 'one of the most hard-fought and interesting battles seen in Christchurch', but expressed concern about the way the fight ended:

> There is considerable comment in Christchurch concerning it having been necessary for Heeney to administer the final punishment after McCleary was obviously in no fit state to continue, or even to defend himself. The popular opinion is that hostilities should have been stopped when Heeney had his man on the ropes after the latter had been down for nine.

There was some argument that, like Whittaker, McCleary should not have been in the ring thanks to football. A week before his fight with Heeney, he had played the inter-island football match, a titanic forward tussle, that resulted in a 6–6 draw, only the second time the honours had been shared.

McCleary retired after the fight with Heeney, but, as boxers do, ruminated on the loss, and at the start of February 1924 *The Sun* newspaper in Christchurch was reporting that:

Both in the boxing and football field [McCleary] is an exponent of the 'do or die' spirit. His fight with Tom Heeney, in which he was robbed of the heavy-weight crown, was to have been his last. But he received a fearful mauling, and he thinks this would be a poor ending to his boxing career. So he contemplates fighting again, and the opponent he most desires to meet is Heeney! Some may call his courage by another name. They still have the vision fresh of McCleary staggering around the ring under a fearful pounding from Heeney, and they have the memory of the weeks he spent in hospital thereafter. They heard no explanation at the time of McCleary's failure, because he is not the sort to put forward explanations. His friends, however, declare that he entered the ring in no condition to fight. The gruelling struggle of the inter-island Rugby match the week before had sapped deeply of his energy, and tiredness weighted his arms from the first round. There were no reserves of motive power to draw upon. Impossible was it for him to succeed against the powerful Gisbornite. In between whiles he keeps himself fit with swimming and shooting excursions, and it is his intention to fix up a ring and throw the gloves about. Should he be selected for the New Zealand Rugby team for England, he shall pack his travelling trunk.

McCleary did return to the ring, and had a title fight for the national light-heavyweight championship in April 1924, before being chosen to tour Britain with the All Blacks.

Of his 23 first-class games, 12 were on the Invincibles tour, where he was very much the epitome of the back-up, midweek player who was never seriously considered for a test team while other players were fit.

A waterside worker, he dropped out of rugby after the tour, but continued to box for several more years. The physical effects of his days in the ring were apparent when he tried to sign up for the Home Guard during World War II. He was found to be suffering from a nasal obstruction and osteoarthritis of both elbows and a knee.

6 February 1917

ENLISTED: **Trooper Charles John Compton FLETCHER (1893–1973)**

AGE AT ENLISTMENT: 22 years, 8 months, 28 days

ARMY NUMBER: 56273

EMBARKATION: Wellington, 13 November 1917; New Zealand Mounted Rifles Brigade, 30th Reinforcements

LENGTH OF SERVICE: 1 year, 292 days

PLAYED FOR: College Rifles and Waimauku clubs; Auckland 1919–20; North Island 1920; North Auckland 1921–24, 1926; Auckland–North Auckland 1921, 1923

ALL BLACK NUMBER: 240

POSITION: Back-row forward

APPEARANCES: 1921; 2 matches, including 1 test

Living and farming at Kaipara Lane in Waimauku northwest of Auckland, Fletcher famously made his way to the city each Saturday morning to turn out for the College Rifles football club. He had been a senior cadet and was a member of the 3rd Auckland Mounted Rifles, but, according to his attestation, he had previously been rejected as unfit to join Crown forces on account of blindness!

Serving with the Auckland Mounted Rifles in Palestine, he was confined to barracks for seven days after failing to attend a parade in March 1918. After recovering from an initial dose of malaria, he again contracted it in the Jordan Valley in the middle of 1918, which brought his active service to an end.

Fletcher, whose late father had been born in Clonmel, Ireland, was selected for the 1920 tour of New South Wales, but broke a small bone in his ankle before the team left, playing for Auckland against the All Blacks in a pre-tour warm-up match. (Jim Moffitt was also injured in the game, but he recovered to play in 9 of the 10 tour games.) For some reason — a proposed team mutiny led by 'Moke' Belliss has been suggested — Fletcher travelled with the team, despite the fact there wasn't even the remotest possibility of him playing.

When he did finally take to the field for the All Blacks, he established an unenviable record. His first appearance was in Christchurch against the touring New South Welshmen of 1921 in a match lost by the All Blacks 0–19. Two weeks later he was called into the side for the third test against the also-touring Springboks in Wellington. That match was drawn 0–0; Fletcher did have a chance to put points on the board when he took a penalty kick but the sodden ball fell just short of the crossbar. So, Fletcher had twice played for the All Blacks and twice lost. But more remarkably, he had twice been in an All Black side that didn't score any points.

He was widely acknowledged as the best player in the 'home' side of Auckland–North Auckland, who lost their match against the Springboks 8–24. Also representing North Auckland in that composite side was Fletcher's old College Rifles teammate, Lynley Weston.

Fletcher continued to represent North Auckland until 1926, and farmed in the north.

ENLISTED: Private Francis 'Frank' Beresford YOUNG (1871–1946)

AGE AT ENLISTMENT: 45 years, 3 months, 27 days
ARMY NUMBER: 53553
EMBARKATION: Wellington, 16 July 1917; F Company, 27th Reinforcements
LENGTH OF SERVICE: 1 year, 279 days
PLAYED FOR: Poneke; Wellington 1894–97
ALL BLACK NUMBER: 66
POSITION: Forward
APPEARANCES: 1896; 1 match

An ironmonger who had been born in Hobart, to a father from Glasgow and a mother from Dublin, Young played his only match for the All Blacks against Queensland in Wellington in August 1896. The home team won 9–0. Three days earlier Young had been in the Wellington team that thrashed the visitors 49–7, scoring a remarkable 14 tries.

On enlistment, his date of birth was recorded as 1877. This would have meant he was only 19 when he made his All Black appearance and just 17 when he made his debut for Wellington, in a season when he was part of a team that defeated the visiting New South Welshmen. It is thus much more likely that he was born in 1871, but believed that declaring himself 46 years of age might affect his eligibility for the army.

In November 1917, he suffered four days of Field Punishment No. 2 for failing to salute an officer. He was wounded in action during the Second Battle of the Somme in April 1918, suffering a gunshot wound to the right side of his face. Two months later, after surgery, doctors at Hornchurch noted that he had difficulty eating a normal diet as, while he could fully open his mouth, the post-injury movement of his jaw saw it deviate slightly to one side. He also suffered attacks of giddiness when undertaking exercise. Classified unfit for further service, he sailed from Plymouth on the *Ulimaroa* four days before the Armistice.

Before the war he had been a self-employed ironmonger; he later became general manager of John Duthie & Co (ironmongers) in Wellington.

As a piece of pure trivia, on the alphabetical list of All Blacks, his has been the final name for nearly 120 years.

12 February 1917

ENLISTED: **Trooper James 'Buster' BARRETT (1888–1971)**
AGE AT ENLISTMENT: 28 years, 11 months, 9 days
ARMY NUMBER: 52363
EMBARKATION: Wellington, 13 December 1917; Auckland
    Mounted Rifles Brigade, 34th Reinforcements
LENGTH OF SERVICE: 2 years, 133 days
PLAYED FOR: City, Ponsonby and Marist clubs; Auckland
    1911–14
ALL BLACK NUMBER: 191
POSITION: Back-row forward
APPEARANCES: 1913–14; 3 matches, including 2 tests

Born in Paeroa to Irish parents, Barrett moved to Auckland to serve an apprenticeship as a wheelwright. He flitted about the Auckland football scene from City to Ponsonby (as a member of their 1910 team that played in Sydney), and then Marist Brothers Old Boys when the club was promoted to the senior club competition in 1911. He played in the second and third tests against Australia in 1913 and was a late call-up for the tour there the following year, but made only one appearance, against Central-Western Districts.

Barrett served with the Auckland Mounted Rifles in the Middle East, where he contracted malaria while fighting in Gaza in July 1918.

Just like Mick Lomas, there is a curious entry on Barrett's service record stating that he left Port Said on 18 March 1919, 'en route for UK on duty (football team)'. Barrett had played with army teams in the desert, but didn't leave for South Africa with the army footballers at the end of May 1919. Instead, he sailed for New Zealand two weeks later. Did he try out for the side, one wonders? Was he deemed not fit enough? While there is no mention of it on his service record, there are suggestions Barrett suffered from a bad knee as the war progressed.

After the war, he spent a couple of years in Ireland and worked on his father's farm at Paeroa, before purchasing his own farm near Morrinsville.

His son James, an only child, played at lock for Waikato between 1967 and 1969.

A SOLDIER'S JOKE

Jones: 'Why are the dungarees we received at Trentham like two places in France?'
Bones: 'Give it up.'
Jones: 'Because they are Toulon and Toulouse!'

19 February 1917

ENLISTED: **Second Lieutenant Robert Gemmell Burnett 'Jimmy' SINCLAIR (1896–1932)**
AGE AT ENLISTMENT: 20 years, 5 months, 19 days
ARMY NUMBER: 49470
EMBARKATION: Wellington, 13 October 1917; Auckland Infantry Regiment, 30th Reinforcements
LENGTH OF SERVICE: 2 years, 42 days
PLAYED FOR: University; Otago 1922–23; South Island 1923; New Zealand Universities 1922; New Zealand Trials 1924
ALL BLACK NUMBER: 270
POSITION: Fullback
APPEARANCES: 1923; 2 matches; 23 points (7 conversions, 3 penalties)

Born in New Plymouth and schooled at the Boys' High, Sinclair served with the A Company of the Taranaki Rifles and the Otago University Officer Training Corp, which was set up in 1916. He had been studying medicine at Knox College prior to enlistment, and suffered a number of ailments in the early months of 1918 including rubella, a sprained ankle while in action, and then another bout of rubella. A second lieutenant, he was variously attached to the reserves of both the Auckland and Wellington regiments and the Cyclist Corps.

In October 1918, having heard that the New Zealand Cabinet had decided that third-year medical students who were at the front should be returned to New Zealand to finish their studies, he wrote (on paper that bore the letterhead of the Church Army Recreation Hut) to the Commanding Officer of the Étaples camp asking for his name to be forwarded to Headquarters in London. He was 'very desirous if possible to return to New Zealand to continue my studies'.

A cable was sent to New Zealand to ascertain when the next university term began. The reply stated that the tertiary year would begin in March and that Sinclair should be returned. He arrived back in New Zealand via the *Athenic* on 19 March 1919, and was immediately demobbed.

After the war he was appointed a lieutenant with the New Zealand Medical Corps and later, when house surgeon at Hawera Hospital, with the 2nd New Zealand (Queen Alexandra's Wellington West Coast) Mounted Rifles.

Sinclair's performance in his first All Blacks match, against New South Wales on his home ground of Carisbrook, was acclaimed for years afterwards as the best debut by a fullback ever seen in this country, surpassed only when one D.B. Clarke made his first appearance against the 1959 Lions.

Sadly, Sinclair — the man of medicine — died only nine years after playing for the All Blacks, as the result of a pulmonary haemorrhage following an operation to remove his appendix.

23 February 1917

ENLISTED: **Lance Sergeant Ernest 'Ernie' Henry DODD (1880–1918)**

AGE AT ENLISTMENT: 36 years, 11 months, 2 days

ARMY NUMBER: 54336

EMBARKATION: Wellington, 16 July 1917; G Company, 27th Reinforcements

LENGTH OF SERVICE: 1 year, 203 days

PLAYED FOR: Wellington College Old Boys; Wellington 1901–05; North Island 1902

ALL BLACK NUMBER: 83

POSITION: Front-row forward

APPEARANCES: 1901, 1905; 3 games, including 1 test

Dodd was the first All Black from the Wellington College Old Boys club. His grandfather, Henry, was a long-serving MP for Wairau, while his father, Mr F.H. Dodd (originally from Bath), of whom he was the only son, was of high standing within the Telegraph Department.

A member of Wellington College Old Boys' first junior team in 1898, Dodd achieved prominence as a member of the Wellington team that defeated the visiting New South Welshmen 17–16 in the first match of their 1901 tour. His selection for the All Blacks in their match against the tourists saw him referred to as 'the lad', as he was the youngest member of the team that won 20–3 at Athletic Park. The All Black lock that afternoon, Bill Cunningham, praised the youngster, saying that Dodd's performance was the best he'd seen by a front-ranker.

In the days when lineout forwards didn't have to stand five metres in from touch for the throw, Dodd took his place as 'first man in', and was a dominant disrupter of his opponents' ball. He played 45 games for Wellington, and virtually retired from the game at the age of only 25.

At the time of entering Trentham, he had been working as a clerk for the New Zealand Shipping Company, and was living towards the top of Cuba Street. Interestingly, he attested that he had spent three years with the College Rifles volunteers before being transferred to Wellington to take up his clerking position.

His preference was for artillery, but he ended up serving with C Company, 2nd Battalion of the 3rd New Zealand Rifle Brigade.

News of his departure saw the rugby football writer for the *Free Lance*, 'Touchline', comment in a column that: 'Twenty years ago Ernie Dodd was one of the outstanding players in Wellington, and as a front-rank forward had probably no superior in New Zealand … A fine stamp of a man — determined and with the fighting spirit — he should make a good soldier.'

The time aboard ship on the way to England was eventful, with Dodd forfeiting three days' pay for some misdemeanour and then spending time in the ship's hospital due to fever.

Once in camp in France, he pulled on a football jersey again, telling one old friend from Wellington club rugby that he had 'two goes in three days … then rousted out at three the last morning to go up the line and do Engineers' fatigue. Oh, hell, what a stiffness in the joints!'

Dodd was wounded in action on 17 April 1918, a bullet grazing his scalp. Four months later he was hospitalised, suffering from scabies.

Rejoining his unit, he was promoted to lance sergeant as the Rifle Brigade prepared for the September assault on Trescault Spur. (See page 260.)

24 February 1917

Due to the cancellation of the visit by the New Zealand Divisional Football Team, the New Zealand Reserve Group team played another match against the Army Service Corps (ASC), who were being referred to as the best team in England due to their continuing run of wins. (Ten of the ASC side were Northern Union players.) The match began after both teams cheered each other and the 'All Blacks' walked to the front of the main stand and offered applause for Prime Minister Massey.

As for the play itself, the ASC won comfortably, 21–3. The referee provided the New Zealand supporters with some mirth when he had to limp off injured and was replaced. One report of the match in the *Chronicles of the NZEF* stated that:

> If Teddy Roberts is given a chance to get together and keep the same team for a few weeks, it is still probable that he will find himself captain of the best team in the British Isles. Maorilanders don't easily get their tails down, and we do not think even a score of 21 to 3 will damp their ardour. Nearly all the New Zealanders in London must have turned out to witness the match, including hundreds of blue boys. If barracking could win the match, there would have been little fear of the result.

28 February 1917

ENLISTED: **Corporal William Charles FRANCIS (1894–1981)**
AGE AT ENLISTMENT: 23 years, 24 days
ARMY NUMBER: 55942

EMBARKATION: Wellington, 23 April 1918; C Company, 36th
Reinforcements

LENGTH OF SERVICE: 2 years, 83 days

PLAYED FOR: Tukapa, Oriental and Wellington clubs;
Wellington 1913–15, 1921; North Island 1914

ALL BLACK NUMBER: 194

POSITION: Front-row forward

APPEARANCES: 1913–14; 12 matches, including 5 tests;
9 points (3 tries)

Francis began playing senior club football as a 17-year-old with the Tukapa club in Taranaki, and then, having moved to the capital, graduated to provincial rugby aged 19. That same season he became (and remains) the youngest forward to play for New Zealand when he took the field against the touring Australians in the second test of 1913, aged 19 years 221 days.

Although the opportunity to represent his country had perhaps been hastened by the fact that an All Black team had to depart for North America, Young proved his selection was no fluke when he was chosen for the 1914 tour of Australia. He missed only 1 of the 11 tour games.

Francis was a plumber living in Upper Hutt. His wife, Ruby, was seven months pregnant when he entered Trentham Camp. He claimed in his medical test that he had rugby football knee, but the doctor assessing him couldn't detect anything symptomatic of problematic joints.

Arriving in Suez in May 1918, he spent two weeks in the Australian Camp, from where he was hospitalised suffering from diarrhoea and then dysentery. He was sent to isolation at Larkhill Camp in England, and from there returned to New Zealand in February 1919.

On discharge from the army in August 1919 he was still only 23, and he joined the regular army as a member of the New Zealand Army Ordnance Corps in 1920. He played only one more first-class game of rugby, for Wellington in 1921.

15 March 1917

The huge popularity among the New Zealand troops of rugby games
was evident in numerous lengthy accounts of matches appearing
in the *Chronicles of the NZEF*. In the report below, the location of
the match was not revealed, indicative of sensitivity around troop
locations and movements:

> The New Zealand (Divisional) Representative Trench Team played
> the 38th Division Team in Belgium, at [censored]. After a strenuous
> game, our boys won by 18 points to 3. Among those present were
> General Sir Herbert C. O. Plumer, commanding Second Army;
> Lieut-General Hunter Weston; Brigadier-General Johnston (New
> Zealand Artillery; Major-General Russell (New Zealand Division);
> Colonel Plugge; and Captain R.I. Dansey.
>
> The game was played on a fine day before five or six thousand
> soldiers. The ground was well within range, and just before halftime,
> Fritz sent his compliments in the form of a couple of H.E. shells,
> which landed about half-a-mile beyond the ground.
>
> The Divisional Band was in attendance and livened the
> proceedings with some fine music.

16 March 1917

ENLISTED: **Sapper Sidney 'Sid' David SHEARER (1890–
1973)**
AGE AT ENLISTMENT: 26 years, 4 months, 21 days
ARMY NUMBER: 53564
EMBARKATION: Wellington, 13 August 1917; New Zealand
  Field Engineers, 29th Reinforcements
LENGTH OF SERVICE: 2 years, 132 days
PLAYED FOR: Oriental, Selwyn and Poneke clubs; Wellington
  1913–14, 1919–22, 1924–25; New Zealand Trials 1921;
  North Island 1922; Wellington–Manawatu–Horowhenua
  1925

ALL BLACK NUMBER: 245
POSITION: Utility forward
APPEARANCES: 1921–22; 8 matches; 3 points (1 try)

Shearer was a registered plumber whose mother had the lovely name Mercy and whose father Alexander had been born in Wick, Scotland. The family lived on Thorndon Quay, and Sid worked for a Mr H.V. Futter of Newtown. Shearer was in the Wellington team that defeated Taranaki for the Ranfurly Shield in the last match before the war-induced four-season hiatus.

In March 1918, Shearer joined a field company of the New Zealand Engineers in France, and a month later forfeited five days' pay for being on leave without a pass.

Part of Poneke's Wellington club-championship winning side in 1921, at the age of 30 Shearer was chosen for the 'second' All Black team that was opposing the visiting New South Wales side while the Springboks were also travelling the country. Fortunately for him, the 0–17 loss was not to be his only match for the team. The following year, after another good showing in the inter-island match, he was chosen for the tour of Australia and played seven matches, including two as a replacement. Unfortunately, the New South Welshmen won the test series 2–1.

In 1922, the *NZ Truth* Wellington football writer 'Tackler' went to the defence of Shearer, and took to the attitude of the more vociferous and parochial sideline supporters of Wellington club football:

> In a recent match at the Park, 'Sid' had the misfortune to be injured and when he went down there was a cheer from a section of the crowd. If that is the sort of sympathy that is passed out to a man who is playing for the love of the game and for the benefit of the spectators, it does not say much for the sporting spirit of some of those who follow our national game.

Shearer's final appearance for Wellington was in 1925, and he finally stepped away from club football in about 1930, at which point he was almost 40.

FROM THE SIDELINES

Overheard at a rugby match at Richmond that a New Zealand team was playing in: 'I wonder if that chap "Digger" is playing today for the New Zealanders? He played a fine open game last week. Everything was "Digger this" and "Digger that". I reckon "Digger" is the mainstay of their team, and if he didn't play the team would absolutely fall to pieces.'

ENLISTED: **Private Leonard Frederick 'Jack' STOHR (1889–1973)**

AGE AT ENLISTMENT: 27 years, 4 months, 3 days

ARMY NUMBER: 3/3651

EMBARKATION: Wellington, 18 February 1918; New Zealand Medical Corps, 34th Reinforcements

LENGTH OF SERVICE: 2 years, 140 days

PLAYED FOR: Tukapa and Stratford clubs; Taranaki 1908–14; North Island 1912, 1914

ALL BLACK NUMBER: 165

POSITION: Centre

APPEARANCES: 1910, 1913; 15 matches, including 3 tests; 73 points (10 tries, 14 conversions, 5 penalties)

In 1909, Stohr set a record for a player scoring all of the points for a winning side when his Taranaki team beat Wanganui, 14–3. The total of 14 (made up of a try, three penalty goals and a conversion) seems small through modern eyes, but it was all the more remarkable as it was the first time a New Zealand footballer had kicked three penalty goals in a first-class game. As a record it wasn't surpassed until R.T. Cundy kicked four penalty goals for Wairarapa against Hawke's Bay in 1927.

Stohr, a chemist by trade, had worked in the eponymous family business in Stratford, and later with Teed and Co. in New Plymouth. He was both a prolific and prodigious goal-kicker. In a match report of the 1911 clash between Wellington and

Taranaki, won by the amber-and-blacks 23–3, the NZ *Truth* reporter wrote:

> Jack Stohr beat 'em by himself with one of the finest exhibitions of place-kicking it has been this city's good luck to see. It wasn't altogether what Stohr got, it was the two or three he didn't get (by a whisker) that shook Wellington's nerve ... Stohr's performance was exceptionally brilliant. To get fourteen points off his own hoof was as much as most cricketers can get off their own bats. Anybody who deliberately gives Jack Stohr a chance with 55 yards [50 metres] and a bit should be attended to by a specialist in brain disorders. On top of which same Stohr played a tremendous fine game for his side ... We have spoken of Stohr. So did 10,000 people in Wellington city alone on Saturday night. I heard 'em.

While undertaking his army training with the Medical Corps, Stohr played in the Awapuni Ambulance football team. He spent much of 1918 in the Ewshot and Aldershot camps, becoming a qualified first-class instructor in anti-gas drills, before crossing the Channel and entering camp at Étaples a month before the end of the war.

Stohr played for the Services football team, top-scoring on the tour of South Africa. While he had been renowned for his long-distance goals in New Zealand, in the rarefied air of South Africa he reportedly kicked a goal from about 70 yards (65 metres), turning the pessimistic jeers of the crowd as he placed the ball to astonished cheers and applause as the leather flew over the crossbar.

Stohr must have been quite taken with South Africa, as a year after the Services tour he moved to the Republic and settled permanently outside Johannesburg.

19 March 1917

ENLISTED: **Rifleman Alfred 'Alf' Lewis KIVELL (1897–1987)**
AGE AT ENLISTMENT: 19 years, 11 months, 7 days
ARMY NUMBER: 56798

EMBARKATION: Wellington, 14 July 1917; Reinforcements
    H Company, New Zealand Rifle Brigade
LENGTH OF SERVICE: 2 years, 138 days
PLAYED FOR: Stratford; Taranaki 1920–30; North Island
    1926; New Zealand Trials 1929
ALL BLACK NUMBER: 375
POSITION: Loose-forward
APPEARANCES: 1929; 5 games, including 2 tests

Kivell was often described by rugby writers as a brilliant forward, but unfortunately for him the peak of his career coincided with that of great loose-forwards such as the Brownlie brothers. The last veteran of the Great War to debut in the All Black jersey, Kivell was selected for the 1929 tour of Australia after almost a decade representing Taranaki, and three years after his only appearance in a North versus South match.

The Karangahake-born farmer, who had undertaken military training in Stratford with the 11th Regiment, enlisted three weeks before his twentieth birthday. He and fellow private Wilfred Johnson were given a grand farewell by the people of Kahouri Bridge (just out of Stratford) at which they were presented with wristlet watches, gloves and good wishes. A programme of numerous musical items was preceded by a main speech given by a Mr J.A. Falder, who hoped that 'both soldiers would in due course return to the district with honour and the knowledge that they had done their duty'. (Johnson survived the war, too, but did suffer gunshot wounds to a shoulder and hand.)

Kivell's service with the New Zealand Rifle Brigade was blighted by illness, including bouts of measles and scabies that saw him hospitalised.

A regular in the annual Taranaki Rugby Union's North versus South match (appearing for the former), he had proven himself to be a player of international potential in 1921 when playing as part of a Taranaki pack who more than held their own against the 'giants' of the visiting Springboks. In 1926 he was one of only two uncapped players in the North Island team that thumped the South 41–9.

The 1929 All Blacks tour of Australia was the least successful by our national team up to that point. Affected by an ever-increasing list of injured players, they lost all three tests for the first time. Kivell himself missed the first 5 games of the 10-match tour due to injury.

In what could be seen as something of a metaphor for the All Blacks' visit across the ditch, when they left Armidale after their match with New South Wales County bound for Brisbane where they would play the Australians in the second test, their train derailed. Six of the eight carriages left the tracks in the Black Mountains, and three collapsed onto their sides. It was early in the morning, foggy and very cold for the passengers who had to disembark. Fortunately, the train had been travelling slowly as it was making its way up an incline, and nobody was injured. The only two carriages not to leave the tracks were the last two, in which the All Blacks were sleeping. Such drama was nothing new to Kivell. When he had been making his way to Wellington to join the team before they sailed, the train he left Stratford on also derailed!

26 March 1917

ENLISTED: **Private David Lindsay 'Scotty' BAIRD (1895–1947)**

AGE AT ENLISTMENT: 21 years, 8 months

ARMY NUMBER: 58963

EMBARKATION: Wellington, 13 October 1917; Otago Infantry Regiment, 30th Reinforcements

LENGTH OF SERVICE: 2 years, 153 days

PLAYED FOR: Star; Southland 1919–21; South Island 1920

ALL BLACK NUMBER: 216

POSITION: Loose-forward and outside back

APPEARANCES: 1920; 9 matches; 17 points (4 tries, 1 conversion, 1 penalty goal)

A member of the 1st Battalion Otago Regiment, the Southland farmer had been rejected as unfit for the Territorial Army and there was concern about a hernia when he enlisted following his name having been drawn in the fifth conscription ballot in March 1917. But it was decided that as he was fit for farm work he was fit for fighting. While at Featherston Camp he forfeited 12 days' pay for extending his leave without authorisation.

Serving in France, he suffered a shrapnel wound to a leg in August 1918, which removed him from active service.

One of the stars of the Southland team in 1920 when they prised the Ranfurly Shield 17–6 from the somewhat accommodating grasp of Wellington (who put the log up for grabs at their matches both home and away), Baird gave a grand 'follow me' performance in front of a crowd that was recorded as the largest ever for a football game in Invercargill. On paper, Baird's task on that cool, windy day looked a difficult one. Wellington had been playing well, and opposing him at wing-forward was Ranji Wilson, while at halfback Wellington captain Teddy Roberts had been controlling play in recent games the way the best halfbacks can.

Once the game kicked off, Baird bore down on or tore after Roberts all afternoon, doing his best to unsettle the champion half. This was a continuation of the form that had seen him chosen for the first post-war tour by the All Blacks, in 1920. On the Australian trip, Baird played in 9 of the 10 matches. He captained Southland against the Springboks in 1921.

In 1947, he died from injuries suffered in a mining accident.

10 April 1917

ENLISTED: **Driver William Richard 'Bill the Bull' IRVINE (1898–1952)**
AGE AT ENLISTMENT: 18 years, 4 months, 8 days
ARMY NUMBER: 50212
EMBARKATION: Wellington, 21 November 1917; New Zealand Field Artillery, 32nd Reinforcements
LENGTH OF SERVICE: 2 years, 133 days

PLAYED FOR: Featherston Liberal, Carterton and Waipukurau
   Rovers clubs; Wairarapa 1920, 1927–30; Hawke's Bay
   1922–26; Hawke's Bay–Poverty Bay–East Coast 1923;
   North Island 1923–26; New Zealand Trials 1924, 1930;
   Wairarapa–Bush 1930
ALL BLACK NUMBER: 280
POSITION: Hooker
APPEARANCES: 1923–26, 1930; 41 matches, including 5 tests;
   21 points (7 tries)

Irvine arrived in Liverpool with the 32nd Reinforcements at the beginning of 1918 and was almost immediately hospitalised with pleurisy. Two months later, after only a fortnight in Ewshot Camp, he was hospitalised with rubella. He finally joined the 7th Battery in the field in April 1918. Eight days before the Armistice, Irvine fell into a shell-hole while on a picket line tending horses, fracturing a rib on his right side.

Having established himself with the champion Hawke's Bay side, he made his debut for the All Blacks against the 1923 New South Welshmen. But it was in the following year that Irvine really made a name for himself as a one of the best front-rankers the game had seen. Technically he was superb in the 2–3–2 scrum, but he was also extremely strong.

Irvine played in 27 of the 30 games on the Invincibles' tour and was described by George Nepia as a 'hard case', particularly after he took a group of the younger team members on 'the sort of expedition soldiers used to make on leave. We returned from it very shaken and [he] laughs at us for [being] a bunch of softies. He is a character, a real character.' He also seemed to take great delight at a dinner in France when several of the team commented on the strange colour of the meat they had been served. 'Bill the Bull' loudly informed his teammates that it was horsemeat. That saw some of the team leave the dining table, and others followed when Nepia asked him about blacks spots in an omelette. Irvine let the young man from the East Coast, affectionately known as 'Hori' by the rest of the team, believe that the 'spots' were from frogs' legs and snails.

Irvine was also wont to call Nepia 'The Smoked Ham', and as the 1924–25 tour progressed he decided that the young fullback, who was garnering constant high praise for his play in the English newspapers, should have a more distinguished name than just 'G. Nepia', as he was listed in rugby programmes and team lists. So, after a bit of thought and a look at some of the multiple initials borne by some of their opponents, Nepia re-christened himself 'H.G.M. Nepia'. Many were the scribes and rugby writers who were caught out by Irvine and Nepia's mischievousness.

Irvine toured Australia with the All Blacks in 1926, playing five games, and was recalled four years later to play the 1930 British Lions. His appearance in the first test was the last by an All Black who had served in World War I.

Irvine's son, Ian, also played for the All Blacks as a hooker, in 1952. Sadly, 'Bill the Bull', who had farmed near Whangarei for some years, had passed away a couple of months earlier.

15 April 1917

A detailed account of the creation of the Divisional 'All Blacks' and how they operated was provided by Malcolm Ross, a war correspondent with the forces in the field:

> La Coupe de la Somme: Une Grande Journée Militaire et Sportive
> A general order to the British Armies in the Field in France, issued some months ago, emphasised the importance of physical training in war. Many of the divisions in the front took that order to heart, and among other exercises, football became the most popular. Boxing, cross-country running, musketry, bayonet and bombing competitions also entered into the scheme.
>
> The New Zealanders, as is their wont, went into the scheme with enthusiasm and thoroughness. Lieut.-Colonel Plugge, who fought on Gallipoli and on the Somme Battle was appointed Director of Physical Training, and at once set to work to get a strong football team together. Names of footballers from the different units of the Division were sent in, and from this list 24 of the best men were

chosen to form the New Zealand Divisional Football Team. The team was housed at the Divisional School, and there put in some hard work in training and in fatigues. It has turned out about five instructors in bayonet fighting, and about four in bombing. Usually the team assembled at 7 a.m. for half an hour's physical exercise. From 9 till 1 they were with the school's instructors. From 2.30 till 4.30 p.m. they were at road work or football practice, and three nights a week they spent some time in the school gymnasium. Since the beginning of February they have been engaged on fatigues from 9 a.m. till 4.30 p.m. seven days a week.

A fine record
During that time they have been in existence as a team they have played nine important matches, and have scored in these 376 points [*sic*, should be 372] to 9. The following is a list of the principal matches:

    A British Division Team 74 – 3
    A British Division Team 44 – 0
    An RE Team 22 – 0
    A Welsh Division Team 18 – 3
    An Irish Division Team 49 – 3
    An RFC Team 82 – 0
    A Welsh Division Team 3 – 0
    France 40 – 0
    NZ Hospital, Amiens 40 – 0

The New Zealand team included players such as Scott, the fullback, from Otago; three-quarter-backs, E. Ryan (Wellington), George Murray (Auckland), G.B. Owles (Canterbury), W. Wilson (Wellington); five-eighths, S. Cameron (Taranaki), J.C. Macintyre (S. Auckland), N.F. Stead (Canterbury); half-backs, C. Brown (Taranaki), F.A. Ross (Auckland); wing-forward, R. Taylor (Taranaki); forwards, R.J. Casey (Auckland), H.G. Whittington (Taranaki), J. Moffitt (Wellington), T. French (Auckland), C. King (Wellington), A. Wilson 'Ranji' (Wellington) and W. Bell (Wellington).

    The strongest team by far that the New Zealanders met was undoubtedly a team from the Welsh Division, all good players, and among them several Internationals. To see this match I motored through part of Northern France into Belgium, and there in a field near Monastery I found a large crowd of British soldiers keenly intent upon every turn of the game. Generals and many officers were present, and a Regimental Band played before and during the halftime interval. Some of the local people who had never seen a Rugby football match were also there, and on the outskirts of the crowd, also interested, but not greatly understanding, were the big tonsured monks in their flowing robes, from the adjoining monastery. Close at hand a great captive balloon swung into the air, and at intervals came the report of a bursting shell flung from the Bosche lines. A Belgian Prince, whose sister helped Edith Cavell and is now in solitary confinement in a German prison on the Rhine, was among the spectators, and to him and to one of the Belgian monks I had to explain the intricacies of the game. The cheering 'Tommies', the two teams fighting their friendly battle in the arena, the Trappist monks in such strange juxtaposition, the excited Belgian youths, and the big balloon swaying in the blue, made up as strange a view as anyone had seen in this war. I had taken with me one of the official cinematographers, so that one day New Zealanders will be able to see something of the movement of the scene thousands of miles away in their own country. For some days before we had been wading knee-deep in mud and water and ice in our own front-line, getting pictures of the shells bursting on the German trenches opposite.

The game itself was an interesting one to watch, for both sides were more evenly matched than the score would seem to indicate, and the passing rushes of the New Zealanders at times were quite brilliant, and drew forth enthusiastic comments from the English and Welsh experts who crowded on the touchline. The return match against this team (played in front of more than a dozen generals) was a closer contest, but it was played on a ground slushy with mud and a greasy ball that made good play almost impossible.

The film Ross describes as having been taken by an official cinematographer matches that held in the National Film Archive, which, according to military historian Chris Pugsley, is believed to be the first moving-image footage of New Zealand trench conditions on the Western Front.

The 14-minute film documents a visit by the Secretary of State for Colonial Affairs, the Honourable Sir Walter Long. Accompanied by Divisional Commander Major General Sir Andrew Russell and Major Peter H. Buck, they inspect the 2nd New Zealand Infantry Brigade and watch a march-past of units, which includes the New Zealand Pioneer Battalion.

Footage then moves to a trench, where firstly a soldier can be seen firing a Lewis gun, the butt of the gun at his shoulder and the barrel resting on top of a sandbag. Next a soldier is filmed firing rifle grenades, loading each, then ducking down behind a low wall of sandbags as the mortar fires. A long, slow pan follows, across an absolutely devastated village in no-man's-land, a wasteland of rubble and dirt. Soldiers are then filmed walking through knee-deep water in a shell-crater. One struggles to retain his smoking pipe and walking stick as he wavers unbalanced, while one or two others smile somewhat amusedly at the camera as they wade past. The film then cuts to a line of soldiers walking along a duckboard through what once would have been forest but is now mere headless tree trunks. Several of the soldiers return with some humour to walk in front of the cameraman again. The next scene is of a field battery of 18-pounder guns firing from concealed positions in buildings in a village, the camera drawn more to the pocked walls of buildings as smoke from the barrage drifts from off camera across the scene. The final images of fighting, shot from behind sandbags, show shells exploding in no-man's-land. The film then finishes with scenes from the football match between the Divisional 'All Blacks' and the 38th (Welsh) Division on 15 March 1917, a game won by New Zealand, 18–3.

The match against France — organised by French newspaper *Le Journal* and L'Union des Sociétés Françaises de Sports Athlétiques — was played at Vincennes, near Paris, on Sunday, 8 April, in front of an estimated 75,000 spectators. The New Zealanders arrived in the city a couple of days before the match and spent their time sight-seeing and visiting the ground they were to play at. (The impression given to their fellow soldiers, however, was that many of the team had been in the trenches as late as the day before 'keeping Fritz busy'.) While the French side were competitive for the first quarter, nine tries were scored by the New Zealanders — Murray (three), Owles (two), and Ryan, Cockroft, Fogarty and Brown (one apiece) — while Ed Ryan converted five of them and added a penalty for the 40–0 score-line.

That evening the players were wined, dined and taken to theatres. Their hosts presented each player with a frosted silver medallion and a tinder box of gold and silver. The team was given a bronze statuette by the sculptor Georges Chauvel, titled *Le Lanceur des Grenades*, better known as *La Coupe de la Somme*. It depicted a soldier arching back with arms outstretched, about to throw a grenade. Just where this prized piece of military history is today is unknown.

17 April 1917

ENLISTED: **Private Samuel William GEMMELL (1896– 1970)**

AGE AT ENLISTMENT: 20 years, 7 months, 20 days

ARMY NUMBER: 19848

EMBARKATION: Wellington, 26 July 1917; Maori Contingent, 20th Reinforcements

LENGTH OF SERVICE: 2 years, 119 days

PLAYED FOR: Te Aute College, Maori Agricultural College, Marist, Hastings, Wairoa Pirates, Mohaka, Waipapa and Tapuae clubs; Hawke's Bay 1921–31; Hawke's Bay–Poverty Bay 1921; New Zealand Maoris 1922–23, 1926–29; North Island 1923; New Zealand Trials 1924

ALL BLACK NUMBER: 265

POSITION: Side-row forward

APPEARANCES: 1923; 1 match

Leaving New Zealand with the 20th Maori Reinforcements, Gemmell spent the first half of 1918 in the field with the Pioneer Battalion in France. At the war's end, while waiting to return to New Zealand, he was absent without leave, forfeiting 15 days' pay.

A member of the Maori Pioneer Battalion football team in

Britain in 1919, he missed the national tour by the side later that year as he was still aboard ship making his way back to New Zealand. He studied at Te Aute College after the war, and became a mainstay in New Zealand Maori sides throughout the 1920s, including the 40-match tour in 1926 that began in Auckland in July and ended in Canada the following February (in between, the side visited Australia, Ceylon, France, England and Wales).

Despite absences when away with the New Zealand Maoris, Gemmell was a regular in the Hawke's Bay side during their famous 24-match Ranfurly Shield tenure from 1922 to 1927. Provincial teammate George Nepia wrote of Gemmell as being

> a great forward. He was a strong, foursquare sort of build, especially powerful in the shoulders, and he hadn't a friend in the world, on the other side at any rate, while he was playing. He really was a rugged hombre, but he never asked a favour on the field and his whole ambition was to get at the ball.

His lone All Black match was against the touring New South Welshmen in the first 'test' in Dunedin in 1923. The All Blacks won the match 19–9, but Gemmell was dropped and never wore the jersey again. Even at the time, it was considered something of a harsh decision from the selectors, given that at the last minute he had been moved to the front row, a position he had never played in before.

For two decades after his retirement, Gemmell held the record for the most first-class games played by a New Zealand footballer. His extraordinary total of 144 matches included 74 for Hawke's Bay and 56 for the New Zealand Maoris.

2 May 1917

A report of results from the *Chronicles of the NZEF* provides a glimpse of just how regularly teams from New Zealand camps in England were taking to football fields.

RESULTS
Pioneer Company
March 7 — D Coy beat A Coy.
March 11 — D Coy defeated C Coy; A and B Coys. a draw
March 18 — D Coy (MAORIES) defeated B Coy. (PAKEHAS) by
26–0.
April 8 — N.Z. PIONEER BATTN. v. 49th BRIGADE (WELSH)
— Pioneers won; Score, 52–0
    N.Z. PIONEER BATTN. v. SOUTH WALES BORDERERS
— Was a walkover for the Pioneers
    O.M.R.
April 1 — OTAGO MOUNTED RIFLES v. 2nd B.A.C. — A hard
game ending in a draw; No Score. A return match a week later gave a
similar result.
April 15 — OTAGO MOUNTED RIFLES v. N.Z. PIONEERS
(BUSH CONTROL) — Otago won by 42–0
    The following members of the O.M.R. team have distinguished
themselves throughout the season: Trpr. Thomas, half; Heade,
five-eighth; and Tpr. Hugh McDonald and Sergt. Cameron, forwards.

Engineers
February 23 — 3rd FIELD CO. v. MACHINE GUN CORPS. —
Sappers won by 16–6.
April 2 — 3rd FIELD CO. v. 12th N.Z. BATTERY — Field Co. won
3–0. The Battery won by the same score a month previously.
April 3 — 3rd FIELD CO. v. 1st FIELD CO. — A run over for the
former. Score, about 100 to nil. A warm game.
    The most prominent players for 3rd. Co. have been Captain
McNab, Corporal Griffin, and Sappers Dufty and D. Dow.

Rifle Brigade
April 17 — 2nd BATTN. v. 1st BRIGADE N.Z.F.A.— Artillery won;
Score 11–3.
April 14 — 2nd BATTN., C Co. v. D Co. A draw, 3-all. Capt. Avery
scoring for C Co. and Webb for D Co. Lance-Cpl. Brogan, an ex-
Wanganui rep. was the mainstay for the D Co. Capt. Avery and Rflmn.
Jaron played well for C Co.

25 May 1917

ENLISTED: **Sapper John Alexander 'Peppy' BRUCE (1887–1970)**

AGE AT ENLISTMENT: 30 years, 14 days

ARMY NUMBER: 63551

EMBARKATION: Wellington, 2 May 1918; New Zealand Engineers, 36th Reinforcements

LENGTH OF SERVICE: 2 years, 84 days

PLAYED AT: St James, Athletic and City clubs; Wellington 1909–10, 1921; Auckland 1911–15; North Island 1909, 1912–14

ALL BLACK NUMBER: 186

POSITION: Back-row forward

APPEARANCES: 1913–14; 10 matches, including 2 tests; 6 points (2 tries)

Bruce played in the inter-island match three times before finally winning All Black selection, for the 1913 tour to North America. He left being the subject of some ribbing from his cobbers, who took delight in a humorous happening on the afternoon their boat was to sail from Wellington. Having been living in Auckland for a couple of years, Bruce had taken the opportunity to catch up with old friends from the capital while the team was waiting to sail. While in the home of acquaintances in Cuba Street, he was alerted to a shipping column in the newspaper and the supposed departure of the All Blacks aboard the *Willochra* at 3 p.m. that day. Bruce was sure that team manager Mr G. Mason had told the team they were leaving at 5 p.m. Looking at a clock on the wall, an increasingly anxious Bruce saw that it was almost five minutes to three. He said hurried farewells and rushed out into the street, where he hailed a taxi, exhorting the driver with the promise of extra financial reward to get him to King's Wharf by 3 p.m. On his arrival at the wharf, the ship was still tied up and there was no urgency from those loading the vessel. A frantic Bruce found he had an hour or two to spare, in which to cool his heels.

During his military medical exam, it was noted that three years earlier he had suffered a cut to the inside of his left leg which had seen him laid up for six weeks. He also complained of having a 'football' knee, which ached sometimes in wet weather but generally did not pain him.

Bruce spent all his army time in England, including almost a month in hospital from the end of October 1918, suffering from influenza. Once he had recovered, his service continued on the football field as a member of the Divisional Football Team and the Services side that toured South Africa.

The last of his 21 games for Wellington was played in 1921, to go with the 24 he had played for Auckland. Bruce also played first-class cricket for Wellington and, a skilled carpenter, was the 'odd-job man' at the National Film Unit later in life.

7 June 1917

† DIED: **Private James Alexander Steenson Baird** †

Baird (see page 143) died of wounds at Messines, having suffered severe injuries to his hands, backside and abdomen. The attack on 7 June began with the early morning detonation of large mines that had been planted under the German lines after months of tunnelling work. Once the mines exploded — with some reports claiming they were heard as far away as London — the New Zealand, Australian and Allied soldiers dusted off the dirt and debris that had rained down on them and advanced from the trenches. They quickly claimed the Belgian village of Messines, but in the early afternoon a German bombardment of their position began. A frightening, relentless hail of bombs fell on the New Zealanders, which killed more than 700 and wounded 3,700 in little more than 48 hours. Baird's casualty form lists his injuries as gunshot wounds (something of a general descriptor for the wounded), but being as extensive as they were, they were no doubt caused by shrapnel.

Baird was buried in the Bailleul Communal Cemetery Extension, one of 252 New Zealanders out of 4,000 from a number of nations who rest there. Two New Zealand brigadier-generals — Earl Johnston and Charles Brown — lie among them.

† DIED: **Private George Maurice Victor Sellars** †

Baird's teammate George Sellars (see page 137) was killed the same day, gunned down as he heroically carried a wounded soldier to safety. His name is inscribed along with 827 other Kiwis on the New Zealand Memorial to the Missing in the Messines Ridge British Cemetery. The memorial reads, 'HERE ARE RECORDED THE NAMES OF OFFICERS AND MEN OF NEW ZEALAND WHO FELL IN OR NEAR MESSINES IN 1917 AND 1918 WHOSE GRAVES ARE KNOWN ONLY TO GOD.' This suggests that Sellars's body was never found, but his active service casualty form notes that he was buried by a Lieutenant McArthur and the location was recorded. However, the cemeteries of the Western Front that we can see today are the product of post-war order and commemoration.

The cemetery was designed by Charles Holden, and saw those buried on nearby battlefields and smaller cemeteries in the area moved to it after the Armistice. Most of those buried there died during 1917.

On the first anniversary of Sellars's death, the *Auckland Star* carried four In Memoriam pieces dedicated to him. The first was from his parents, brothers and sister. It read:

We often think of you, dear George
Ne'er again your dear face shall we see
But as long as life and memory last
We will remember thee.

The second was from another brother:

For duty and his country's call
He went both true and brave
Upon a battlefield to fall
and fill a soldier's grave.

An aunt and a good friend contributed the other two.

Such notices in memory of George Sellars continued until World War II.

20 June 1917

† DIED: **Lance Corporal Reginald Taylor** †

Lieutenant Sydney Paul (see page 60), who had refereed the match between 'Australia' and 'New Zealand' at Lemnos in 1915 and spent time at the front with his former Taranaki team-mate Taylor, wrote in a letter from Sling Camp to a friend in Waitara that

> it was very hard luck about poor old Reg. Taylor going west as he was a real good sort. I don't know his people, but you can tell them from me that he was one of the best and keenest soldiers in our forces, always ready to do anything at any risk, and that he was of the sort that New Zealand could ill afford to lose. The death caused quite a gloom among the boys as they all thought so much of Reg.

Taylor lies in the Underhill Farm Cemetery, one of 39 New Zealand soldiers buried there. Red Lodge and Underhill Farm were two buildings near Ploegsteert Wood, which were used as dressing stations. Commonwealth soldiers were interred there between June 1917 and January 1918. It was taken by the Germans, named 'The Military Cemetery at the foot of Nightingale Hill', and was occupied until

September 1918. Allied soldiers were buried there again the following month.

Taylor's parents, Barbara and Thomas, placed annual memorial notices in the local newspaper, such as this from 1919:

> *A loving son, so true so kind*
> *No one on earth like him we'll find*
> *Two years have passed and none can tell*
> *The loss of one we loved so well.*

Sydney Paul was killed in battle several weeks after Taylor's death.

21 June 1917

† DIED: **Private James 'Jim' McNeece** †

The father of James McNeece (see page 138) — also called James — received a letter from the commander of McNeece's platoon, written on hearing of the young man's death. It outlined his last hours:

> During the time your son had been with the Battery he endeared himself to us all by his unfailing cheerfulness, and his capacity for work was unrivalled. We all feel his loss very deeply, and I wish to convey on behalf of members of this Battery our very deep sympathy with you and your family in the irreparable loss you have sustained in losing one so near and dear to you.
>
> I do not know whether Jim was able to write to you after he was wounded, but in any case you will doubtless be glad of some particulars as to how he was wounded.
>
> He comprised one of the gun teams under my care in the advance on Messines. We reached an objective

and consolidated on 7th June. There was but little sleep for the next 48 hours, but at the end of that time things had cooled down somewhat and as I was living in a very deep shell hole I sent him (Jim) and another (Lynch) into my hole to have a sleep. They were there for some hours and then the Bosches started shelling very heavily. Your son stood up to see what was doing when a shell burst nearby and a piece of it entered his shoulder up close to the neck. We tied him up and in a couple of hours got him away. He was quite able to walk and none of us thought that the wound would be fatal, so it was a big surprise when I yesterday received the official advice of his death. Your loss is a great one, but you have the satisfaction of knowing that Jim died while doing 'his little bit' — and well he did it, too.

McNeece is buried in the St Sever Cemetery, which, along with its extension, holds in excess of 10,000 graves. New Zealanders total 188. His brother Alex had left New Zealand in April 1917, and was severely wounded on the Western Front. He returned to New Zealand but died in 1935, his death attributed to wounds he had suffered during the war.

22 June 1917

From this day on, Maori men were no longer exempt from conscription.

The Divisional XV was continuing to provide physical benefits, as well as boost morale, as Major-General Sir A.H. Russell wrote to Defence Minister Sir James Allen:

I can report that the Division is in first-class fighting trim. I have never seen the men look so well as they do today. The sick rate is low. If it were not for mumps it would be exceptionally low. All the Division institutions are running very well. We have first-class variety entertainment. The Divisional football team has been winning laurels on a more peaceful field by playing other divisional teams over here, so far with an unbeaten record.

23 June 1917

In the Christchurch club competition, Marist and Linwood played each other at Linwood Park. Though it was a 0–0 draw, it was reported that eight players were knocked out. *The Star* newspaper condemned the physicality of the game:

> The game was an appalling travesty labelled Rugby football, showing to what depths of degradation a noble sport may be dragged. Too many players discarded all sportsmanlike feelings, and played the man instead of the ball with a ferocity that would have been better employed against the ravagers of Belgium.

27 June 1917

ENLISTED: **Private Donald Cameron HAMILTON (1883–1925)**
AGE AT ENLISTMENT: 34 years, 5 months, 8 days
ARMY NUMBER: 3/3778
EMBARKATION: Wellington, 9 May 1918; New Zealand Medical Corps, 37th Reinforcements
LENGTH OF SERVICE: 2 years, 8 days
PLAYED FOR: Pirates; Southland 1906–08; South Island 1908
ALL BLACK NUMBER: 154
POSITION: Wing-forward
APPEARANCES: 1908; 1 test

A registered chemist from Bluff, Hamilton's only match for the All Blacks was the second test of 1908 against the Anglo-Welsh in Wellington, a game that was the last for one of the finest fullbacks the game has seen, Billy Wallace. Hamilton had been the stand-out player on the park when the visitors played Southland in their fourth tour match. He starred in the loose, as well as kicking a penalty and a conversion in the 8–14 loss, and on the back of that form justifiably earned an All Black cap.

The All Blacks had won the first test in Carisbrook 32–5, so the selectors made a number of changes, among them Hamilton. Unfortunately, this self-confidence backfired on the selection panel of Messrs Gallaher (Auckland), Harris (Otago), Kelly (Wellington) and Wilson (Canterbury). The day dawned wet, rain was unrelenting throughout the afternoon, and the ground was slushy at best. The élan with which the All Blacks had played the week before was gone, and passing a large bar of soap may have been easier than handling the sodden, mud-coated pig's bladder. Quickly the pattern of play was established: the ball would be kept at the feet of the forwards, who would use dribbling rushes to make their way upfield, or if the ball did get to the backs, they would kick it long. The Anglo-Welsh revelled in such tactics, and were perhaps unlucky not to win the match, which was drawn 3–3. (It was the second drawn test in three matches for the All Blacks, after the 5-all final test against Australia the previous season.)

Taking note of the fright the All Blacks had received, the selectors reverted to a less experimental line-up for the third test in Auckland, and recalled George Gillett (who had played as a forward and a back on the 1905 Originals tour) in place of Hamilton at wing-forward.

Controversy brought Hamilton back to prominence in the sporting pages the following year when, just like Ned Hughes, he was suspended from the game by the Southland Union when he was part of the Pirates team that, along with their opponents Britannia, refused to play a match because of dreadful weather conditions. So, when the two teams played a festival game under Northern Union rules, to a man they were banned from rugby union because they were deemed to be professionals.

Hamilton fared better in summer sport, where he starred for the Southland cricket side in 1910. He scored a century against Rangitikei as captain for the southerners in their first Hawke Cup match.

During the war he was posted to the New Zealand Medical Corps and spent nine months at Trentham. Four weeks before he embarked on the *Maunganui* to head overseas with the 37th Reinforcements, he married Ethel Harrington in Bluff. He was also able to play a final first-class rugby match when he turned out for the Trentham team.

In England, he went from camp at Aldershot to working at the 3rd NZ General Hospital, treating men suffering from venereal disease and other sores. Once posted to France, he worked for two months after the Armistice with the New Zealand Field Ambulance. While the war had officially ended, thousands of casualties still needed tending to.

11 July 1917

ENLISTED: **Lance Corporal Alfred 'Alf' Henry Netherwood FANNING (1890–1963)**

AGE AT ENLISTMENT: 27 years, 3 months, 10 days

ARMY NUMBER: 68801

EMBARKATION: Wellington, 27 July 1918; H Company, 41st Reinforcements

LENGTH OF SERVICE: 2 years, 7 days

PLAYED FOR: Marist and Linwood clubs; Canterbury 1913–14

ALL BLACK NUMBER: 204

POSITION: Lock

APPEARANCES: 1913; 1 test; 3 points (1 try)

Fanning hailed from a well-known footballing family in Canterbury: one of his older brothers, Bernie, had played in the first international played by the All Blacks, in Australia in 1903. Bernie was a tall, solid muscular man, and it was claimed that one of his party tricks was striking a match on the rough palms of his hands! Another brother, Leo, was a pressman and in 1910 wrote one of the first books on players and personalities in the New Zealand game.

The much younger Alfred played one test for the All Blacks in 1913, the lost third test against the visiting Australians. In all, he played only 14 first-class football games.

A carpenter who worked for the New Zealand Railways, living just across the road from the Christchurch rail yards in Moorhouse Avenue, Fanning had been part of the Railway Corps military cadets. His name was drawn in the ninth conscription ballot in June 1917.

A member of the Canterbury Infantry Regiment, he didn't arrive in London until October 1918, where almost immediately he was admitted to the 3rd New Zealand General Hospital. With the war at an end and awaiting embarkation to New Zealand, he worked on agricultural duty in Torquay. Later he served on the Junior Advisory Board of the Canterbury Rugby Football Union.

16 July 1917

ENLISTED: **Private Jack Douglas SHEARER (1896–1963)**
AGE AT ENLISTMENT: 20 years, 10 months, 27 days
ARMY NUMBER: 63682
EMBARKATION: Wellington, 21 November 1917; F Company, 32nd Reinforcements
LENGTH OF SERVICE: 2 years, 36 days
PLAYED FOR: Selwyn and Poneke clubs; Wellington 1919–25, 1927–29, 1931; North Island 1919; New Zealand Trials 1921
ALL BLACK NUMBER: 228
POSITION: Utility forward
APPEARANCES: 1920; 5 matches; 3 points (1 try)

Like his brother, Sid, Jack was also a plumber, and he too worked for H.V. Futter in Newtown. He had cadet training with the Thorndon Senior Cadets and entered Trentham four months after his younger brother. He was passed fit, but the medical examiner noted that both sides of his chest, below the nipple line, were flattened as the result of a bad case of pleuro-pneumonia nine years earlier.

Shearer joined the New Zealand Engineers Battalion in France in March 1918, and was then attached to the 27th Company. Early in August he was taken to a casualty clearing station suffering from dysentery, and was also treated for scabies at the base depot hospital at Étaples. After a month he rejoined his unit in the field, and for a month after the Armistice was appointed company cook.

He arrived back in New Zealand in July 1919, and two months later had been chosen to represent the North Island in the annual inter-island match, which, due to the steady stream of soldiers returning after what would have been the normal start to the football season, was played in September rather than in June or July as it had been in the years immediately before the war.

His inclusion in the All Black team to Australia in 1920 came after Mick Cain's withdrawal, and he played five games at back- or side-row. Despite eventually playing over 60 matches for Wellington, he was never selected for the national side again.

Part of Poneke's Wellington club-championship-winning side in 1921, along with brother Syd, Beet Algar and Ned Hughes, he was club captain from 1927 to 1932.

17 July 1917

ENLISTED: **Corporal Henry Morgan TAYLOR (1889– 1955)**

AGE AT ENLISTMENT: 28 years, 5 months, 12 days

ARMY NUMBER: 78723

LENGTH OF SERVICE: 1 year, 110 days

PLAYED FOR: Christchurch High School Old Boys; Canterbury 1910–14; South Island 1913–14

ALL BLACK NUMBER: 183

POSITION: Halfback and wing

APPEARANCES: 1913–14; 23 matches, including 5 tests; 60 points (20 tries)

A shop manager employed by Taylor and Oakley, gas engineers, Taylor appeared in 22 games across two seasons for the All Blacks. It says something about his pace and passing skills that he could play halfback or as an outside back, and amassed 20 tries for the All Blacks. Fifteen of those touchdowns were on the Australian tour, and five of those were in the match against Central–Western Districts won 59–10.

Three years after debuting for Canterbury (whom he had also represented at cricket in 1912–13), he made the All Blacks in the first test of 1913 against Australia in Wellington, although his first start was somewhat blemished by having to leave the field with an injury.

He competed for team selection in North America against Wellington's great halfback Teddy Roberts, but on the 1914 tour of Australia moved to wing to cover for an injured George Loveridge, and finished the tour with 15 tries to his name.

Taylor's name, like that of a fellow 1913 All Black from Christchurch, Alf Fanning, was drawn in the ninth conscription ballot in June 1917, but he does not appear to have entered camp until April 1918. His entire service was spent in New Zealand, at Trentham and Featherston camps, which meant he turned out several times for their army football teams.

After the war, Taylor didn't add to his tally of 46 first-class football games, but he did turn out for Canterbury again in his cricket whites in 1920–21. He served on the New Zealand Cricket Council, and was the manager of the Dominion XI when a team from the M.C.C. (Marylebone Cricket Club) toured New Zealand in 1936.

27 August 1917

ENLISTED: **Rifleman Lancelot Matthew JOHNSON (1897–1983)**
AGE AT ENLISTMENT: 20 years, 18 days
ARMY NUMBER: 71040

EMBARKATION: Wellington, 23 April 1918; A Company, 36th
   Reinforcements
LENGTH OF SERVICE: 1 year, 281 days
PLAYED FOR: Wellington and Celtic; Wellington 1923–25,
   1927, 1929, 1930, 1932; Hawke's Bay 1926; North
   Island 1927, 1929; New Zealand Trials 1927, 1930
ALL BLACK NUMBER: 307
POSITION: Five-eighth
APPEARANCES: 1925, 1928, 1930; 25 matches, including
   4 tests; 19 points (3 tries, 5 conversions)

Johnson was at Southland Boys' High School when the war began, and played for the college First XV in 1915. On turning 20, he was employed as a clerk when he attested at Trentham, and finally joined active service in France a year later in September 1918. He had arrived there via a short stint in the Australian camp in Suez, then sailed from Alexandria to Southampton, from where he went into camp again at Brocton, then across the Channel to Étaples before being posted to the 3rd Battalion of the 3rd New Zealand Rifle Brigade. He had to wait until June 1919 before again walking up the gangway of a ship, only this time to come home.

It was four years before he debuted for the Wellington team and, with members of the Invincibles who had recently returned from the Northern Hemisphere not eligible for the 1925 tour of Australia, Johnson won a place in the side, playing in all eight games, with three starts at first five-eighth and five at second five-eighth.

He wasn't required for home tests against New South Wales late in 1925, or for the tour to Sydney and Victoria in 1926, but he did turn out for Hawke's Bay in several of their Ranfurly Shield defences. Come 1928, he was chosen for the 29-man party which would be the first All Black squad to visit South Africa, and played in 16 of the 23 tour games, including 3 of the test matches.

Johnson had one last game for the All Blacks in 1930, when the team warmed up for the series against the Lions with a match against North Otago, and he served as a selector for Canterbury in 1949–50.

7 September 1917

ENLISTED: **Private James Burt DOUGLAS (1890–1964)**

AGE AT ENLISTMENT: 27 years, 1 month, 27 days

ARMY NUMBER: 69063

EMBARKATION: Wellington, 18 February 1918; A Company,
Auckland Infantry Regiment, 34th Reinforcements

LENGTH OF SERVICE: 1 year, 335 days

PLAYED FOR: Southern; Otago 1912–13, 1915; South Island
1913

ALL BLACK NUMBER: 188

POSITION: Utility forward

APPEARANCES: 1913; 9 matches; 24 points (8 tries)

With a complexion described as 'swarthy' on his army discharge certificate, Douglas certainly had the appearance of what one might call the stereotypical Southern man. But he was also a man prone to injury, and his one tour with the All Blacks (to North America) was interrupted by niggles that meant he played in only 9 of the 16 games.

A hundred years on from that tour, rugby medicine and the welfare of players who have suffered head-knocks is a high priority for those that run the game around the world. Sadly, in 1913, that was not the case. In the match against Victoria B.C., the home fullback Peter Ogden was knocked out early in the first half when fearlessly attempting to stop an All Black forward rush. A purely accidental knee to the side of the head left him lying out cold on the pitch. A few minutes later he came round, stood up and, despite being urged to leave the field, insisted on carrying on. At halftime, the All Black captain Alex McDonald urged the Victoria captain to replace Ogden, but again Ogden himself resisted any attempts to have him removed. Later in the game he was again concussed, and this time, though he continued to play, he did look decidedly dazed. Two minutes before the game ended, he was tackled by Douglas and both men crashed to the ground. Douglas got up and followed play, but Ogden lay prone on the ground for the third time. He was taken to the dressing room where a medic diagnosed 'severe concussion of the brain' and the inquiring All Blacks were told he was slowly coming around again. But, at 7 p.m., the All Black manager, Mr George Mason, was advised that Ogden had died. According to one All Black, 'All festivities were, of course, abandoned, the sad and sudden calamity casting a gloom over the whole city.' Poor Douglas was particularly disturbed by the news and had the very unnerving experience of having to attend a coroner's inquest.

Having begun training at Trentham, Douglas complained of having painful varicose veins in his lower left leg when marching, but this wasn't substantiated by the medical board. He served in France with the Otago Infantry Regiment throughout 1918, falling victim more than once to dysentery.

He played for the Divisional XV and in the King's Cup, which was no doubt a welcome return to rugby after he had been suspended by the Otago Union for allegedly accepting a bribe in a case of rugby match-fixing in 1915.

After the war, he hoped that he might be able to return to the domestic rugby ranks, as many who had turned to league before the war were being welcomed back, but his reinstatement was not allowed.

13 September 1917

ENLISTED: **Rifleman Richard 'Dick' William ROBERTS (1889–1973)**
AGE AT ENLISTMENT: 28 years, 7 months, 21 days
ARMY NUMBER: 81286
EMBARKATION: Wellington, 27 July 1918; F Company, 41st Reinforcements
LENGTH OF SERVICE: 1 year, 177 days
PLAYED FOR: Kaponga, Okaiawa and Hawera clubs; Taranaki 1909–15, 1920–22; North Island 1912–14
ALL BLACK NUMBER: 181
POSITION: Wing

APPEARANCES: 1913–14; 23 matches, including 5 tests,
9 games as captain; 102 points (22 tries, 15 conversions,
2 penalties)

No relation to Teddy Roberts, Dick Roberts was an outside back who had it all: swerve, side-step, a keen tactical eye, a strong tackle and the ability to kick goals. He starred in Taranaki's first-ever Ranfurly Shield win, over Auckland in 1913. On a sunny August afternoon, with a light breeze puffing across Alexandra Park, a crowd of 8,000 saw just what an electrifying player Roberts could be. With barely five minutes gone on the clock, Taranaki were on attack and Roberts received the ball. He kicked over the defending Auckland backs and chased through to force the ball for a try. Then, with the holders leading 11–9 and only a few minutes left on the clock, a sweeping Taranaki move took the ball close to an Auckland corner. The ball came to the midfield where Norkey Dewar ran on to it at pace and, with Roberts on his shoulder, flicked a short pass for the latter to drop over the line for the winning score.

Roberts was one of those wings who would go looking for work across the field. He would call for a pass from the maul, ruck or dribbling rush, and use his speed to get in behind the close-in defenders.

Having shown such dash since his debut for Taranaki in 1909 and made the North Island side in 1912, it was only the simple fact that the All Blacks didn't have any fixtures in the 1911–12 seasons that meant his debut had to wait until 1913, when he was part of the squad to North America. He played in 12 of the 16 high-scoring romps, and scored 14 tries, a total only bettered by 'Tiger' Lynch. With the addition of 9 conversions, his tally of 60 points was the second-highest on tour (behind Otago's goal-kicking forward James Graham, who notched up 66 points, including 24 conversions).

The following year Roberts was appointed captain for the tour of Australia, but he missed the farewell game against Wellington because he hadn't arrived in the capital from up the line. Of the remaining 10 games he played in 9, scoring 7 tries.

Legend has it that 'to a man' the 1914 All Blacks all volunteered for service when they returned to New Zealand. Proof that this was not the case is shown by the fact that Roberts's name was drawn in the tenth conscription ballot, as a reserve from the Wanganui Recruiting District.

A farmer from Aukopae on the Wanganui River, he arrived in London on 4 October 1918 and was posted to Brocton Camp with the New Zealand Rifle Brigade Reserve. Thirty-eight days later the war was over.

He played Services football in the King's Cup and in South Africa, and when home again captained Taranaki for three seasons.

With World War II under way and plans for another army rugby team being made, the *Auckland Star* looked back at the Services players from World War I, and wrote of Dick Roberts as

the type one sees perhaps [once] in a decade — the type that brings the grandstand to its feet by suddenly opening up play from the loose and going over himself, or sending someone else over for a splendid try. This is Rugby in excelsis, although it gives most fullbacks the 'jitters' and others caught on the 'hop'. Old time Rugby fans well remember this player.

4 October 1917

† DIED: **Sergeant David 'Dave' Gallaher** †

On 3 October, Gallaher (see page 145) was with his men as they prepared for an attack on Gravenstafel Spur, an approach to Passchendaele Ridge. The enemy had been silent during the day, but that changed as night descended and sporadic barrages fell around the New Zealand and Australian troops.

Those pre-dawn hours awaiting orders in the trenches are best described by Ormond Burton, who wrote of his time with the Auckland Regiment that during the night a drizzling rain commenced to fall. Through the miserable hours of waiting, men huddled together in the shell-holes, without overcoats, shivering under their oilsheets. All night the German guns searched the slopes, and towards morning their fire became very intense. In the darkness officers and N.C.O.s moved around seeing that all was in place and giving the last instructions. Breakfast was an unappetizing meal of bully beef, dry bread and water, nerves on edge after the ordeal of the night, very tired, counting off the moments until the barrage, half-eager for it to come, yet fearful of the coming, for all know that many must die when the hour strikes. On the other side German soldiers were also waiting to attack ...

At five-thirty in the morning, German artillery began bombarding the Anzac lines, but fortunately much of it was misdirected and fell some distance from where the troops were readying themselves to advance.

At zero hour New Zealand and Australian guns opened fire, providing cover for the infantry to hop the bags and attack the German lines. That shelling decimated large numbers of German infantry. But the advance was not a walkover. The Germans retaliated with a determined charge of their own, one of the few times both sides met with bayonets drawn, and their guns were let loose on the lines of slowly advancing Anzac soldiers.

Burton also recalled the German barrage on the paths the Kiwi soldiers were following:

To either side and clear in view lay dead men blackened by the explosions. Shell after shell shrieked down and burst a few feet on either side, flinging columns of black mud into the air. The nervous strain was a terrible one because it was impossible to hurry and the screaming missiles fell with a machine-like regularity.

It was under this torrent of shelling that Gallaher was struck and fell. As he led his platoon over the top and towards the enemy lines, a shell exploded in front of him. He suffered severe wounds to his face and head, but, like so many that day, he did not die immediately.

The two sides called a truce later in the day, allowing each to tend to their injured and attempt to clear their dead. Private Monty Ingram wrote in his diary that

> enemy Red Cross men can plainly be seen gathering in the dead and wounded on our front. All about us are our own dead and dying, lying in the mud in the drizzling rain. God knows when they will be removed as a vast sea of mud lies between us and the habitable rear from whence the stretcher bearers must come. Most of our own stretcher bearers have 'gone West' and we are physically incapable of removing them ourselves ... A few yards behind our trench lies one of our wounded in delirium. He is on his back, his head resting in his helmet which is a basin of blood; he is making awful grimaces and appears to be choking. Someone goes over to him and discovers that his denture is stuck in his throat and he is certainly choking. The denture is relieved but not before the fingers of the Good Samaritan are severely bitten by the delirious man. We go about tending our wounded, endeavouring to make them more comfortable, though God knows our efforts are but poor relief. All we can do is lay them on a groundsheet, cover them with another sheet and leave them in the drizzling rain and gathering darkness, alone with their thoughts and pain.

In Gallaher's case, he was carried from the battlefield to the 3rd Australian Casualty Clearing Station. His wounds, gruesomely described by one eyewitness as looking as if the side of his head had been kicked in by a horse, were so severe that he passed away before he could be moved off to a field ambulance. He was one of 320 New Zealand soldiers to die that day.

He was buried in the Nine Elms British Cemetery. The cemetery got its name from a small group of trees that was a geographical feature of the area's no-man's-land for the duration of the war. Burials began at the site in September 1917, when the area was used by the 3rd Australian and 44th Casualty Clearing Station.

Gallaher's 1905 teammate Ernie Booth wrote a tribute to his former captain which journalist E.H.D. Sewell included in his 1919 book *The Rugby Football Internationals Roll of Honour*:

> The news of the sad and sudden death of my old skipper 'Dave' has distressed me beyond measure … his last letter came almost simultaneously with the notification of his end. In the letter he states with his usual philosophy (and he was 'some philosopher'), 'Here I am in good health and spirit among the boys; it's like old times again. So far I have a whole skin, though life here, on the whole, is a matter of chance. So long "Old Horse." Heaps of luck and good wishes from your old pal Dave Gallaher.'
>
> In the huge list of fallen International Rugbyites in this gigantic match of 'Right v Might' the name of 'Dave' Gallaher stands out pre-eminently clear for all time.

Later in the month, the Auckland Rugby Union's management committee convened and messages of condolence to Gallaher's wife, Nellie, from the Canterbury and Otago rugby unions were read. The committee members, among them 1905 teammate and fellow Ponsonby personality George Nicholson, then stood as a tribute from the Auckland Rugby Union was read.

11 October 1917

ENLISTED: **Rifleman Alexander James 'Jimmy'**
RIDLAND (1882–1918)
AGE AT ENLISTMENT: 35 years, 7 months, 8 days
ARMY NUMBER: 72271
EMBARKATION: Wellington, 9 May 1918; A Company, 37th
Reinforcements
LENGTH OF SERVICE: 1 year, 1 month
PLAYED FOR: Invercargill Star; Southland 1907–10, 1912–13;
South Island 1909–10, 1913
ALL BLACK NUMBER: 164
POSITION: Utility forward
APPEARANCES: 1910; 6 matches, including 3 tests

The Invercargill blacksmith, who was club captain of Star in 1913, played 22 games for Southland over 6 seasons but never had the opportunity to play in a Ranfurly Shield match, as Southland's only challenges around that time were against Auckland in 1906 (lost 12–48) and Taranaki in 1914 (lost 0–6).

In 1908, Ridland gave a good account of himself in the Southland side that hosted the Anglo-Welsh team at Rugby Park in Invercargill. Following fine form for his club and province in 1909 and 1910, playing in several different forward positions, he participated in the inter-island matches in both those years before being selected for the All Blacks tour to Australia in 1910. Three of his six appearances were in the test matches.

At the annual meeting of the Invercargill Star football club in March 1913, Ridland won the trophy for most consistent player in the 1912 season, with comment being made during the presentation that if 'every player put the same vim into his play as Mr. Ridland did, the team would be at the top of the ladder'.

When, after a hiatus of two seasons, the All Blacks did again assemble for matches, Ridland was controversially omitted not only from the 1913 tour to North America but from the two other test teams which faced the visiting Australians, comprising players who also had not sailed to California. That Ridland was not considered for a front-row position remains puzzling to this day.

When Southland faced the Australians in a midweek match four days after they had lost the first test by 5–30, Ridland proved that he was more than worthy of being in the All Black side for the next test. He was an outstanding participant on a day when Australia battled valiantly to stay in a physical game but ultimately were beaten 8–14.

After his name was drawn in the tenth conscription ballot at the beginning of October 1917, the *Southland Times* reported on his last visit to the factory of his employer, James Macalister Limited. His former workmates

> assembled in the show-room when the horn blew at midday on Saturday to say good-bye to one of their mates, Mr. James Ridland, who leaves for Trentham today. Mr. Ridland was the recipient of a beautiful wristlet watch and pocket shaving outfit from the firm and employees. Mr. John Grant, foreman blacksmith, made the presentation and spoke highly of Mr. Ridland's many good qualities as a workman and shopmate. Mr. Macalister said he had never had a better man in his employ. Jim was an honest and reliable worker, and he was one of Southland's best men at football, so that if he got in a scrum with the Huns he would let them know he was there and do his credit to his country. Mr. Dunbar and Mr. Willets also spoke in hearty terms of Mr. Ridland, who feelingly replied he would try and do his bit.

The day before he left camp in England for France, the 35-year-old had completed a New Zealand Expeditionary Force will form, writing, 'I do not desire to make a will.'

Ridland marched into camp at Étaples on 23 September 1918, and four days later was posted to A Company of the New Zealand Rifle Brigade's 1st Battalion. On 4 November 1918, he was reported missing. (See page 225.)

12 October 1917

Noted military historian Glyn Harper has written of Passchendaele being 'the single bloodiest day in New Zealand's military history'. The New Zealand Division attacked an area known as Bellevue Spur, near the small Belgian village of Passchendaele. The plan was for soldiers to attack German lines following artillery bombardments that cut holes in the defensive lines. But the rain that had been falling for days turned the area into a quagmire and the shelling proved ineffective. When the whistles blew for the soldiers to leave their trenches and attack the enemy, the rain was at its heaviest and waves of men were slowed by having to wade through boggy mud and then got caught up in, or were stopped by, the tangled nests of wire. They were left exposed to gunfire from German pill-boxes and slaughtered.

In the first four hours of the attack, which began at 5.25 a.m., 846 New Zealand soldiers were killed. The dead, wounded and missing totalled more than 2,700 by the end of the day. Stretcher-bearers, medics and other soldiers spent nearly three days clearing casualties from where they had fallen.

Among the wounded was Tom French, who had played for Buller from 1911 to 1913, New Zealand Maoris in 1911 and 1913, and Auckland in 1914. He had been part of the initial Divisional Football team squad, but his days playing rugby ended at Passchendaele when he lost an arm.

15 November 1917

ENLISTED: **Gunner Wallace Frankham SNODGRASS (1898–1976)**
AGE AT ENLISTMENT: 20 years, 6 months, 22 days
ARMY NUMBER: 78780
EMBARKATION: Wellington, 2 October 1918; New Zealand Field Artillery, 43rd Reinforcements
LENGTH OF SERVICE: 1 year, 174 days

PLAYED FOR: Nelson College Old Boys; Hawke's Bay 1917;
    Nelson 1919–32; Nelson–Marlborough–Golden Bay–
    Motueka 1921; South Island 1923, 1927, 1928; New
    Zealand Trials 1924, 1927; Seddon Shield Districts 1926;
    Nelson–Golden Bay–Motueka 1927
ALL BLACK NUMBER: 271
POSITION: Wing-three-quarter
APPEARANCES: 1923, 1928; 3 matches; 13 points (1 try,
    5 conversions)

An all-round sportsman also adept with tennis racquet or oar in hand, Snodgrass was born in Nelson but made his provincial rugby debut for Hawke's Bay in 1917 as a 19-year-old, having been posted to Hastings as a clerk with the Bank of New South Wales.

Later that year he went into camp at Trentham, training for almost a year before finally sailing for England. Once there he was transferred to 41st then 45th then 43rd New Zealand Field Artillery as a gunner, but spent all his time at Sling and Ewshot camps.

After the Armistice, he had a long wait to return to New Zealand, not sailing until September 1919. The frustration obviously became too much for the 21-year old, who was absent without leave for a week from 23.45 hours on 14 June until 03.00 hours on 21 June. The forfeiture of seven days' pay was probably well worth the time he spent away from army routines, though.

Snodgrass returned to provincial rugby in 1920 and faced the 1921 Springboks with the combined Nelson–Marlborough–Golden Bay–Motueka side, taking his place in the XV not as a wing but as a wing-forward.

The first hint that higher honours might be close came in 1923 when Snodgrass was selected for the South Island team, at wing. Weeks after the inter-island encounter, a 6–6 draw, he made his debut for the All Blacks against New South Wales in Dunedin. The match was won 19–9, but wholesale changes were made for the second and third matches and Snodgrass was not used again. Despite playing a trials game in 1924, Snodgrass was not chosen for the trip to Great Britain and returned to club and provincial football. He continued to play with great consistency and made the South Island team again in 1927.

With international tours inbound and outbound in 1928 — the All Blacks to South Africa and New South Wales visiting New Zealand — Snodgrass was named in the team for the first match against the Australian side at Athletic Park, five years after his last appearance. A leg injury caused his withdrawal, but he was back to full fitness in time for the next match the following Saturday. Four days later he took to the field in Greymouth with the All Blacks, who made a very rare appearance on the West Coast, playing a combined West Coast–Buller side. The national side ran way with the game, 40–3. Snodgrass scored 13 points, dotting down for a try and then converting 5 of the 10 tries.

Snodgrass was chosen for the South Island for the third time in 1928, and continued playing for Nelson until 1932.

14 December 1917

ENLISTED: **Corporal Francis 'Frank' Turnbull GLASGOW (1880–1939)**
AGE AT ENLISTMENT: 37 years, 3 months, 27 days
ARMY NUMBER: 79577
LENGTH OF SERVICE: 356 days
PLAYED FOR: Athletic, Hawera, Eltham, Waipawa and Star
   clubs; Wellington 1899–1900; Taranaki 1901–04;
   Hawke's Bay 1906; Southland 1908–09; North Island
   1905
ALL BLACK NUMBER: 117
POSITION: Hooker or side-/back-row forward
APPEARANCES: 1905–06, 1908; 35 matches, including 6 tests;
   43 points (10 tries, 5 conversions, 1 penalty)

When Glasgow's name was drawn out of a conscription ballot in November 1917, he was working as the manager of the Bank of New Zealand (BNZ) in Ohura, outside of Taumarunui. He signed his certificate of enrolment under the Military Service Act of 1916 on 11 July 1917, a month before his thirty-seventh birthday. By that time, he had been transferred by the bank to Kaikohe in the Far North. He finally went into camp to join the 45th Reinforcements in May 1918. (Glasgow's father, James, may well have been from a military family, given that he was born in India.)

The teenage Frank made his provincial debut for Wellington in 1899, having secured a job with the BNZ at Te Aro when was 16, and a year later married Kathleen Davis. Due to his burgeoning career with the BNZ, the couple began a life of regularly being shifted about the country. But wherever he went (Taranaki, Hawke's Bay, Southland), Frank represented that province at football when available. In club matches, he was occasionally known to turn out playing in the backs.

His call-up for the All Blacks came in 1905. That was a year when he does not appear to have played provincial rugby, but the names of potential members of the squad to tour Great Britain had been made at the end of the 1904 season, and after the inter-island match he was included in the party that played matches in Australia and New Zealand, playing in all seven matches, before departing for 'Home'. One of the most consistent players on tour, gradually being used more as a side-row forward than a hooker, Glasgow played in 27 of the 35 games, which was the third-highest tally behind 'Bronco' Seeling (30) and vice-captain Billy Stead (29). He scored nine tries as well as proving handy with the boot, kicking five conversions and a penalty goal.

His final appearance for the All Blacks was as a hooker against the Anglo-Welsh in 1908. He was called into the side for the final of the three tests, at Auckland's Potter's Paddock, having been back playing for only several weeks after recovering from an injury suffered the previous season. The game was easily won, 29–0, with Glasgow being one of the try-scorers, his touchdown coming as the result of an All Black scrum close to the visitors' goal-line.

In September 1918, his final first-class appearance was when he turned out for a Trentham team against Wellington in a match refereed by another 1905 tourist, George Nicholson. Two weeks earlier he had been part of a soldiers' team that had beaten

Canterbury in a Red Cross benefit match at the Christchurch Show Grounds along with fellow All Blacks Henry Morgan and Teddy Roberts. The soldiers won 14–8, reversing a 12–27 loss they had suffered at the hands of the home side in Wellington three weeks earlier.

Glasgow loved sport generally; he was happy to take the referee's whistle, was handy with tennis racquet, golf club or cricket bat in hand, and was known for bowling a slow-break ball that was once described as an 'insidious terror to batsmen'. At the age of 43, while the manager of the Raetihi BNZ, he turned out in a football match between Old Timers and Returned Soldiers and gave a great display of some of the skills that had seen him regarded as one of the country's best when at his peak.

Glasgow remained involved with rugby as the King Country Union delegate and in roles with the national union. As a member of the management committee from 1931 until 1936 he was quite vocal in his opposition to the increasingly used tactics of illegal obstruction and shepherding. When the 1937 Springboks toured he was the liaison officer and served as a member of the NZRFU executive committee. Sadly, he and his parents all died within five years, with James passing away in 1934, then Annie, and finally Frank in 1939. At the time, he was manager of the BNZ in Te Aro and was aged just 58. Teammates of 1905, Billy Wallace, Mona Thomson, Jim O'Sullivan and Alex McDonald, were among those who attended his funeral.

Several years before he died, a Taranaki newspaper wrote of him as

> one of the cleverest forwards Taranaki has known. The forward game was an open book; he could handle like a back and was one of the best dribblers ever. He was never known to play a bad game, his football being of the hard, clean type, and he was a tiger for work. [He] will long be remembered in Taranaki for his sterling play and his popularity on the field. He seemed to always be smiling when playing, and no player found more joy in the game than he.

26–31 December 1917

At the end of 1917, three New Zealand camp teams — A, B and C — played fund-raising matches against English, Welsh and Australian army and navy sides. Vernon Haydon, who had been a reporter with the *Manawatu Daily Times* prior to the war and served with the Medical Corps, met some of the players when he visited Ewshot Camp in Hampshire, England, as he reported in a letter to *The Free Lance* newspaper:

It is snowing outside and bitterly cold, so much so that I sought the comforting warmth of the canteen fire. When I arrived, I 'lobbed' into a nest of Infantry visitors temporarily quartered in the camp. There were five or six of them and I thought their faces were familiar. I had another look and saw the dark, smiling dial of 'Ranji' Wilson grinning at me and next to him Teddy Roberts. They told me they were off on the morrow to play Wales at Swansea on Boxing Day and were going to do their best to avenge the All Blacks.

With 'Ranji' and Roberts were Bilkey, the Auckland rep.; Fitzgerald, another Queen City man who has worn the blue and white on the rep. field; Dan Sullivan, the Melrose player who has been out for a long time and was smacked at Messines; Snowy Adams, an old Athletic player — he had an attack of French fever which confined him to hospital for a little while, but he is well and strong again now; also there were McCarlie, an old Athletic player; Ned Hughes, Southland and New Zealand rep.; Ward Udy and Tom Price from Petone and one or two others.

Some of them had only come over from France on Christmas leave and others have been resting in England. 'Ranji' tells me that the team is a strong one and will give a good account of itself. Five of the seven backs are drawn from the ranks of the Artillery A team here, which has an unbeaten record here and has accounted for several good teams here by large margins. Despite the fact that all these boys have been through the mill, they are fit and well, but all speak of the good time coming when they board ship for the long trail home to New Zealand ... I'm sorry I will not be able to see this game, but I'm off to France to-morrow, and by the time this gets [to] you I will be well in the thick of it.

On Boxing Day, the A side played South Wales at Swansea, in front of 12,000 spectators, winning 8–3 and the B side played the Cardiff Football Club at Cardiff, 14–0. The C team travelled to Northampton to play Australian Headquarters and lost 3–14.

An A and B selection played Newport, losing 5–15. The New Zealanders fell foul of the referee who took 'every opportunity of penalising, especially when their efforts looked as if they would result in a score'. Newport won 15–5, but, more importantly, £200 was raised for the local military hospital.

Those players then travelled to London where they joined the C team and a team was chosen to travel up to Wigan to play the Wigan Football Club. Wigan identity Seeling played tour guide, and the players had the experience of going into a mine as part of their sightseeing. That was probably the best place to be, as the weather during the match, won by the New Zealanders 9–6, was atrocious.

1918

14 January 1918

ENLISTED: **Staff Sergeant Major Frederick 'Fred' Elder Birbeck IVIMEY (1880–1961)**
AGE AT ENLISTMENT: 37 years, 9 months, 17 days
ARMY NUMBER: SA 7913/1st NZEF 66203
EMBARKATION: Wellington, 5 June 1918; B Company, 38th Reinforcements
LENGTH OF SERVICE: 1 year, 329 days
PLAYED FOR: Dunedin, Union, Gore Albion and Invercargill clubs; Otago 1907–10; Southland 1911, 1913; South Island 1908
ALL BLACK NUMBER: 172
POSITION: Side-row forward
APPEARANCES: 1910; 1 match

Ivimey was born in the greater London area. His 1904 attestation for the New Zealand Permanent Force as a member of the Royal New Zealand Artillery lists his date of birth as 27 March 1879, while forms from World War I record it as 1880 (which was later verified by a copy of his birth certificate).

Ivimey served with the Dunedin Engineers Volunteers for three years prior to sailing with the 9th Contingent to the Boer War, and remained attached to the regular army on his return to New Zealand. He worked as a timber tallyman and clerk for John Murdoch and

Company in Dunedin, when not engaged in military affairs in Wellington as a physical and recreational fitness instructor. Moving between the two cities undoubtedly postponed his representative football career until he spent a settled four years in Dunedin and turned out for Otago 17 times. One of the highlights was the 9–6 win over the touring Anglo-Welsh side at Carisbrook in May 1908.

He was included in the 1910 All Black side to tour Australia, but it was a hugely frustrating trip for him, in which, due to recurring injury, he was mainly a spectator, his participation being limited to a single run-on, the least of any of the 22 tourists. His sole appearance was the fourth match in Australia, the second played against Queensland. The All Blacks won 21–3.

Ivimey moved to Invercargill and turned out a couple of times for Southland in 1911 and 1913. In July 1914, he married Flora Mackay, and they had a daughter, Dora, who was 15 months old at the time of her father's enlistment.

Holding the rank of staff sergeant major, warrant officer first-class, he spent two months at Sling before crossing the English Channel and joining troops at Étaples and then at the front.

A confidential report written by his lieutenant colonel in January 1919 remarked that Ivimey

> has served under my command since 16th October, 1918. He is a hard worker, thoroughly conscientious and reliable, and a very able instructor. He was in two engagements, in which he showed great coolness and courage and sound judgement, and had the war continued, I would certainly have recommended him for a commission.

Ivimey sailed from Liverpool for New Zealand in July 1919, and remained with the army, employed as an instructor. In 1922, a report on officers who had undertaken specialist training with the Hotchkiss gun noted that Ivimey was 'very attentive and pain-staking. Good style when teaching.'

When the world again went to war in 1939, Ivimey was still employed by the New Zealand Army and signed up for temporary staff service in New Zealand, his third answering of the call to duty.

31 January 1918

ENLISTED: **Rifleman William Rognvald FEA (1898–1988)**

AGE AT ENLISTMENT: 19 years, 3 months, 26 days

ARMY NUMBER: 74721

EMBARKATION: Wellington, 10 July 1918; 40th Reinforcements Specialist Company

LENGTH OF SERVICE: 1 year, 353 days

PLAYED FOR: University; Otago 1920–23; New Zealand Universities 1920–22; South Island 1920, 1922

ALL BLACK NUMBER: 248

POSITION: Five-eighth

APPEARANCES: 1921; 1 test

Fea listed his occupation as 'farmer' when he enlisted nine months short of his twentieth birthday. The son of parents born in Scotland's Orkney Islands, he served as a rifleman in the New Zealand Rifle Brigade. On the way to Britain with the 40th Reinforcements aboard the troopship *Tahiti*, a boxing match was organised. In one corner was Fea, in the other a fellow rifleman and budding pugilist by the name of Tom Heeney. Given that at the time Fea was 3 inches (8 centimetres) shorter than Heeney and 15 pounds (7 kilograms) lighter, it must have been an interesting contest!

Fea arrived at Larkhill in September 1918, and two weeks later was hospitalised for almost a month suffering a severe case of dysentery. He recovered to play for the army football team contesting the King's Cup, and from there was selected for the New Zealand Services side — he was, in fact, the youngest member of the team that visited South Africa. His military career ended when he was discharged due to illness, having become sick with enteritis after the South Africa trip.

After the war, he studied medicine, and his university commitments ultimately cut short his rugby career. He debuted for Otago in 1920, and the following year made a single appearance for the All Blacks, in the scoreless third test against the Springboks. Playing outside him was another gifted one-test All Black, Karl Ifwersen.

One of the consistent criticisms of Fea's provincial play was his at times excessive use of short kicks behind defenders, but he was nonetheless an exciting five-eighth with ball in hand, who seemed to break past the first tackler or two with ease.

It is fair to say that All Black fans did not see the best of Fea, who in 1922 captained his club, his province, the South Island team in the annual inter-island match (won 9–8) and the New Zealand Universities team. Unfortunately he had to declare himself unavailable for all rugby after the 1923 season as he worked towards completing his studies at the end of 1924.

Upon graduation he moved to private practice in Timaru, but still found time to coach Timaru High School Old Boys from 1926 to 1930. The following year-and-a-half was spent in London doing post-graduate work, and after returning to Timaru he won the New Zealand squash championship in 1936 and 1937 before moving to Hamilton in 1938.

In May 1939, he volunteered for the Royal New Zealand Army Medical Corps and served as lieutenant colonel with the 8th Field Ambulance. He was involved in rugby during World War II when he selected the 7th Brigade Group team in 1942.

2 February 1918

In the Middle East, as the weather began to cool, organised rugby resumed and a Brigade Tournament was played in Palestine. The following account appeared in the *Chronicles of the NZEF*, on 13 March 1918:

Auckland Wins Divisional Championship
Operations in general are of a peaceful nature at present, and, of course, football is the long suit. Saturday, February 2, saw the finish of the Brigade Tournament, Auckland gaining the honour. The Aucklanders played well throughout in some well-contested games;

and, considering they only had one win of 3 to nil (against Canterbury) marks well the evenness of the Brigade teams.

The results of the Tournament are:

Auckland	13 points
Composite	10 points
Canterbury	10 points
Wellington	8 points

Conspicuous among the Aucklanders were Lieut. Hatrick, Cpl. Alexander; Tprs. Finlayson, Waldron and Nelson; and Farrier Dwyer made a very efficient captain.

For Composite, Lieuts. Picot and Brownlea were responsible for splendid work.

For Canterbury, Sgts. Burns and Gleeson defended well the honours of their team.

Wellington produced two sound players, in Sgts. Scott and Whibbley.

We are now playing a Divisional Tournament, and great interest is being taken. The first two matches were played on the 6th; A.M.R. v. 1st A.L.H., a draw, after a real hard game; and 6th A.L.H. v Composite, a win for the former by 3 to nil, after a good game.

A great crowd watched these games, the G.O.C. among them. The A.M.R. Band gave us good music in the intervals.

17 February 1918

Rugby teams of the French and New Zealand armies met for the second time in Paris. The result was nothing like the 40–0 victory for New Zealand in the first meeting. This time the Kiwis, who had warmed up with a 14–3 win over the 38th Welsh Division, scraped home by 5–3, with Lieutenant Colonel Plugge admitting afterwards that 'The better team lost.' Captaining France was the Algerian-born Maurice Boyau. He had represented France as a flanker immediately before the war, leading the side in two of his six tests. During the war, having started his service as a driver, he trained as a pilot and became a flying ace, decorated with the Médaille Militaire and the Légion d'Honneur for shooting down several dozen enemy planes and observation balloons. Seven months after the rugby match, he was killed in action. A statue of Boyau in his aviator uniform stands outside the stadium named after him in Dax, in southwest France.

Jean-Jacques Conilh de Beyssac, a tank commander, was a five-test veteran playing as lock or a side-row forward. One of the stand-out home players on the cold afternoon, he was killed in action on 13 June 1918.

The daughter of General Russell started the match by kicking off, and the referee was a Lieutenant Muir of the US Army. He played only 30 minutes in the first 'half', so 45 minutes was played in the second period.

There is an old story that after one of the matches in Paris in 1918, 'an older All Black' woke early in the morning to find himself with what felt to be a beautiful but stone-cold woman. He got the fright of his life. Was she dead? More light revealed that it was a large statue of Venus that his teammates had seconded from the hotel foyer and put in bed with him when they had tucked their mate into bed after a late night.

Meanwhile, in England the New Zealand Field Artillery team were proving to be the strongest of the New Zealand camp teams, which drew attention to it but also criticism of their play from E.H.D. (Edward Humphrey Dalrymple) Sewell, a former first-class cricketer turned journalist who had devoted much ink to the 1905 All Black tour. In a report on their match against Public Schools he wrote for the *Winning Post*:

> It is not that the 'official' programme did not profess to be punctilious, for it advertised the kick-off for 2.35; the odd five minutes, doubtless, being chucked in to allow for lateness of postal and train services. The kick-off took place at 3.10 or thereabouts, which was really pretty good considering practically the whole of both teams was present at 2.30.
>
> Trolly [referee] was very 'whistly.' He seemed to have made up his mind that the N.Z. people had made up theirs to beat him with 'foot up.' A great many of his numerous 'frees' were well deserved and none more than a glaring kick-out (which seemed likely to have beaten

him, in such a way was it worked), but I saw a clear half-dozen cases of 'foot-up' in which the Schools and not N.Z. ought to have been penalised!

His 'running' of the game was a little on the lines of that Dallas at Cardiff, in N.Z. v Wales, Dec., 1905, and the game suffered in consequence.

As against this it must be said that the wing-forward, N.Z. shape, will always be a source of whistling over here with ninety and nine per cent of our referees. We have often said we do not see eye to eye with them as to this position, and we never shall.

Experienced people tell me the N.Z. wing-forward properly played is Rugby football. Well, then, I have never seen it played properly.

On Saturday the wing was actually 'handling off' the Schools' half when the ball was on the ground! That is not, and never was, Rugby football.

My experienced friends will tell me that this wing-forward was not a good player. In my ignorance he was as good a player in the position as the departed David Gallaher. Does N.Z. think D.G. played the wing-forward game properly? I presume so.

Anyway, on the form of Saturday this N.Z. 'unbeaten' team is not in the first four now playing.

On that form it would lose every time to the Royal Naval Division, Devonport, to the R.N.D., Crystal Palace, to the Australian Headquarters side, and presumably, therefore to the Welsh Guards, who beat the Crystal Palace lot (who were without J.J. Coughlan I believe) on Saturday, 3 tries to nil. The C.P. side is running stale and may have had enough of it for a bit.

The incessant punting into touch on Saturday was a thing no good N.Z. side is ever guilty of. The N.Z. onlookers thought so — and said so — too, often advising their men to have a go for the line; advice I have never before known to be necessary in the case of these highly educated Rugger players.

Perhaps the whistle put them out of humour with themselves. Anyway, two flashes, the all-round backing up, fire, and dash of their forwards, and one glorious pass in the first-half (this pass won the match for them) apart, it was not N.Z. Rugger that we saw in this booting-into-touch competition.

Nonetheless, the New Zealand Field Artillery team would go on to win the Aldershot Command Rugby Tournament, defeating the Canadian Infantry Reserve (Bramshott), 22–0.

On the same weekend the New Zealand Rifle Brigade team lost to Public Schools at Richmond, the New Zealand Field Artillery B team defeated the Royal Airforce Factory team at Farnborough, and the New Zealand Headquarters team defeated an Australian team at Norbury.

6 April 1918

Canterbury played Returned Soldiers at a now potato-free Lancaster Park, a benefit game for the Salvation Army and the Lady Liverpool War Comforts fund. The Cantabrians won, 27–0.

9 April 1918

† DIED: **Sergeant Hubert Sydney 'Jum' Turtill** †

While serving with the 422nd Field Company of the Royal Engineers in the defence of Givenchy, Turtill (see page 36) was killed by a burst of shrapnel. He is buried in the Brown's Road Military Cemetery.

Although he had changed rugby codes, he was not forgotten by old friends in Christchurch, and at a meeting of the Canterbury Rugby Union in June 1918 an adjournment was called in his honour.

After the war, Turtill's wife, Mabel, and son, Alan, returned to their old hometown of Christchurch, where one of Turtill's brothers was still living in Riccarton, while another was in Greymouth.

The tragedy of global conflict struck the family again during World War II when son Alan, a New Zealand army captain, lost his life in North Africa in 1941.

30 April 1918

† DIED: **Trooper 'Dean' Eric Tristram Harper** †

The *Official History of the Canterbury Mounted Rifles* records what happened on this day in the Middle East as:

> a strong reconnaissance developed into a big fight. The object was to envelop the right of the enemy forces at Shunet Nimrin and capture Es Salt. The troops engaged were the 60th Division, the Australian Mounted Division and the Anzac Division. The infantry were to attack Shunet Nimrin while the Australian Mounted Division ascending the hills to Es Salt attacked the strong force of Turks holding the foothills at Shunet Nimrin. The advance over the plain was made under heavy shellfire from Shunet Nimrin, and both the infantry and the Canterbury Regiment were held up by strong posts of the enemy in the foothills. Casualties were heavy and the Regiment lost forty-five horses, besides a number slightly wounded.

It was while attempting to calm beloved horses during a night barrage that Harper (see page 165) was killed by an exploding shell. His name is listed on the Jerusalem Memorial, within the Jerusalem War Cemetery, along with 3,300 Commonwealth servicemen who have no known grave, but at the time of Harper's death a burial was carried out by a Reverend A. McDonald at Es Salt, near to where he had been killed.

When news reached New Zealand of his death, formal tributes and condolences were offered to Harper's father, George, by a number of Christchurch organisations, including the Automobile Association and the Spreydon Borough Council, for whom he was borough solicitor.

In the Christchurch courts, *The Press* reported that:

Mr TAB Bailey SM said that before beginning business he would like to express on behalf of his colleague and himself deep sorrow at the loss that the legal profession had sustained in the death of Trooper Eric Harper. Trooper Harper, he said, was a young man of great promise, and he could not let the occasion pass without expressing sympathy with his parents, widow, and family. Members of the legal profession present stood in silence during the time that the Magistrate was making his remarks.

9 May 1918

ENLISTED: **Corporal Alexander 'Alex' McDONALD (1883–1967)**
AGE AT ENLISTMENT: 35 years, 16 days
ARMY NUMBER: 87771
LENGTH OF SERVICE: 6 months, 15 days
PLAYED FOR: Kaikorai; Otago 1904, 1906–09, 1911–14, 1918–19; South Island 1904–07, 1913; Otago–Southland 1904
ALL BLACK NUMBER: 128
POSITION: Side- or back-row forward
APPEARANCES: 1905–08, 1913; 41 matches, including 8 tests; 14 games as captain; 50 points (16 tries, 1 conversion)

The final All Black to enlist, McDonald's involvement came via a conscription ballot.

One of the most-capped All Blacks prior to World War I, McDonald made his debut in 1905 — playing 20 games on the Originals tour — and then continued to represent his country through the tour to Australia in 1908 and a home test against the Anglo-Welsh in 1908. Some eyebrows were raised when he was not only recalled to the team in 1913 for the tour to North

America, but chosen to captain the side, which he did in 14 of the 16 unbeaten games.

McDonald had first played senior club football aged just 17, and captained Otago for 9 seasons including their 9–6 win over the 1908 Anglo-Welsh side. Having suffered a season-ending leg injury in 1909, McDonald considered retirement, but was convinced to turn out again for Kaikorai and his return to full fitness saw further provincial and national honours bestowed on him.

When captaining Otago against South Island Country in August 1911, he allegedly directed an 'insulting expression' at the referee, 'Mr Otago Rugby' himself, Jimmy Duncan. The matter only came to light when Duncan — former captain of the All Blacks and controversial 'coach' of the 1905 Originals — caught the ear of an Otago Rugby Union official at the dinner following the game. McDonald was initially suspended from playing by the Otago union until the end of 1912. The dispute went to the NZRFU and the suspension was eventually overturned.

Employed by J. Speight & Co as a cooper, this son of parents from Inverness in Scotland had his army medical examination in May 1918. McDonald wrote that he had suffered a back injury 11 years prior, and 9 years earlier had an injury to his right leg which had troubled him ever since. That injury kept him out of football in 1910, the only year between 1904 and 1914 that he didn't turn out for Otago.

The doctor examining McDonald commented on the examination form that he: 'Complains of pain and loss of power [in] right leg and foot resulting from old injury. Purely subjective. Examination of limbs reveals nothing.'

He was classified C1 — likely to become fit for active service after special training — and at the start of September McDonald made his way north from Dunedin to Trentham. After being in camp for only four days, he was again examined by a doctor who wrote on his record that 'He is an "All Black footballer".'

On the day of the Armistice being declared overseas, McDonald was admitted to Trentham hospital suffering from influenza and he was kept there for 11 days. Several days after his release from hospital, he was discharged from the army. An undated handwritten note in his file reads: 'Never complains. Seems fit. A very good man.'

Once his playing days were over, McDonald remained heavily involved in the administration of the game. He served on the Otago Rugby Football Union management committee (1920–28) before moving to Wellington, where he coached Wellington College Old Boys in their championship win of 1933. His roles with the NZRFU included selector (1929–32, 1944–48), member of the management committee (1935–36), council member (1937–50) and assistant manager of the All Blacks (Australia 1938, and South Africa 1949). Such dedication to the union saw him made a life member in 1951, making him one of the most respected men involved in the New Zealand game.

11 September 1918

† DIED: **Lance Sergeant Ernest 'Ernie' Henry Dodd** †

The Battle of Trescault Spur, part of the ferociously contested Hindenberg Line in northern France, saw the New Zealand Rifle Brigade (NZRB) making a preliminary attack on German lines on 9 September in preparation for a greater assault by the New Zealand Division and Allied forces three days later. The area, including the ominously named 'Dead Man's Corner', was a mix of wooded areas and trench systems, and from their points of slight elevation German machine gunners ruled over the area. The battle on the night of 9 September was fierce, with the NZRB being repelled by German artillery, the aforementioned machine gunners and even some bombs dropped from a plane. It was during two days of relative calm, for want of a better term, and the solidification of NZRB positions that Dodd (see page 200) was killed, a sniper's bullet piercing his throat.

Dodd is one of 43 Kiwis buried in the Metz-en-Couture Communal Cemetery.

27 October 1918

The Divisional Team played another match in Paris against France, winning 14–0. At a dinner reception in the evening, the New Zealanders were toasted as being 'the champions of the world'. Each player received a pocket wallet from the French Rugby Union, and the team was presented with a vase valued at 2,000 francs (this sounds like a lot but the war had greatly devalued the French currency).

Further matches were played against Tarbes and Bordeaux. Two long days were spent at Amiens train station, waiting 15 hours the first day and 10 hours the next for a train to return them to Divisional Headquarters at Beauvois.

5 November 1918

† DIED: **Rifleman Alexander James 'Jimmy' Ridland** †

Ridland (see page 239) was the thirteenth and final former All Black to be killed in World War I. In the thirteenth month of service since his enlistment, he was reported missing on 4 November 1918, as the New Zealand Rifle Brigade famously liberated the walled village of Le Quesnoy in France. Having surrounded the ramparts, they then scaled them with ladders and overwhelmed the enemy stationed within.

The following day Ridland was found barely alive, having been shot in the head. He was taken to the 3rd Casualty Clearing Station, where he died shortly after. Ridland is buried in the Caudry British Cemetery, one of 53 Kiwis there. Meticulous Western Front historian Ian McGibbon has observed that in that cemetery there are 23 men who died in the last week of the war.

11 November 1918

Armistice Day. The war was officially over. It had claimed the lives of 18,166 New Zealanders. In the eight-month campaign at Gallipoli 2,779 died, of whom 1,684 have no known grave. Sinai and Palestine saw the deaths of 381. The Western Front of France and Belgium was to be the final resting place for 12,483 Kiwis. A third of them have no known grave. Others died in training, while serving with other forces, or of injuries suffered while on active service.

After the War

28 November 1918

A New Zealand Expeditionary Force (NZEF) Sport Control Board was formed to be 'responsible for the organising of inter-unit sport — football (Rugby and Association), hockey and boxing — during the armistice and demobilisation period in the depots'.

The board also decided that the 'All Black' team — which would contest a series of international matches against England, Scotland, Wales, Ireland, Australia and South Africa — should be selected from the whole of the NZEF in France and the United Kingdom. The very best players were needed to 'uphold the reputation of New Zealand'.

Ten trial games were played before two NZEF United Kingdom teams — A and B — were chosen. From those 30 players a final XV was selected to play the Divisional Team from France. The final NZEF XV would be chosen from those two teams. However, the players from France were delayed in making it across the Channel, so the United Kingdom team faced Wales (a side itself containing 12 former internationals) in what had become an annual Boxing Day match, with the beneficiary of the gate-takings to be the Welsh Fund for Widows and Orphans.

The side warmed up with wins over the Royal Navy (Harwich), 30–6, and Public Schools Services, 16–0. The match against Wales, at Swansea, drew a crowd of 30,000, which proved difficult to keep from encroaching on the playing field, particularly when a Welsh winger scored the only points of the match for a 3–0 win to the home team.

1 January 1919

On New Year's Day 1919, the NZEF United Kingdom XV again played Wales. The home side had only three players from the previous match, whereas the 'All Blacks' had only two changes to personnel. Bad weather spoiled any chance of an open game and it ended 3–3, both teams having scored a try.

Following their return to Hornchurch, the players who had been based in England joined with the players who had represented the Divisional XV in France to prepare for matches to be played around Britain.

Lieutenant Ernest 'Ernie' Booth, who had played for the All Blacks in 1905–07 and then for New South Wales in 1908–09, was working for the YMCA in English army camps and as a journalist during the war. Thinking that, with rugby's general hiatus at an end, it would be the perfect time to make some changes to the rules of the game, he wrote an article titled 'Rugby football as it might be', which appeared in the *Chronicles of the NZEF* at the start of 1919. It is interesting to see which of Booth's ideas (not solely held by him) were later included in the rules of the game, and which remain sources of contention.

> Peace has brought to all and sundry a fitting time and opportunity for reconstruction. Among all players and the football public generally there is a demand for improvements and alteration in the present much too complex laws of the game.
>
> As an old player, and theorist, and one who has keenly watched the evolution of the game in Britain, New Zealand, Australia, and America, I here set forth what appears to be the most popular and rational recommendations. Their adoption would certainly promote better understanding, give standardisation, make more open, spectacular play, suppress illegalities, and give fuller advantage to a trained team.

1. That the number of players on both sides be reduced to fourteen men — seven forwards, seven backs.

2. That the scrum be standardised by the universal adoption of the New Zealand style, 2-3-2 being the best for the following reasons:
    (a) Rapidity of formation, i.e. 'packing'; (b) it is unequalled for wheeling and screwing; (c) there is less liability for 'foot up' trouble; (d) every man can see the placing of the ball in the scrum; (e) it prevents present 'loose head' troubles; (f) it prevents centre-row front-rankers 'swinging' across, i.e. a movement introduced here by the Wallabies in 1908–09.

3. That the playing time be divided into four equal quarters of not less than twenty minutes' duration; quarter and three-quarter time merely constituting time to change ends. (This will equalise all possible climatic advantages.)

4. That the referee shall put the ball in all scrums. This procedure is the best for these reasons:
    (a) It is most equitable for both sides; (b) it prevents illegal 'putting in'; (c) it leaves scrum-halves in equal position; (d) it keeps referees up with play.

5. That three points only be allowed for a dropped-goal, and that one point be granted for every two 'force downs'.

6. That the throw-in from touch be at least five yards, and that a disjointed line of demarcation (spots, small-length lines), be made the length of the field running parallel with touch-line.

7. That a 'free-kick' be so literally; i.e. —
    (a) No charge permitted; (b) kicker can be placer; (c) kicker can kick over mark; (d) kick must be taken ten yards back; (e) modicum of time allowed.

8. That wing forward be abolished.

9. That no player on either side shall advance past an imaginary line parallel with the rear of the scrum.
    (a) This prevents illegal work on the part of the scrum-halves.
    (b) Gives distance between outstanding halves.

10. That unintentional 'knock-ons,' provided the player recovers the ball before it touches the ground, be permitted, and constituting — in the case of a fair catch — a fair mark.

11. That any fair catch immediately claimed as a 'mark' by the catcher, even if he should be off the ground, be allowed.
12. That 'passing off the ground' be allowed. (The present ruling is merely an unnecessary hindrance to continuance of play.)
13. That any player pushing an opponent with one or both hands, except in case of 'finding' in running, be penalised by a free kick.
14. That one man of either side in position constitute a scrum, the referee to at once place ball between them.

There is need for universal ruling in the following cases. The Colonial interpretation is as follows:

Any player taking a pass ball thrown forward by one of his own side is adjudged off-side, and a free kick is awarded.

All 'lying on the ball' is penalised by free kick. Players in possession on the ground must immediately part with ball or play with his feet.

Recommendations:
The 'Advantage Rule' should be more liberally dealt with, and small technical illegalities pass without stoppage of play.

That for important matches an extra ball be held in readiness on each touch-line.

That the goal-post be erected at least three yards back from the goal-line, with frontal 'outriggers' or extensions carrying continued upright posts. This is an American idea, and saves collisions with goal-posts.

That touch-line umpires have power to report rough play or infringements.

January to April 1919

Despite the war being at an end, tens of thousands of men were still under the employ of their respective armies and awaiting their demobilisation, not only back to New Zealand, but to the other countries in the Dominion. In the case of New Zealand, ships had been able to traverse the seas from south to north and north to south carrying the latest month's reinforcements or returning those whose service had been ended by disability, but there simply wasn't the availability of vessels to move all the men virtually at once.

So they remained in camp, with reluctance and frustration. Forfeiture of pay was no deterrent to being absent without leave, particularly when the reason the men had joined the army — to fight — was no longer part of their thinking. The restless, waiting men had to be distracted and entertained, and organised sport was one way to do that. (As it happened, drunken New Zealand troops at Sling Camp rioted over several days in March 1919.)

The War Office mooted the idea of an 'Army Football Competition (Rugby)' in January 1919, and the following month representatives of the various national forces met in London to plan a tournament of fixtures to be played around Britain. They would be a celebration, for players and spectators, of unity, mateship, sport and the end of hostilities. The British Army side (made up of English, Welsh and Scottish soldiers) played under the moniker of 'Mother Country', while the Royal Air Force were just that. The Royal Navy couldn't muster a team of sufficient quality to be included.

The ear of rugby fan King George V twitched when he heard of the plans, and he offered to donate an eponymous cup, thus elevating the competition to something more than a mere festival of matches. National pride was now at stake back on the sporting field, and although the NZRFU had no involvement, the reputation of the game they governed was under threat.

The Maori Pioneer Battalion were based at Larkhill, and there a football team was selected that played three matches: against the Royal Naval Division, Devonport, won 6–3; against Swansea at Swansea, won 9–0; and against Llanelli, lost 0–6.

The New Zealand Services team had already begun playing matches in and around England against both services and club teams. In fact, two teams were being fielded, made up of the players listed below, and on more than one occasion the 'All Blacks', as newspapermen called them, would be playing at the same time but on different grounds. (The players and matches that constituted the King's Cup are in *italic* below.)

Pte. P. Allen, Sgt. F.P. Arnold, Rfn. E.A. Belliss, Gnr. R.W. Bilkey, *Sgt. C. Brown, Sap. J.A. Bruce, Pte. M. Cain, Bom. C.H. Capper,* Lieut. E.A. Cockroft, *Sgt. E.L.J. Cockroft,* Sgt. A. Cooke, *Pte. J. Douglas, Rfn. W.R. Fea, Sgt. R. Fogarty, Rfn. W.A. Ford, Gnr. A. Gilchrist,* Sgt. E.C. Grey, Cpl. F.M.H. Hansen, *Gnr. E.W. Hasell, Pte. W.L. Henry,* Sgt. F. Juno, *Sap. J. Kissick, Gnr. A.A. Lucas,* Bom. C.A. McCombie, Lieut. D.A. McGibbon, *Lieut. G.J. McNaught, Sgt. J.E. Moffitt,* Lieut. A. Munro, Cpl. H.V. Murray, *Sgt. E.J. Naylor, Sap. J.G. O'Brien, Bom. G. Owles, Rfn. R.W. Roberts, Cpl. E. Ryan, S.S.M. J. Ryan [Captain], Pte. D.M. Sandman, Sap. R. Sellars, Pte. A.P. Singe, Gnr. S.J. Standen, Pte. L.B. Stohr, Sgt. P.W. Storey, Sgt. C.W. Tipene,* Cpl. P. Tureia, *Sgt. E. Watson, Drv. A.H. West, Cpl. H.G. Whittington, Sgt. A. Wilson,* Cpl. G.A.T. Yardley.

  25 January v Royal Naval Division, Devonport 0–0
  1 February v Monmouthshire, Cross Keys 22–3
  8 February v United Services, Torquay 9–0
  19 February v Canadian Forces, Chiswick 12–0
  20 February v South African Forces, Richmond 26–5
  22 February v Coventry RFC, Coventry 14–0
  26 February v Australian Imperial Forces, Richmond 9–0
  1 March v Royal Air Force, Swansea 22–3
  8 March v Canadian Forces, Portsmouth 11–0
    v Yorkshire, Bradford 44–5
  15 March v a British XV, Leicester 11–3
  19 March v Royal Air Force XV, Richmond 3–0
  22 March v Gloucester RFC, Gloucester 15–12
  29 March v South African Forces, Twickenham 14–5

This last match was the first time a New Zealand team played at Twickenham. The 1905 All Blacks had played at Crystal Palace, with estimates of the crowd side ranging wildly from 40,000 to 100,000. In 1906, similar crowds flocked to see the first Springbok side to play in London. Then, after nearly 40 years of playing international rugby, the English Rugby Union decided that it was time to buy land for their own venue. The land that was purchased in south London in 1907 was a market garden, best known for its cabbage production, giving the venue its first nickname, 'The cabbage patch'.

The stadium, with a capacity of 24,000, had opened in January 1910, with an international between England and Wales, and it became the home of the Harlequins rugby club. The major criticism was the location of the ground, some distance from central London.

With the advent of war, the English Rugby Union suspended play and the arena became a horse paddock, the long, low stands on the eastern and western touchlines looking out on a weedy terrain where horses grazed the days away.

> 29 March v Cardiff RFC, Cardiff 0–0
> 2 April v Maesteg, Maesteg 8–3
> *5 April v Mother Country, Edinburgh 6–3*

The ground at Inverleith, Edinburgh, was the home of Scottish rugby from 1871 to 1925. Although it was the first purpose-built home ground for a member of the Home unions, after sitting disused during the war, apart from the occasional army rugby game, it was looking a bit shabby. Still, with war over, an enormous crowd packed the ground to watch the King's Cup matches.

> 8 April v Abertillery RFC, Abertillery 3–0
> *9 April v Australian Imperial Forces, Bradford 5–6*

The only loss for the New Zealand side came against the Australians, a team that was captained by Nelson-born Bill Watson, who had represented Australia from 1912 to 1914. He had played in four test matches against the All Blacks (three in 1913 and one in 1914). During the war he was awarded the DCM and MC and bar.

Another New Zealand-born player was 43-year-old Jim Clarken. Originally from Thames, he had visited New Zealand with the 1905 Australians and had faced the All Blacks in Australia in 1910. He toured California and British Columbia with the Australians in 1912.

> 9 April v Cross Keys, RFC, Cross Keys 6–0
> 12 April v Pill Harriers RFC, Newport 0–0

15 April v Ogmore Vale RFC, Newport 12–7
16 April v Mother Country, Twickenham 9–3

English newspapers' sports pages gave the matches, and the New Zealand team's victory, great coverage as sampled below:

Morning Post
New Zealand laid its plans admirably, and in astuteness and generalship one has never seen tactics so admirably carried out, not even by the Welsh teams ... They set out to play a particular game and played it. They had a sterling set of forwards, who could shove and break quickly, and could hold the ball if they chose. And they never gave the brilliant Mother Country back division a chance.

Daily Mail
The victors played their typical game to perfection, especially in the second half, and they rushed and bustled our men off their legs. They succeeded and have now achieved their supreme ambition, the winning of the King's Challenge Cup. The Army's backs, clever as they were, did not get many chances and they spoiled some of those by knocking on.

Daily Telegraph
We would have no rugby football that was not all iron; this about which I write was tremendous in its insistence that there should not be a single breather. It was a succession of bangs, and to the mind, not more than ordinarily imaginative, it supplied the secret of many of the imperishable stories the war has given us. There were moments when the two packs set one alight with enthusiasm. They ran and worked like Trojans. The New Zealanders did not suggest a perfect machine; most of their movements were plain and conventional — their backs especially did not bring out the poetry of Rugby football — but as a team brimful of determination and indifferent to all else except to finish winners of the most memorable tournament in the history of a great, great game, they were giants every one of them.

Sporting Life
The Army did well at times, but there were practically none of
the passing bouts which had caused so much trouble to previous
opponents. The black-garbed men saw to that. As a matter of fact,
no latitude was allowed on either side ... Spectators saw a dour,
determined struggle between two sides with but a single thought —
the winning of the championship, and incidentally, the trophy.

With the cup competition complete, the New Zealanders, as winners,
returned to Twickenham to play the French Army side. Before the
game, King George V presented James Ryan with the cup, officially
called the Inter-Services and Dominion Forces Championship Rugby
Football Challenge Cup.

19 April v French Army, Twickenham 20–3

The side then continued on their way around the British Isles,
winning all but their final game.

19 April v Neath RFC, Neath 15–0
21 April v Wales, Swansea 6–3
22 April v Abergavenny RFC, Abergavenny 20–0
23 April v Ebbw Vale RFC, Ebbw Vale 28–0
    v Coventry RFC, Coventry 47–0
27 April v Queen's University, Belfast 18–0
    v United Services, Salisbury 20–7
3 May v Devonshire, Torquay 14–0
4 May v Tredegar RFC, Tredegar 8–0
    v A French XV, Colombes 16–10
5 May v Monmouthshire, Ebbw Vale 3–4

Although it was widely regarded as the New Zealand Army side, the
team did not include players who had been stationed in the Middle
East. (The service records of two men, Mick Lomas and James
Barrett, who had been serving in Palestine, show that there was some
intention to make the team a truly inclusive NZEF team. They
travelled back to England but were not included in the final squad.)

Indeed, the fact that no one serving outside of England or France was included was of some annoyance to those in the desert who read of the team in troop newspapers and considered themselves worthy of selection.

The troops in the desert did play their own competitions, of course, one of which has had lasting resonance in New Zealand football. At Ismaïlia in January 1919, a tournament was established featuring five Australian teams, four British teams and one New Zealand team. At stake was the Moascar Cup, a trophy which included in its base part of a propeller of an enemy plane that had been shot down in the desert.

The Kiwis won with a record of 9 wins and 1 draw, scoring 147 points and only conceding 3. Further matches were played against South African and Welsh teams. One story has it that the match reports were lost somewhere on the return to New Zealand, but fortunately the cup was not.

The members of the team that won the tournament and the trophy were: H.A. Quartermain (*captain*), J. Jobson, H.J. Higgs, W.G. Smith, A.D. Higgie, C.S. Smith, G.W. Conrad, J. Jenkins, A.G. Macauley (Wellington Mounted Rifles), G. Carter, R.N. Snow, H.J. Ward, R.G. Buyers, T.W. Gleeson (Canterbury Mounted Rifles), C.H. McManus, R.G. Halstead, H.W. Waldron, L.H. Wynyard, O. Finlayson, L.H. Alexander, C.G. Brown (Auckland Mounted Rifles), A.H. McAldon, V.H. Thomas, G.J. Oliver (1st Machine Gun Squadron), L.A. Harris (2nd Machine Gun Squadron).

May to October 1919

Following the King's Cup success, New Zealand Army Headquarters in London accepted an invitation from their South African counterparts, at the urging of the Transvaal Rugby Union, for the Services side to play in the Republic on their way back to New Zealand. All players received temporary promotion to sergeant, sergeant-major or staff sergeant.

The team was: Sgt. E.A. Belliss, S./Sgt. C. Brown, Sgt. J.A. Bruce, Sgt. M. Cain, S./Sgt. E.L.J. Cockroft, Sgt. W.R. Fea, S./

Sgt. R. Fogarty, Sgt. W.A. Ford, Sgt. A. Gilchrist, S./Sgt. E.W. Hassell, Sgt. W.L. Henry, Sgt. J. Kissick, Sgt. A.A. Lucas, Lieut. G.J. McNaught, Lieut. J.E. Moffitt, S./Sgt. E.J. Naylor, S./M. J.G. O'Brien, Sgt. R.W. Roberts, Sgt. E. Ryan, S./M. J. Ryan, Sgt. D.M. Sandman, Sgt. A.P. Singe, Sgt. S.J. Standen, Sgt. L.B. Stohr, S./Sgt. P.W. Storey, Sgt. A.H. West, S./Sgt. H.G. Whittington.

However, two players originally selected were not allowed to take part on account of their colour: Ranji Wilson and Parekura Tureia. It appears their inclusion in the team for matches in the Republic was granted in South Africa but vetoed in London, where the South African High Commissioner refused necessary documentation to allow the players to travel with the team. One excuse for Tureia not being part of the side was that he 'missed the boat'.

The 19-match tour began with games in France and ended in Auckland six months later.

8 May v Selection Français, Pau 16–6
10 May v Northern Command, Headingley 33–0
11 May v Selection Français, Toulouse 14–13
24 July v Western Province Country, Cape Town 8–6
26 July v Cape Town Clubs, Cape Town 3–3
29 July v South Western Districts, Oudtshoorn 23–0
2 August v Eastern Province, Port Elizabeth 15–0
6 August v Orange Free State, Bloemfontein 16–5
9 August v Griqualand West, Kimberley 3–8
13 August v Witwatersrand, Johannesburg 6–0
16 August v Rand Mines, Johannesburg 24–3
20 August v Pretoria Clubs, Pretoria 5–4
23 August v Transvaal, Johannesburg 5–3
27 August v Natal, Durban 17–3
3 September v Western Province Universities, Cape Town 8–9
6 September v Western Province, Cape Town 6–17
12 September v Western Province, Cape Town 20–3
16 September v Natal, Durban 11–4
18 October v Auckland, Eden Park 16–6

The manager of the 1919 South African Services side was Percy Day. He later wrote that: 'In my considered opinion the best XV of the Services' team was superior to the best XV the 1928 All Blacks could field. Being ex-soldiers their team-work and team spirit were alike admirable, and they blended into a most workmanlike side.'

Back Home

1919

The Pioneers Battalion team reassembled and undertook a tour of New Zealand on their arrival back in the country in 1919, playing three of their nine games in front of big crowds on the East Coast. The team was: Lieut. A. Auhana; Sgt. R. Amohanga; Sgt. A. Apanui; Sgt. F. Barclay; Sgt. W.P. Barclay (MM); Sgt. T. Carroll; Corp. M. Edwards; Lieut. G. Gardner; Capt. J. H. Hall (*captain*); Pvt. H. Hingston; Pvt. L. Hingston; Lieut. H. Jacob; Sgt. W. Mapu; Lieut. J. Ormond; Corp. F. Pirihi; Sgt. G. Rogers; Sgt. P. Te Urupu; Capt. R. Vercoe; Lieut. H. Wilkinson. (Rogers and Hall had been part of the 1913 New Zealand Maoris XV that defeated Australia at Alexandra Park, Auckland, in 1913.)

17 May v Hawke's Bay, Napier 8–3
24 May v Otago, Dunedin 6–9
28 May v Southland, Invercargill 18–8
31 May v Canterbury, Christchurch 6–16
3 June v Wellington, Wellington 3–3
7 June v Auckland, Eden Park 11–22
11 June v Manawatu, Palmerston North 22–9
14 June v Hawke's Bay, Napier 25–6
21 June v Poverty Bay, Gisborne 24–12

In Christchurch, Canterbury and a Returned Soldiers side played a second match in front of large crowds at Lancaster Park. During halftime, with the Soldiers ahead 9–0, the New Zealand Rugby Football Union president, Mr D. Evans, hosted an afternoon tea for the players and officials. After the break, Canterbury caught up with their somewhat lethargic opponents and led by a point, until a last-gasp penalty goal gave the ex-servicemen the win.

In August 1919, Wellington dusted off the Ranfurly Shield, which had sat idle for five seasons, and accepted a challenge from Canterbury. Among the 10,000 spectators who witnessed a fast, competitive game won by Wellington 21–8 was the Earl of Liverpool.

1920

A true sense of normality finally returned to New Zealand football in 1920. The men came back, nobody talked about 'the war', and the unspoken expectation was that veterans would slot back into the lives they had left. Rugby clubs therefore became an important place for ex-servicemen to congregate.

Members of the Mounted Rifles team that had won the Moascar Cup presented it upon their return to the New Zealand Rugby Football Union for it to be used in a secondary schools' competition. Christchurch Boys' High School defeated Palmerston North Boys' High School in a match at Athletic Park to become the first holders of the trophy.

In May 1920, Wellington played a New Zealand Army XV in front of His Royal Highness the Prince of Wales (the future King Edward VIII). Nearly £1,000 was raised and donated to Wellington City, which developed the Prince of Wales Park as a rugby ground in his honour. As part of his programme, the Prince — who himself had served in France — attended a military review at Newtown Park, where he spoke to and shook hands with many recently returned soldiers and visited the Trentham Military Hospital. *The Dominion* newspaper doffed its hat to him, saying that he had 'shown that the men of the NZEF are all his comrades and that his interest extends to the lads and young men who fill the ranks of the Territorial Army and the Cadets today'.

South Africa were unable to accept an invitation from the NZRFU to tour in 1920, but acknowledged the interest created by the Services team and the delight the union and fans got from the way the army team played the game; they committed to arriving in 'Maoriland' the following year. Instead, the All Blacks visited New South Wales, playing seven matches, and winning all. As rugby in Queensland was in some disarray, the All Blacks did not face a composite side representing Australia. Rather, they played New South Wales three times. While the men of the sporting press referred to the games as 'tests', the NZRFU did not consider them full internationals, so no test caps were awarded to those who played in them.

The 1920 All Black side contained five men who had played for the team before the war — Chas Brown, Nut Hasell, Jack O'Brien, Teddy Roberts and Jim Tilyard. A sixth, Mick Cain, had to withdraw. All but Tilyard had served during the war, as had a further 10 players in the 21-man squad.

Captaining New South Wales was Bill Watson DCM, MC and bar, who had captained the Australian Imperial Forces team in the King's Cup.

1921

In July 1921, the South African football team arrived in New Zealand for the first time, to play 19 matches. Of the 29 members of the touring party, 23 had served in World War I. They visited and were made honorary members of Returned Services Associations throughout the country. When the Springboks and the All Blacks met in the first test at Carisbrook in August 1921, it was almost seven years to the day since the All Blacks had last played a test — the longest hiatus in the history of the game in New Zealand.

Parekura Tureia, who had 'missed the boat' when the New Zealand Services side sailed to South Africa, played against the tourists twice. His first game was as part of the combined Hawke's Bay–Poverty Bay team; four days later he captained the New Zealand Maoris.

Also in the Maori side was Wattie Barclay, who had been awarded
the Military Medal during the war and played for the Maori Pioneer
Battalion team in 1919. (He would lead the New Zealand Maori side
to France, England, Wales, Ceylon, Australia, Canada and matches
in New Zealand in 1926.)

On 21 August 1921, at a meeting of the Auckland Rugby Union
management committee, it was proposed that 'at [the] annual
meeting of delegates 1922 season it be a recommendation that
either a Challenge Shield or Cup be given for senior competition
to perpetuate the memory of the late D. Gallagher [sic]'. Thus the
Gallaher Shield came into being. (Since 1922, Ponsonby have won
it over 30 times, more than any other Auckland club. Not having
'Dave', as the Shield is known at the club, leaves a noticeable gap on
one of the clubroom walls.)

1923

In 1923, at the request of the Citizens' Committee of the Auckland
War Memorial Museum Fund, the Auckland Rugby Union agreed to
play a match to raise funds for the proposed museum. In what was the
final match of the season on 6 October, Auckland and Hawke's Bay
met at the Auckland Domain. (The two sides had met in Napier two
weeks earlier in a Ranfurly Shield fixture, with the Bay successfully
repelling the Aucklanders' challenge, 20–5.) Great sporting unity
for the cause was shown by management from both Auckland Rugby
League and Auckland Football, who decreed that there would be no
afternoon league at Carlaw Park or soccer matches throughout the
city in an effort to boost the gate-takings at the rugby game.

Auckland won the match, which featured seven war veterans
among the playing teams, 17–9. Cyril Brownlie scored a try for
the Bay, while Karl Ifwersen kicked a penalty and a conversion for
Auckland.

A total of £1,019/1/7 was donated to the museum fund, at least
twice the average gate receipts for inter-provincial matches at Eden
Park that season. However, the benefits in playing the match close
to the central city were negated by the fact that the grandstand was

small, restricting the number of premium tickets that could be sold, and preventing people from watching the match without paying was almost impossible in the vast bowl that is the Domain. It is estimated as many as 3,000 people may have ducked over, under or through cordons without paying.

1924–25

When the All Blacks of 1924 undertook their first post-war tour of Britain (and Ireland, France and Canada), they were following in the footsteps of the 1919 Services side as much as Gallaher's men of 1905. Of the 14 backs, 3 were under the age of 20: George Nepia, Handley Brown and 17-year-old Lui Paewai. A dozen of them were 25 or younger. The 15 forwards, although only slightly older in average age, included 10 veterans of World War I. They returned to Britain and France as old soldiers as well as footballers.

In the modern world of sporting statistics, the experience of an international rugby team is measured in the number of test caps a XV has in total. The 10 old-soldier forwards of the 1924–25 team (4 were debutants that year) had played a total of 86 games for the All Blacks by the time they arrived in Britain, of which 38 were appearances in the precursor trip to Australia and games against Auckland and Manawatu–Horowhenua. Test caps totalled just six, from three players who had met the Springboks in 1921 (those being the days when the NZRFU did not credit 12 matches against New South Wales between 1920 and 1924 as internationals). However, the average war service of the veterans was more than three years.

The 1905 team had sailed from Wellington into the unknown. Long sea journeys were foreign to most of the team, and by the end of the tour some were tired of the travel. Prime Minister Seddon saw the importance of the endeavour, and so an army veteran — Gallaher — was installed as captain. He knew what demands lay ahead in terms of travel, preparation, fitness and health.

The war veterans in the 1924–25 team had previously experienced long-distance travel as part of 'a team'. There was no culture shock for them, few unknowns and, while looking to emulate the record of the 1905–06 team, who suffered only one loss, they went through their tour unbeaten, earning the moniker 'the Invincibles'. (Although it must be noted that the Scottish rugby union, still sour after the 1905 game, did not host a test match at a time when they were the strongest of the Home unions.)

They Invincibles were wined and dined wherever they went, a far cry from their service days of rationed water and dry biscuits, of endless days in the heat of the desert or the mud of Europe, of sickness, injury and the sight of dead mates, of keeping company with lice and rats, of weeks without a change of uniform or even a bath. Compared with war, the rugby lark was fun.

In his 1959 autobiography — *I, George Nepia* — the man who had been the sensation of the 1924–25 tour wrote of his days as a tourist with the Invincibles. Notably he often mentioned that individual teammates were old soldiers. When the team set sail for Britain, less than six years had passed since the Armistice, and being a veteran was an important facet of a person's make-up and, it seems for Nepia, character. He was far too young to have served, of course, having been born in 1905, but he could vividly recall in his later years the welcome home the Maori Battalion had received at the old Awatere racecourse in 1919. For George, there was a more personal connection to the war, too. His wife's father, Lieutenant Kohere, had died of wounds sustained in action on the Western Front in September 1916. George and Huinga Kohere were wed in the Tikitiki memorial church, which had been built to commemorate Maori who had lost their lives at the front.

Read Masters kept a diary of the tour which was published in 1928. He wrote of a day spent touring sites on what had been the Western Front:

> We motored along Menin Road (known during the War as 'The Strand'), Ploeg Street, around 'Hyde Park Corner', past Hill 63 to Messines Ridge, where, with all reverence we inspected the beautiful New Zealand Monument, which stands on the German front line, in memory of New Zealanders who lost their lives in their gallant fight for, and capture of Messines. We then proceeded to

Ypres via Kemmel, Dicky Bush, La Clytte (where New Zealanders were encamped), Reninghelst (N.Z.A.S.C Headquarters), and Poperinghe. At Poperinghe we broke our journey to enable Cliff Porter and Fred Lucas to place wreaths on Sergeant David Gallaher's grave, whose body lies in the Nine Elms' Cemetery. Porter's wreath was from 'Members of the 1924–25 All Blacks' and Lucas' from his club in Auckland, to which Gallaher belonged. We saw many cemeteries in and near Poperinghe, including the largest in France or Belgium, which contains 11,000 graves of soldiers. The cemeteries were kept in perfect order, the lawns between the tombstones being nicely mown and trimmed. At Ypres, where we had lunch, we saw the remains of the Cloth Hall and hundreds of buildings that had been blown to pieces. Unfortunately darkness prevented us from visiting Paschendaele [*sic*]. We returned to Lille and caught the train for Paris, having spent the most memorable day of the tour.

When the Invincibles finally left London, they were farewelled at a dinner hosted by the London Olympic Association. Among those there to honour the All Blacks were sporting heroes such as Harold Abrahams, who had won the 100 metres in the 1924 Olympics.

Veterans of the Great War were in attendance, too, including General Sir Ian Hamilton, General Sir William Birdwood and General Sir Alexander Godley. Given the disdain in which those officers had been held by soldiers under their command — particularly those who had survived Gallipoli and the Western Front — one wonders what the feeling of some of the more cynical members of the touring party was regarding the presence of these men.

1930

In 1930, two war veterans appeared in All Black sides. Lance Johnson played in the match against Otago before the series against the visiting Lions. But the last appearance for the All Blacks by a former soldier of the Great War was by 'Bull' Irvine 13 years after he had enlisted in the army.

While rugby football at the senior level had slowly ground to a halt in New Zealand as the war progressed, those who had enlisted to fight carried the game on while away overseas. It became a crucial part of New Zealand soldiers' relaxation and recuperation. On makeshift football fields, the rules of engagement were well known and understood. When players tracked their way through sand or mud chasing the leather, little rectangles of foreign lands became, for an hour or so, temporary pieces of New Zealand where the mateship and unity seen in country paddocks and provincial rugby parks were celebrated once more. The raging conflict was sometimes so close that the thunder of artillery moaned in the background, drowning out sideline cheers.

As games became more organised, they naturally became more competitive and the enemies on the football field were, as they had been in peacetime, teams from other New Zealand provinces and then those from Australia, Wales and England, albeit made up of members from the services, though some had been international representatives. The army footballers were charged with maintaining the reputation of the nation, no small challenge.

At war's end, the quality of the New Zealand Services team, and their winning results, meant that when they returned home the New Zealand senior domestic competition fully resumed with arguably more interest than had been seen at the end of the 1914 season. The Wellington rugby team of 1919–20, which is still considered by many to be the best the province has seen, was made up of returned soldiers who had played for successful army teams. That union's generosity in declaring that in every match it played, whether in Wellington or away, the Ranfurly Shield would be up for grabs sparked life into the competition and, from there, all levels of rugby in the country.

Contact with South African teams had suddenly become frequent, so it was almost a foregone conclusion that the perceived giants of the Republic, some of whom had been seen in the flesh in Britain and later South Africa, would quickly land on New Zealand shores for what many deemed to be the world championship. That they did in 1921, and there has been no greater rival for the men in black since.

While the relaxed nature of weekly winter football was embraced by many returned servicemen, 13 shadows lay dark across the game for many years. Those former All Blacks who lost their lives at Gallipoli, France, Belgium and Palestine were remembered on the anniversaries of their deaths, year in and year out.

So, 100 years later, we remember them (and the other 80 men who wore khaki and the black jersey). The game of rugby football was all the better for their having been part of it. But New Zealand's spirit was dulled somewhat, by their passing, along with those of thousands of their mates.

Their short lives are commemorated on headstones or on monuments, here and overseas. Their names endure as part of our national game. But we must always remember that, in light of their sacrifice, war is not sport and rugby, even in the professional age, is just a *game*.

Bob Luxford, *Alex the Bruce : The Story of J. Alex Bruce, 1913–14 All Black and Wellington Representative Cricketer*, Rugby Museum Society of New Zealand, Palmerston North, 1994.

J.H. Luxford, *With the Machine Gunners in France and Palestine*, Whitcombe and Tombs, Auckland, 1923.

Winston McCarthy, *Haka! The All Blacks Story*. Pelham Books, Bristol, 1968.

Andrew Macdonald, *On My Way to the Somme: New Zealanders and the Bloody Offensive of 1916*, HarperCollins, Auckland, 2005.

Ian McGibbon, *Gallipoli: A Guide to New Zealand Battlefields and Memorials*, Penguin, Auckland, 2014.

——*Kiwi Sappers: The Corps of Royal New Zealand Engineers' Century of Service*. Reed, Auckland, 2002.

——*The Western Front: A Guide to New Zealand Battlefields and Memorials*. Penguin, Auckland, 2015.

Don Mackay (ed.), *The Troopers' Tale: The History of the Otago Mounted Rifles*, Turnbull Ross, Dunedin, 2012.

Morrie Mackenzie, *Black, Black, Black!* Minerva, Auckland, 1969.

Norman McKenzie, *On With the Game*, A.H. & A.W. Reed, Wellington, 1961.

Terry McLean, *Great Days in New Zealand Rugby*, A.H. & A.W. Reed, Wellington, 1959.

——*New Zealand Rugby Legends: Fifteen Reflections*. Moa Publications, Auckland, 1987.

R.R. Masters, *With the All Blacks in Great Britain, France, Canada & Australia 1924–5*, Christchurch Press, Christchurch, 1928.

Paul Neazor, *100 Years of College Rifles, 1897–1997*. Celebrity Books, Auckland, 1997.

——*Provincial Giants*. Celebrity Books, Auckland, 2006.

George Nepia and Terry McLean, *I, George Nepia: The Golden Years of Rugby*, A.H. & A.W. Reed, Wellington, 1963.

New Zealand Division, *New Zealand at the Front: Written and Illustrated by the Men of the New Zealand Division*, Cassell, London, 1918.

Sergeant C.G. Nicol, *The Story of Two Campaigns: Official War History of the Auckland Mounted Rifles Regiment, 1914–1919*, Wilson and Horton, Auckland, 1921.

Tim O'Donoghue, *Athletic Park: A Lost Football Ground*, Tim O'Donoghue Publications (in association with the Wellington Rugby Football Union), Wellington, 1999.

Officers of the New Zealand Cyclist Corps, *Regimental History of New Zealand Cyclist Corps in the Great War, 1914–18*, Whitcombe & Tombs, Auckland, 1922.

Ron Palenski, *New Zealand Rugby: Stories of Heroism and Valour*, Cumulus, Auckland, 2002.

Jock Phillips (ed.) with Philip Harker and Susan Harper, *Brothers in Arms: Gordon and Robin Harper in the Great War*, NZHistoryJock, Wellington, 2015.

Matt Pomeroy, *Kiwi Cameliers: A Nominal Roll of the Men of the 15th and 16th New Zealand Companies of the Imperial Camel Corps in the Great War 1914–18*, Fair Dinkum Publications, Christchurch, 2009.

Pounding Battle: Match Report, Canterbury v South Africa Played at Lancaster Park, Christchurch, Saturday, 30 July 1921, Nag's Head Press, Christchurch, 1995.

Colonel C.G. Powles, *The History of the Canterbury Mounted Rifles, 1914–1919*, Whitcombe and Tombs, Christchurch, 1928.

Christopher Pugsley, *Fighting for Empire: New Zealand and the Great War of 1914–18*, Auckland Museum/David Bateman, Auckland, 2014.

——*On the Fringe of Hell: New Zealanders and Military Discipline in the First World War*, Hodder & Stoughton, Auckland, 1991.

John Robertson, *With the Cameliers in Palestine*, A.H. & A.W. Reed, Dunedin, 1938.

D.H. Rowlands, *For the Duration: The Story of the Thirteenth Battalion The Rifle Brigade*. Simkin Marshall Limited, London, 1932.

Larry Saunders, *The Canterbury Rugby History, 1879–1979*, Canterbury Rugby Football Union, Christchurch, 1979.

E.H.D. Sewell, *The Rugby Football Internationals Roll of Honour.* T.C. & E.C. Jack, London and Edinburgh, 1919.

Maurice Shadbolt, *Voices of Gallipoli*, Hodder & Stoughton, Auckland, 1988.

Shell Shocks by the New Zealanders in France, Jarrold, London, 1916.

Tim Shoebridge, *Featherston Military Training Camp and the First World War*, Ministry for Culture and Heritage, Wellington, 2012.

S.J. Smith, *The Samoa (N.Z.) Expeditionary Force 1914–1915: An Account Based on Official Records of the Seizure and Occupation by New Zealand of the German Islands of Western Samoa*, Ferguson and Osborn, Wellington, 1924.

R.A. Stone, *Rugby Players Who Have Made New Zealand Famous*, Scott and Scott, Auckland, 1938.

Richard Stowers, *Bloody Gallipoli: The New Zealanders' Story*, David Bateman, Auckland, 2005.

A.C. Swan, *History of New Zealand Rugby Football, 1870–1945*, A.H. & A.W. Reed, Wellington, 1948.

The Kia Ora Coo-ee: The Official Magazine of the Australian and New-Zealand forces in Egypt, Palestine, Salonica & Mesopotamia, A.I.F. Headquarters, Cairo, 1918.

Christopher Tobin, *Gone to Gallipoli: Anzacs of Small Town New Zealand Go to War*, Bosco Press, Timaru, 2001.

F.M. Twistleton, *Letters From the Front — World War I*, Dick Twislteton, Gisborne, 2009.

Major A.H. Wilkie, *Official War History of the Wellington Mounted Rifles Regiment, 1914–1919.* Whitcombe & Tombs, Auckland, 1924.

Selected websites

Archives New Zealand: http://archives.govt.nz/

Auckland Museum Cenotaph database: www.aucklandmuseum.com/war-memorial/online-cenotaph

Australian Defence Force records: www.naa.gov.au/collection/explore/defence/service-records/army-wwi.aspx

The British Army in the Great War: www.1914–1918.net

British Pathé, historical films: www.britishpathe.com/
The Encyclopedia of New Zealand: www.teara.govt.nz
www.militarian.com
New Zealand Electronic Text Centre: http://nzetc.victoria.ac.nz/
New Zealand Film Archive www.ngataonga.org.nz/
New Zealand History: www.nzhistory.net
New Zealand Rugby Museum: http://rugbymuseum.co.nz/
Nixon Pictures, production company: www.nixonpictures.co.nz/
Papers Past: http://paperspast.natlib.govt.nz/cgi-bin/paperspast
St Helen's Rugby League club: www.saints.org.uk
World War 100 centennial website: www.ww100.govt.nz

Acknowledgements

For the most part, writing such a book would be a much more laborious and drawn-out process were it not for the access that Archives New Zealand provides to service records from World War I (which can vary in length from 3 to 300 pages). Auckland Museum's Cenotaph database, now revamped, is similarly invaluable.

Thanks to Finlay Macdonald, publisher at HarperCollins, who offered me the project; editors Scott Forbes (Sydney) and Kate Stone and Eva Chan (Auckland); Keith Giles, Photograph Collections Librarian, Sir George Grey Special Collections, Auckland Library; the staff of Glenfield Library; Matthew Tonks, WW100.

More personal thanks to Marie-Louise and Selby Gouldstone; David, Erin and Fred Bremford (Kazakhstan and Birkenhead); and Tony Holden.

Special thanks as always to my wife, Melissa; son Peter ('Tea's ready!'); and to Murray (for his ongoing interest).

Index

Numbers

1st Auckland Battalion 160–161

1st Canterbury Battalion 160–161

1st Otago Battalion 160–161

2nd Battalion 139

13th Battalion 120–121

27th Reinforcements Specialists Company 184–185

55th 2nd West Lancashire Division 38

422nd Field Company, Royal Engineers 37, 38, 256

A

Abbott, Harold ('Bunny') 7, 87

Abrahams, Harold 281

Aitken, George 18

Akers, Clive 39

Aldershot Command Rugby Tournament 256

Alexandra Park 8

Alf West Memorial Trophy 86

Algar, Beethoven ('Beet') 79–83, 229, 283

Alhambra 44, 156

All Blacks

  1883–1914 record 8

  1897 Australian tour 117

  1903 Australian tour 6

  1904 'Great Britishers' 130

  1905 British Isles, France and North America tour 6–7, 27, 37, 50, 67, 87–88, 147, 166, 167, 226, 244, 258, 279

  1908 Australian tour 258

  1910 Australian tour 33–34, 55–56, 239, 250

  1913 Australian tour 30–31, 45, 66, 73

  1913 North American tour 6, 7, 28, 44, 46, 53, 115–116, 219, 232–233, 234, 258–259

  1914 Australian tour 12, 24, 53, 58, 65, 66, 107, 108, 116, 178, 203, 230, 234

  1920 Australian tour 62, 72, 84, 133, 185, 210, 229, 277

  1922 Australian tour 15, 99, 152, 205

  1924–25 Britain, Ireland, France and Canada tour 2, 279–281

  1924–25 Britain, Ireland, France and Canada tour: team members 19, 27, 84, 85, 100, 102–103, 105, 111–112, 152, 157, 160, 186, 191, 194, 211–212

  1925 Australian tour 105, 231

  1926 Australian tour 103, 212

  1928 South African tour 231

  1929 Australian tour 96, 208–209

  1949 South African tour 160

  1996 South African tour 153

  first international 6, 15, 147

  first test match 6

  inauguration 5

  uniform 1

Allan, James 9

Allen, Fred 282

Allen, Sir James 11, 78, 169, 224–225

Alpers, Oscar 168

American football 7

American Women's War Hospital
50
Anglo-Welsh 7, 27, 50, 127, 225–
226, 239, 244, 259
Anzac (Australian and New
Zealand Army Corps) 1, 257
apartheid 127, 273
Apia 32
Apiata, Willie 2
Armistice Day 262
army discipline 48–49
Army Football Competition
267–272
Army Service Corps 71, 131,
186–187, 191–192, 202
Arneil, John 68
The Arrower 29
Asher, Albie 17
Athletic 57, 59–60, 126, 128,
219, 243–245
Athletic Park 282
Atkinson, Henry 30
Auckland 5–6, 8, 16, 18–19, 42,
52–54, 55, 65, 69, 70–71, 73,
104–105, 106, 135–136, 137–
138, 142, 145–146, 176–177,
179–180, 185–186, 195, 197–
198, 219–220, 278–279
Auckland Electric Power Board
20
Auckland Infantry Battalion 55,
63–64, 72, 135, 137–138,
142, 145, 147
Auckland Infantry Regiment 175,
179–180, 199–200, 232
Auckland Mounted Rifles 104,
195, 197–198
Auckland War Memorial Museum
93, 278–279
Auckland–North Auckland 16,
65, 104–105, 195–196

Australian Imperial Force 116, 117
Australian tours see under All
Blacks
Austria-Hungary 10
Avery, Henry Esau CMG, CBE,
DSO 32–36
Avery, Henry (son) 34
Avery Motors 36
Avery's Book Depot 36

B
Badeley, Bert 186
Badeley, Cecil Edward Oliver
('Ces') 184–186
Badeley, Vic 19, 185
Badeley, William 185
Bailleul Communal Cemetery
Extension 221
Baird, David Lindsay ('Scotty')
98, 209–210
Baird, James Alexander Steenson
143–144, 220–221
Bank of New Zealand 243–245
Barclay, Wattie 40, 278
Barrett, James ('Buster') 197–198,
271
Barrett, James (son) 198
Baskerville, Albert 131
Baverstock, Private 161
Bay of Plenty 110–111
Beck, Captain 148
Bedell-Sivright, Dr David
('Darkie') 147
Belgian Relief Fund 54
Belgium 204
Belliss, Ernest Arthur ('Moke')
97–99, 195
Belliss, Peter 99
Birch Hill Station 10
Birdwood, General Sir W.R. 63–
64, 281

Black, Robert Stanley ('Bobby') 106–107, 162–163
Blacklock, Private 109
Blunt, Roger 43
Boer War 6, 7, 95–96, 131, 145–146, 147, 249
Bolt, George 170
Booligal Bob 102
Booth, Ernest ('Ernie') 238, 264–266
boxing 113, 151, 192–194, 251
Boyack, Nicholas 80
Boyau, Maurice 253–254
Britannia 130, 131
British Army 267–272
British Lions 212, 231
Brown, Brigadier-General Charles 221
Brown, Charles ('Chas' or 'Charlie') 56, 61–63, 277
Brown, Handley 279
Brownlie, Anthony ('Tony') 100, 102
Brownlie, Cyril James 93, 96, 100–104, 107, 152, 278
Brownlie, Jack Lawrence 102, 151
Brownlie, Maurice John 27, 93, 96, 102–103, 150–154, 191, 192
Brown's Road Military Cemetery 256
Bruce, John Alexander ('Peppy') 219–220
Bryant, W.H. 95–96
Buck, Captain 40
Buck, Major Peter H. 215
Buller 21, 24, 106–107, 183
Burton, Ormond 54, 148, 235–236
Bush 169, 172

C
Cain, John 140
Cain, Michael Joseph ('Mick') 139–141, 229, 277
Calcinai, Dave (Duilio) 128
California Rugby Union 7
camels 80–81
Canada 41, 256
Canterbury 24, 37, 68, 90–91, 112, 132–133, 134–135, 154–155, 159, 165–166, 190–191, 227–228, 229
Canterbury Infantry Battalion 21, 49, 50, 67, 94, 95, 107, 184, 227–228
Canterbury Mounted Rifles 32, 34, 35, 257–258
Canterbury Regiment 107, 162–163
Canterbury–South Canterbury–West Coast 165, 167
Carson, Bill 282
Carterton 210–211
casualties (New Zealand)
 total 262
 Western Front 158, 163, 221, 224, 238, 241, 260, 261, 262
Caterpillar Valley Cemetery 163
Caudry British Cemetery 261
Cavell, Edith 214
Celtic 66, 93, 131, 231
Centennial Exhibition (1940) 36
Chauvel (sculptor), Georges 216
Chester, Rod 1
Christchurch 24, 37, 165–166
Christchurch High School Old Boys 134, 159, 229
Churchill, Winston 42
Churton, M.A. 109
City 176, 197–198, 219
civil register 86

Clark, A.J. 77

Clarke, D.B. 200

Clarken, Jim 269

Clifton 42, 56, 60, 140

Cobden, Donald 282

Cockroft, Eric Arthur Percy 107–110, 116, 144, 155

Cockroft, Les 109

Cockroft, Samuel 9, 108

Codford Camp 59

Coffey, Reverend Richard 33

College Rifles 12–13, 16, 32, 65, 69, 70, 195

Collins, W.J.T. 177

colour patches 22

compulsory military training 9

conscription 150, 175, 224

Cooke, Bert 172

Corfe, Arthur 146

Costello (winger) 50

Cotton, Lieutenant 32

cricket 43, 57, 168, 226

Crystal Palace 268

Cundy, R.T. 206

Cunningham, Bill 60–61, 201

Cupples, Errol 111

Cupples, Leslie Frank ('Les') MM 110–112

Cuthill, John Elliott ('Jock') 45–47

Cyclist Company 22

D

Daniel, Joe 77

Dave Gallaher Memorial 283

Day, Percy 274

de Beyssac, Jean-Jacques Conilh 254

Dean, Stan 27

Deans, Bob 6–7, 91, 103

Deans, Colin 91

Defence Force Act (1909) 9

Democratic Labour Party 175

Dempster, Charlie 43

Denniston, George 168

Department of Maori Affairs 41

Dernancourt Communal Cemetery Extension 161

Dewar, Henry ('Norkey') 27–29, 53, 60, 77–79, 234

Dewar, Mrs (mother) 77–78

Die Hards 61

Distinguished Conduct Medal (DCM) 134

Distinguished Service Order (DSO) 134

Dodd, Ernest Henry ('Ernie') 30, 37, 176, 200–202, 260

Dodd, F.H. 200

Dodd, Henry 200

Douglas, James Burt 232–233

Downing, Albert Joseph ('Doolan') 51–54, 76–77, 78

Draper, Alice 34

Duleepsinhji 43

Duncan, Jimmy 144, 259

Dunedin 249

Dunedin Engineers Volunteers 249

E

Eagle, Private 163

Eastern Maori (electorate) 1

Eden Park 8

Edward, Prince of Wales 103, 136

Edward VIII, King 276–277

Edwards, Captain 14

Ellesmere 154

Ellis, Roy 13–14, 74–75

Eltham 243–245

Encyclopaedia of New Zealand Rugby 1

English Rugby Union 268–269
Étaples 124, 148
Evans, Cyril Edward ('Scrum')
    134–135
Evans, Don 97, 276
Excelsior 149

F
F Company 196
Fache, George 68
Fair, Mr Justice 20
Falder, J.A. 208
Fanning, Alfred Henry
    Netherwood ('Alf') 227–228,
    230
Fanning, Bernie 227
Fanning, Leo 227
Fea, William Rognvald 18, 251–
    252, 283
Featherston *see under* training
    camps in New Zealand
Featherston Liberal 210–211
Feilding Technical College Old
    Boys 178
Fell, Nolan 123
Field, Harry 14
Firth, J.P. 33
Fitzpatrick, Sean 153, 154
Fletcher, Charles John Compton
    195–196
Fogarty, Richard MM 69–71, 84
Ford, William August ('Jockey')
    90–91
France
    1913 All Blacks tour 6
    1919 New Zealand Services tour
    273
    Divisional All Blacks 215–216,
    253–254, 261
    World War I 10, 21–23 *see also*
    Western Front

Francis, William Charles 144,
    202–203
Franz Ferdinand, Archduke 10
Fraser, Malcolm 175
Freethy, Albert 103
French, Tom 241, 283
Freyberg, Bernard 33–34

G
Gallaher, Charles 148
Gallaher, David ('Dave') 6–7, 53,
    55, 126, 137, 145–148, 166,
    226, 235–238, 279, 281
Gallaher, Douglas 148
Gallaher Shield 278
Gallipoli 50
    1914–15 1, 13–14, 21, 25,
    34–35, 56
    1915 landings 63–64, 94–95
    Chunuk Bair 40, 46, 60, 76–77
    Chunuk Bair Memorial 78–79
    evacuation 35
    New Zealand casualties 262
Geddes, William McKail MC
    73–75
Gemmell, Samuel William 93,
    216–217
George V, King 31, 267, 271
Germany
    British army of occupation 36
    declaration of war 10
    German Samoa 15, 32
    in Pacific 24, 38
Gibbon, Colonel C.M. 169
Gillespie, Charles Theodore MC
    29–31
Gillett, George 226
Gilray, Colin MacDonald MC,
    OBE 37, 118–122
Glasgow, Francis Turnbull
    ('Frank') 87, 243–245

Glasgow, James 244
Glebe (Sydney) 116, 117
Glenn, William Spiers ('Billy') MC 86–89, 167
Godley, General Sir Alexander 9, 10, 11–12, 281
Goode, Jack 181
Gore Albion 249
Grafton 42
Graham, James 234
Grammar 185
Grammar Schools' Old Boys 16, 18
Great Britain 10, 11–12, 36, 147
Green, Clem 58
Grimmett, Clarrie 43, 57

H
Haig, Field Marshall Sir Douglas 36
Hall, George 125
Ham, William 51
Hamilton, Donald Cameron 131, 225–227
Hamilton, General Sir Ian 281
Hancock, Edith 37
Hanlon, Myrtle 59
Hardcastle, William Robert 116–118
Hardham, William 6, 27, 29, 30
Harper, Anthony 168
Harper, Eric Tristram ('Dean') 88, 133, 165–168, 257–258
Harper, George (brother) 95, 166
Harper, George (father) 166
Harper, Glyn 241
Harper, Leonard 168
Harper, Robin 151, 166
Harris (selector) 226
Harris, Jack 282

Harry Jacob Memorial Trophy 41
Hart, George 282
Hasell, Edward William ('Nut' or 'Nuts') 132–133, 141, 277
Hastings 100, 102, 151, 216
Hautapu 97
Hawera 27, 69, 84, 86, 233–234, 243–245
Hawke Cup 43
Hawke's Bay 52, 93, 100, 103, 104, 151, 153, 187–188, 210–211, 216, 231, 242, 243–245, 278–279
Hawke's Bay–Poverty Bay 93, 151, 216
Hawke's Bay–Poverty Bay–East Coast 93, 100, 151, 210–211
Haydon, Vernon 246–247
Hayson, Bert 56, 162
Heeney, Tom 151, 192–194, 251
Hill, James 61
Hill, Lance-Corporal 76–77
Hodder, Florence and Gordon 19
Holden, Charles 221
Hore, Jack 153
Horowhenua 11, 39–41
Hospital Ship Fund 54
Hughes, Edward ('Ned') 129–132, 167, 229
Hull Kingston Rovers 37
Hunter, George MP 170
Hunter, Jimmy 59, 67, 87, 167
Hutchinson, Ella 158

I
Ifwersen, Karl Donald 16–21, 252, 278
Imperial Camel Corps 80–81
Incomparables (1996) tour see under All Blacks
Ingram, Monty 237

Invercargill 249
Invercargill Star 239
Inverleith, Edinburgh 269
Invincibles (1924–25) tour see under All Blacks
Irvine, Ian 212
Irvine, William Richard ('Bill the Bull') 188, 210–212, 281
Irwell 154
Ivimey, Frederick Elder Birbeck ('Fred') 7, 249–250

J
J Company 183
Jacob, Hohepa ('Harry') MC 39–41, 98
Jacob, Lucy 41
Jacob, Ranfurly 41
James Macalister Limited 240
jazz band 191
Jerusalem War Cemetery 257
John McGlashan College 122
Johnson, Lancelot Matthew 230–231, 281
Johnson, Wilfred 208
Johnston, Brigadier-General Earl 75, 160, 221
Johnston, William ('Massa') 88

K
Kahouri Bridge 208
Kaikorai 258–259
Kaponga 233
Karamea 183–184
Kelly (selector) 226
King, W.W. 20
King Country Union 245
King George V Cup 283
King's Cup (1919)
  New Zealand Services win 267–272

team members 62, 70, 90, 92, 98, 127, 133, 149, 155, 178, 233, 251
Kingstone, Charles Napoleon ('Nipper' or 'Nap') 42–43
Kinvig, George 282
Kitchener, Lord 9, 63
Kivell, Alfred Lewis ('Alf') 207–209
Kohere, Lieutenant 280

L
La Coupe de la Somme (sculpture) 216
Lancaster Park 150, 256
Larkin, Ted 146–147
Lee, John A. 173–175
Lemnos Island 96–97
Levin–Wanderers 39
Lindsay, Andrew 123
Lintott (front-rower) 105
Linwood 227
Liverpool, Earl of 11, 276
Logan, Colonel Robert 15
Lomas, Albert Robert ('Mick') 104–106, 271
Lomu, Jonah 188
London Olympic Association 281
London Scottish 118
Long, Sir Walter 215
Loveridge, George ('Bear') 108, 115–116, 230
Lowry, Tom 97
Lucas, Freddie 191
Lynch, Thomas William ('Tiger') 54, 59, 65–67, 234
Lynch, Tom (father) 66

M
McArthur, Lieutenant 221
McCarthy, Winston 69–70, 85, 99, 107

McCaw, Richie 2, 154
McCleary, Brian Verdon 191–194
McClymont, Scotty 17
McDonald, Alexander ('Alex') 232, 245, 258–260
McGibbon, Ian 261
McHugh, Captain 22
McKenzie, Ernie 99
McKenzie, Lieutenant J. 56
Mackenzie, Morrie 26
McKenzie, Norman 52, 93, 104, 153
McKenzie, Richard John ('Jock') 54, 142–143
Mackenzie, Sir Thomas 187
Macky, John Victor 179–180
McLean, Charles MM 21–24
McLean, Les 70
McLean, Terry 153–154
Maclear, Basil 147
McLeod, Mr 78
McMillan, Neville 1
McNab, John Alexander 92–94, 96
McNeece, Alex 224
McNeece, A.M. 138–139
McNeece, James ('Jim') 138–139, 223–224
McNeece, John 139
Macky, John Victor 179–180
Mahia 187
Major, Charles T. 13
Manawatu 178
Manawatu–Horowhenua 39, 40–41
Manawhenua 39
Maori Agricultural College 216
Maori Contingent 38, 39, 40, 123–124, 187–188, 216, 280
Maori Pioneer Battalion 216–217, 267

Maori XV 62
Marama (hospital ship) 66, 67
Marist 52, 112, 113, 135, 142, 191, 197–198, 216, 227
Marlborough–Nelson–West Coast–Buller 49, 50
Martin, Hugh 119–120
Marylebone Cricket Club 43, 230
Mason, George 219, 233
Massey, William 11, 38, 89, 187, 202
Masters, Frederick Harold ('Skin') MM 12–15
Masters, Read 280–281
Meads, Colin 154
medals/honours 134
medical conditions, illnesses and wounds 3
 ametropia 131
 bullet wounds 75
 dental health 139
 hookworm 17
 medical treatment 82, 171–172
 Number 9 Pill 141
 poison gas 22, 60, 131, 150
 PUO 121
 shell-shock 25–26
 trench mouth 116
 varicose veins 155
Mediterranean Expeditionary Force 14, 35
Melbourne University 122
Meldrum, Lieutenant-Colonel W. 28–29, 77, 89
Melrose 27, 116
Merchant Navy 66, 67
Merivale 90, 132–133
Messines Ridge British Cemetery 221
Metz-en-Couture Communal Cemetery 260

Middle East *see* Palestine; Sinai
Military Cross (MC) 134
military districts 9
Military Medal (MM) 134
Millton, Edward 10
Millton, Captain William 10
Millton, William 10
Mitchinson, Frank 66
Moascar Cup 272, 276
Moawhanga Huia 97
Moffitt, James Edward ('Jim') MM
    71–73, 80, 195
Moffitt, Joe 72
Mohaka 216
Monro, General Sir C. 14, 35
Morkel, Gerhard 91
Morris, G.N. 20–21
Mortland, J.P. 97
Mudros West 96–97
Mumm, Bill 183
Munro, Henry Gordon ('Abe')
    190–191
Murray, Harold Vivian ('Toby')
    96, 154–155
Mynott, Harry 87

N
National Film Archive 214–215
National Film Unit 219
Nelson 49, 50, 94, 95, 183, 242
Nelson (club) 49, 94
Nelson College Old Boys 183, 242
Nelson–Golden Bay–Motueka 49,
    242
Nelson–Marlborough–Golden
    Bay–Motueka 94, 242
Nepia, George 57, 84, 103, 128,
    152, 211–212, 217, 279, 280
New Zealand Alpine Club 168
New Zealand Apple and Pear
    Board 160

New Zealand Army Ordnance
    Corps 203
New Zealand Army XV 276–
    277
New Zealand Base Depot 116
New Zealand Brigade tournament
    252–253
New Zealand Cricket Council
    230
New Zealand Cyclist Corps
    22–23
New Zealand Defence Force 33,
    34, 36
New Zealand Division 36, 158
New Zealand Divisional
    Ammunition Column 84
New Zealand (Divisional)
    Representative Trench Team
    204
New Zealand Divisional XV 61,
    70, 127, 178–179, 189–190,
    212–216, 219, 224–225, 233,
    261 *see also* New Zealand
    Reserve Group
New Zealand Expeditionary Force
    army discipline 48–49
    British requirement for 10, 11
    Dardanelles campaign 42
    departure on transport ships
        38–39
    first combat 51
    initial force 11–12
    Samoa 15
    Sport Control Board 263
    uniform 1
New Zealand Field Ambulance
    227
New Zealand Field Artillery 29,
    32, 42–44, 73–74, 84, 91–93,
    132–135, 177, 210–211,
    241–242

New Zealand Field Engineers 12, 13, 61, 62, 64, 65, 112, 115, 204–205, 219, 229

New Zealand (Infantry) Division 123–124

New Zealand Machine Gun Company 108–109, 154–155, 190

New Zealand Maoris 39, 137, 216, 217, 275, 277–278, 283

New Zealand Medical Corps 110–111, 206–207, 225, 227

New Zealand Military Forces 9

New Zealand Mounted Rifles 9–10, 17, 22, 156, 159, 165–166, 168

New Zealand Permanent Force 249–250

New Zealand Permanent Militia 30

New Zealand Pioneer Battalion 40, 188, 215, 216, 275–276

New Zealand Reserve Group 124, 167, 180–181, 186–187, 202 *see also* New Zealand Divisional XV

New Zealand Rifle Brigade 69, 70, 90, 97, 98, 118, 120, 126, 130, 163, 171, 201–202, 208, 231, 235, 240, 251, 260, 261

New Zealand Rugby Football Union 1–2, 5, 6, 68, 131, 160, 245, 260

New Zealand Rugby League 7, 16, 17, 37
  Legends of League 21
  as Northern Union 7, 37, 131, 190, 226

New Zealand Services 2, 284 *see also* King's Cup (1919); South Africa (1919)

1914–18 team members 54, 71, 72, 84, 85, 96–97, 136, 140–141, 178, 207, 219, 235, 251

1945 Kiwis team 282

2015 'Defence Blacks' team 283

New Zealand Trials 12, 15, 39, 42, 43, 57, 69, 84, 90, 91, 93, 94, 100, 104, 110, 149, 151, 156, 159, 183, 185, 190, 191, 199, 208, 216, 231, 242, 204–205, 210–211, 227–228, 231

New Zealand Universities 45–46, 169, 190, 199, 251–252

New Zealand Volunteer Force 9, 50

New Zealand Wars 61, 87

Newman, Dr A.K. 88–89

Newman, Frank 88

Ngata, Apirana 188

Nicholls, Ginger 59

Nicholson, George 54, 238, 244

Nielson, A.E. 18

Nine Elms British Cemetery 238, 281

North Auckland 20, 65, 185, 195–196

North Island (team) 12, 27–28, 29–30, 32, 34, 39, 42, 52, 55, 57, 60, 61, 65, 71, 73, 79, 84, 86, 93, 97, 100, 102–103, 104, 105–106, 110, 115, 116, 126, 137, 140, 142, 145–146, 151, 169, 175, 176, 178, 185, 195, 200, 203, 204–205, 206–207, 208, 211, 216, 219, 228, 231, 233–234

North Island Country 3, 52

Northern 66

Northern Maori 187–188

Northern Union *see* New Zealand
  Rugby League
NZEF *see* New Zealand
  Expeditionary Force
NZMR *see* New Zealand
  Mounted Rifles
NZRFU *see* New Zealand Rugby
  Football Union

O
O'Brien, John Gerald ('Jack') 116,
  135–137, 277
O'Connor, Corporal 162–163
Ogden, Peter 232–233
Okaiawa 233
Oldham Infirmary 133
O'Leary, Joe 115, 136
Omana, Tiaka *see* Ormond
Oriental 29, 30, 31, 71, 72–73,
  203, 204–205
Originals (1905) tour *see under*
  All Blacks
Ormond, John ('Jack') / Tiaka
  Omana 187–188
O'Sullivan, Jim 87, 245
Otago 44, 45, 69, 106, 108, 118–
  119, 143–144, 156, 190–191,
  199, 232, 249–250, 251–252,
  258–260
Otago Infantry Battalion 45, 46,
  57, 59, 60, 61, 138–139, 143–
  144, 148, 209–210, 233
Otago Mounted Rifles 25, 100–
  101, 106–107
Otago Province 68
Otago Rugby Football Union 260
Otago University 45, 119
Otago–Southland 258
Otaki Maori Racing Club 41
Oxford University Blues 118,
  119–120

P
Pacific Ocean 24, 38
Paewai, Lui 188, 279
Pahiatua 169, 172
Palenski, Ron 3
Palestine 1, 252–253, 262, 271
Palmer, A.C. 120
Parata, Wiremu ('Ned') 137
Parker, James Hislop MM, CBE
  157, 159–160
Parsons, Linda 87
Paul, Sydney 54, 56, 60–61, 96,
  97, 222, 223
Pearson, Lieutenant Colonel W.R.
  95
Pepper, Cyril 282
Perry, Arnold 157
Petone 83, 91, 116, 142, 178
Pienaar, P.J. 95–96
Pirates 106, 108, 131, 156, 176,
  225, 226
Plugge, Lieutenant Colonel Arthur
  51, 63–64, 189–190, 212, 253
Poneke 79, 83, 92, 130, 196,
  204–205, 227–228
Ponsford, Bill 43
Ponsonby 55, 137, 145, 146, 197–
  198, 278
Ponsonby Cricket Club 55
Port Ahuriri 53
Porter, Cliff 27, 99, 157, 160, 186
Potter's Paddock 8
Poulton, Ronald 119–120
Prince of Wales Park 276–277
Pugsley, Chris 214
Purdue, Charles and Edward
  ('Pat') 50

R
Raetihi 175
Ranfurly, Earl of 5

Ranfurly Shield 5–6, 7, 11, 27–28, 36, 40, 52, 58, 127, 136, 147, 179, 210, 217, 234, 276
Rangitikei (electorate) 89
Ranjitsinhji 127
Redwood, Charlie 117
Reform Party 89
Rhodes Scholars 119
Richardson, Brigadier-General 187
Richardson, Johnstone ('Jock') 27, 103, 156–158, 191, 283
Richardson, Vic 43
Ridland, Alexander James ('Jimmy') 44, 131, 139, 239–240, 261
Riley, Sid 117, 147
Ritchie, William Traill 123
Roberts, Edward James (Teddy) 54, 56, 57–60, 80, 96, 116, 125, 167, 181, 202, 210, 245, 277
Roberts, Fred 27
Roberts, Harry 57
Roberts, Len ('Little') 59
Roberts, Richard William ('Dick') 28, 58, 59, 127, 233–235
Ross, Malcolm 212–216
Rouen 124
Royal Aero Club 170
Royal Air Force 267
Royal Field Artillery 88–89
Royal Flying Corps 169–170
Royal Navy 267
Royal New Zealand Artillery 249
rugby football
  changes to rules 264–266
  concussion 157, 186, 232–233
  corkscrew punt 57
  'Digger' 206
  dribbling rushes 8
  Egyptian rugby 54, 56
  kicking 8
  knocked-out players 225
  match-fixing 233
  scrum formation 8
  tactics 245
  venues 8
The Rugby Football Internationals Roll of Honour (Sewell) 238
Rugby Football: Some Present Day New Zealand Methods 109
Rugby Park (Invercargill) 158
Rugby Players Who Have Made New Zealand Famous (Stone) 180
Rugby World Cup 283
Russell, Major General Sir Andrew 34, 61, 88, 124, 215, 224–225
Russia 10
Ryan, Edmond 91–92
Ryan, James 62, 92, 140–141, 178–179, 271

S
Sacred Heart First XV 100
St Helen's rugby league club 37
St James 57, 71, 219
St Sever Cemetery 224
Samoa 1, 15, 16
Saunders (winger) 50
Schultz, Dr 32
Scotch College 122
Scotland 118, 120, 123, 269
Scott, Bob 282
Seddon (Prime Minister) 279
Seddon Shield Districts 183, 242
Seeling, Charlie Edward ('Bronco') 53, 88, 98, 126, 176–178, 186–187, 244
Sellars, George Maurice Victor 54, 116, 137–138, 221–222

Sellars, Percy Roy 137
Selwyn 204–205, 227–228
Sewell, E.H.D. 254–255
Shearer, Jack Douglas 228–229
Shearer, Sidney David ('Sid') 204–205, 229
Sherwood, Sergeant 109
Siddells, Stanley Keith 168–172
Sinai 1, 262
Sinclair, Richard 84–85
Sinclair, Robert Gemmell Burnett ('Jimmy') 199–200
Singer family 50
Skinner, Kevin 154
Smith, William Ernest 49–50, 95
Smyth, Bernard Francis ('Frank') 112–113
Snodgrass, Wallace Frankham 241–243
Snow, Ashley 94, 95
Snow, Eric McDonald ('Fritz') 94–96
Snow, Roy 94–95
South Africa (1919)
  New Zealand Services tour 272–274
  team members 62, 70, 90, 92, 98, 127, 133, 149, 153, 207
South African Super Rugby 40
South Auckland 68
South Canterbury 66, 108, 109, 149, 150
South Country 3
South Island (team) 21, 23, 24, 26, 37, 44, 45–46, 49, 66, 90, 94, 106–107, 108, 112, 113, 118, 130, 132, 134–135, 138, 149, 154, 156–157, 159, 165, 190, 191, 199, 209–210, 225, 229, 232, 239, 242–245, 249–250, 258

South Island Country 94
South Island Minor Unions 183
Southern 232
Southland 24, 66, 130, 131, 138–139, 156, 158, 209–210, 225–226, 239–240, 243–245, 249–250
Southland–Otago 130
Spencer, Carlos James 39–40
Springboks
  1921 test 277–278
  1921 test: team members 15, 18, 24, 26–27, 43, 59–60, 70, 72, 84, 90–91, 98–99, 111, 132, 133, 135, 150, 151, 156, 185, 242
  1937 test 20, 245
Springfield 154
squash 252
Star 27, 61, 209–210, 243–245
Stead, Billy 130, 244
Steel, Jack 160
Stohr, Leonard Frederick ('Jack') 206–207
Storey, Percival Wright ('Percy') 148–150
Stowers, Richard 77
Stratford 12, 27, 206–207, 208
Stratford War Relief Association 78
Suez Canal 51
Swan, Arthur 107
Swannell, Blair 147
Sydney Grammar School 15
Symes, Lance Corporal F.Q. 141
Symon, Lieutenant-Colonel 31

T
'Tackler' 205
Taieri 45
Taihape 97

West Coast–Buller 183
Western Front 1, 2, 35, 40, 117
  All Blacks tour sites 280–281
  Battle of Flers-Courcelette
    160–161
  Battle of Pilckem Ridge 38, 142
  Battle of the Ancre 120–121
  Battle of Trescault Spur 260
  cemeteries 161, 163, 221–223,
    224, 256, 260, 261, 281
  film of 215
  Givenchy 256
  Le Quesnoy 261
  Messines 14, 220–221, 223–
    224
  New Zealand Field Artillery
    74–75
  New Zealand Machine Gun
    Company 108–109
  Passchendaele 31, 149, 235–
    238, 241
  the Somme 25, 46–47, 59, 112,
    158, 162–163, 197
  Vierstraat line 22–23
Weston, Lynley Herbert 9, 16, 54,
  64–65, 196
Westport 21
Whangarei High School Old Boys
  185

Whangarei United 65
White, Andrew ('Son') 24–27, 84
White Star 106
Whittaker, Cyril 192–193
Wigan 177
Williams, Peter 43–44
Willochra 28, 76, 140, 219
Wilson (selector) 226
Wilson, Billy 127–128
Wilson, Frank Reginald 54, 55–
  56, 124–125, 160–162
Wilson, Nathaniel Arthur ('Ranji')
  126–128, 167, 210, 273
Woodfull, Bill 43
World War II
  All Blacks 282–283
  Home Guard 1, 47, 63, 75, 116,
    184, 194
Wynyard, Jim 282

Y
YMCA 132
Young, Frances Beresford ('Frank')
  196–197

Z
Zingari 149
Zingari–Richmond 143–144